The Great British Book of BAKING

The Great British Book of BAKING

120 best-loved recipes, from teatime treats to pies and pasties

RECIPES BY LINDA COLLISTER
PHOTOGRAPHY BY MARK READ

MICHAEL JOSEPH
an imprint of
PENGUIN BOOKS

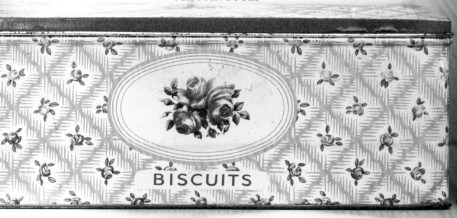

MICHAEL JOSEPH

Published by the Penguin Group

Penguin Books Ltd, 80 Strand, London WC2R 0RL, England

Penguin Group (USA) Inc., 375 Hudson Street, New York, New York 10014, USA

Penguin Group (Canada), 90 Eglinton Avenue East, Suite 700, Toronto, Ontario, Canada M4P 2Y3
(a division of Pearson Penguin Canada Inc.)

Penguin Ireland, 25 St Stephen's Green, Dublin 2, Ireland (a division of Penguin Books Ltd)

Penguin Group (Australia), 250 Camberwell Road,
Camberwell, Victoria 3124, Australia (a division of Pearson Australia Group Pty Ltd)

Penguin Books India Pvt Ltd, 11 Community Centre,
Panchsheel Park, New Delhi – 110 017, India

Penguin Group (NZ), 67 Apollo Drive, Rosedale, North Shore 0632, New Zealand
(a division of Pearson New Zealand Ltd)

Penguin Books (South Africa) (Pty) Ltd, 24 Sturdee Avenue,
Rosebank, Johannesburg 2196, South Africa

Penguin Books Ltd, Registered Offices: 80 Strand, London WC2R 0RL, England

www.penguin.com

First published 2010

3

Photography copyright © Mark Read, 2010

Additional photography copyright © Tara Fisher, 2010 on pages: 9 *(bottom centre)*,
10 *(third down, left)*, 11 *(second down, left; bottom left; bottom centre)*,
21 *(top left; top right; bottom right)*
234–5, 247, 252, 260, 272–3, 288 *(top)*, 289 *(top left)*

Additional photography copyright © Alistair Richardson, 2010 on pages: 16, 35 *(bottom centre)*, 84, 142

Picture of Mary Berry and Paul Hollywood, page 11, copyright © Vicki Couchman 2010

Text and recipe copyright © Love Productions 2010

BBC and the BBC logo are trademarks of the British Broadcasting Corporation
and are used under licence. BBC logo © BBC 1996.

Recipes written by Linda Collister

Main introduction and chapter introductions written by Sheila Keating

Set in Scala Sans, The Serif, Grocers Script, SignPainter House Script and Industrial Gothic

Printed and bound by Firmengruppe APPL, aprinta druck, Wemding, Germany

Colour reproduction by Altaimage

A CIP catalogue record for this book is available from the British Library

HARDBACK ISBN: 978-0-718-15711-1

Contents

A Word from Mel and Sue

Our Mums are two of the finest bakers we know. Ann Perkins's Lemon Drizzle Cake, partnered with a cup of Earl Grey, is one of the finest fits since Ray Alan put his hand up Lord Charles. It's so good that, for a brief moment when she serves it, you're transported from a Croydon semi-detached to a Sicilian citrus grove. Sadly, once it's finished, you're transported back again. Rosemary Giedroyc's Upside-Down Ginger Pudding is not only a feat of engineering but dances on the tastebuds like a spicy Fred Astaire. Before you enquire, the recipe is a family treasure; you'd sooner break Colonel Sanders into revealing his secrets than Mrs G.

Neither parent was Cordon Bleu-trained, neither learned their skills from the forty-three thousand hours of cookery programmes littering the television schedules each and every week. They learned how to bake from watching their Mums, certainly, but most importantly, they learned through trial and error and they learned on the job. Just ask our Dads, who have developed cast-iron constitutions as a result . . .

Since mankind discovered fire, we've been trying to perfect what we cook with it; from the chewy Beltane loaves of Iron Age man to the semolina-crusted sourdoughs of the modern artisan baker. Baking runs in our blood, it's as quintessentially British as football and disappointment. What's sad is that we have started to lose our basic baking skills; instead choosing to waste our cash on mass-produced cakes, pastries and biscuits from the supermarkets. We are part of this generation, who turned away from the wholesome and homespun in pursuit of all things easy and processed; so much so, we've all but forgotten what a really good, home-cooked sponge in all its buttery glory tastes like.

But times are thankfully changing, and now many of us, ourselves included, are running back to the floury arms of our ancestors, begging for forgiveness. There is regret, of course. Why did we not watch our Mums more closely as they pored over their Be-Ro cookery cards? Why did we never learn how to roll out, fold over, crimp, prink and bake our own pasties? Why didn't we write down Granny's recipe for vodka scones? But all is not lost. Thankfully there are thousands of extraordinary men and women (a lot of them in their twenties and quite the little saucepots) who have retained and developed these skills, and who can pass the seeded baton on to us. Thanks to them, Sue can now bake a fourteen-tiered classic wedding cake and Mel is the proud owner of several icing bags.

So next time you fancy something sweet, eschew the vacuum-packed, flavour-enhanced pallor of the supermarket muffin and whip up something awesome yourself. It's fun, it's therapeutic, and when you get it right it can make you very, very popular with friends, family and prospective in-laws.

Let's get Britain home-baking again. It might still be naughty, but it's a hell of a lot nicer.

Mel and Sue

IN THE SUMMER OF 2010, ten home bakers took part in *The Great British Bake Off*, a Love Productions series for BBC2. Each week, the series explored a different part of our great baking heritage and along the way featured some of the wonderful people keeping these traditional skills alive.

In each place – from Scone in Scotland, to Sarre in Kent and Mousehole in Cornwall – the bakers were set challenges by *The Great British Bake Off* judges, Mary Berry and Paul Hollywood. Throughout the book you'll come across recipes from the home bakers – each marked with a steaming teapot.

Annetha

Miranda

Jonathon

Ruth

Jasminder

Edd

David

Louise

The Judges

Cakes   Scones

Lea

Mark

Tips from the judges

This country has a strong baking heritage dating back hundreds, even thousands, of years and during this time many changes have taken place, from the evolution of ovens to modern milling techniques. The home baker today has everything needed to produce a perfect loaf, cake or scone, and the experience of baking for the first time is something never to be forgotten – and is much talked about!

There are a number of points the home baker needs to take note of before starting to bake at home. Whether the recipe is a family one, borrowed from a friend or from a recipe book, the ingredients must be looked at carefully. Never put an ingredient into a bake that you don't like and follow the recipe to the letter until you become familiar with it. Then you can add your own touches.

My second point about baking is your oven. Ovens nowadays have many settings and can overcomplicate an otherwise simple procedure. I would recommend that most baking be done in the middle of your oven, as this is where an even temperature is achieved. Temperature is the key. A longer bake should be baked at a lower temperature, a shorter bake at a higher temperature. This will ensure that your Victoria sponge stays moist!

The third, and probably the most important, rule is consistency. There may be a problem following a recipe because different flour brands will require more or less liquid to attain the ideal consistency. This is where my experience as a baker has been of great benefit. I rarely follow a recipe's liquid content: instead, I will use touch to determine whether the mix is correct or not. My point is, when baking at home, initially follow the recipe: try it, and, if you feel it's too wet or dry, alter the mix the next time you make it, taking careful note of the brand of flour used.

An organized kitchen when baking is an absolute necessity. Clear the tops of anything that may find its way into your mix – a clean kitchen generally means a good finished product!

Baking can be fun for all ages. My son Joshua, aged eight, is an avid pizza-base maker, while my mother-in-law bakes bread and cakes for grateful grandchildren. My advice to you is to start making bread at home first, because creating a great loaf builds confidence and spurs you on to other baking delights. Bread is particularly good for understanding the liquid content in doughs, as it is allows you to feel the dough between your fingers.

TOP TIP: When kneading dough on a surface, use olive oil on the surface and your hands, as adding flour will tighten the dough and give you a very dense loaf . . . Happy baking!

My advice for a novice baker is to bake what you and your family like. There's nothing worse than baking something that you don't want to eat. Make sure you give yourself enough time – don't rush things. And *enjoy* baking.

First of all, choose a really good recipe – it helps to have a picture. Read through the method right to the end and make sure you understand everything. Check that you have all the right ingredients and equipment. One of the major pitfalls in baking is using the wrong-sized tin, so always check that your tin is exactly what the recipe asks for. And it's a good idea to go down the ingredients list and weigh all the items out first – like you see on the telly. That way, you won't forget anything. If you do that and follow the recipe properly – don't freestyle the first few times – you will have success in the kitchen.

It's very exciting to see people around the country keeping these wonderful traditional skills of baking going – and baking is a lovely thing to share. If you have recipes in your family, make sure you jot them down, because otherwise they'll be gone. Keep them and perfect them.

People's lives are very, very busy, but it's important that we teach our children how to cook – and clear up! It does make a mess, but it's essential. I've always cooked with my children and grandchildren. From a very early age, children can start helping in the kitchen. I never do anything big that they're going to be frightened of and won't eat. So if we're going to do cakes, when they're very small I do little fairy cakes. If they are enthused, then they get good results that they're proud of. And the thing they enjoy most, of course, is decorating them and licking out the bowls!

In terms of ingredients, I always used the best available. I go for free-range eggs every time. You've only got to break a budget egg and you'll see the yolk is a pale yellow in comparison. For normal family cooking I buy the supermarket own-brand of flour and for baking I would either use butter or a baking spread.

If I'm judging a cake, I look at it and see if it is tempting to eat. If it's a sticky gingerbread, then it wants to be so sticky and so moist that you just want to poke your finger in it and you can't wait to cut a piece from it. It has to look inviting. And it has to be the best of its type.

For me, my ultimate cake at teatime is a perfect small *éclair*, but you can't beat a chocolate cake in winter, or a lovely sticky gingerbread . . .

TOP TIP: After you've cooked a recipe once, it's a very good idea to make a note of what you should do next time to improve on it. Every oven varies, so maybe it needs ten minutes more in your oven. Or perhaps you think it could do with more sugar, or fewer sultanas. Put your own stamp on it.

Introduction

Britain and baking: the two are irrevocably intertwined. So much so that around the world there is a perception that everyone in Britain stops what they are doing at 4 p.m. and sits down for tea and cake – and perhaps we should. After all, there is something so calming and restorative about teapots and milk jugs and the passing round of plates of home-made biscuits and cakes. Tea therapy is what the British do best.

It's frequently said that while cooking is an art, baking is a science. It is about performing small miracles with a few ingredients, which by following a precise formula can be transformed into something entirely different. Throw an extra glass of wine or handful of herbs or spices into a casserole and you are unlikely to ruin the dish, but alter the proportions of butter or flour when you are baking and you could end up with a biscuit instead of a cake. That said, there is nothing clinical about British baking. Far from it. If we now know the exact formula for a perfect wholemeal loaf or Victoria sandwich, it is thanks to centuries of experimentation that began with the earliest 'breads', mixtures of grain and water baked on a stone in Neanderthal times, and was perfected in the home by generations of housewives, mothers and grandmothers. It is a tradition that may be founded on the principles of chemistry, but owes more to flowery pinnies and gingham tablecloths than the white coats of scientists or pastry chefs.

In Europe, it is the custom to go to the *boulangerie* to buy the daily loaf and to the *pâtisserie* for something special and elaborate for Sundays, feast days or holidays. In Britain, by contrast, we have enjoyed a long tradition of home-made bread and would be more likely to make a fruit tart, crumble or bread and butter pudding to follow Sunday lunch than go out and buy fancy pastries.

Ask an artisan baker or anyone who makes their own bread and cakes and they will talk in emotional terms about baking with love and passion, about the warm feelings that accompany the taking of a loaf or cake from the oven, and the simple joy of cutting into it to share with family or friends. That is what British baking is all about.

It may not always be sophisticated but British baking has a substance and heart that is born out of centuries of necessity and making do with whatever ingredients were to hand. In the grand houses, tables may have been groaning with food, but for the vast majority of people, working the land and later toiling in the mills and factories, baking was about hearty pies and pasties to keep out the cold and release energy while working in the fields or down the mines, or simple cakes made from adding a little dried fruit to a scrap of dough for a treat.

British baking charts a rich social and geographical history, told through many different stories, some undoubtedly true, some the stuff of popular legend. It gives us a view of people's spiritual lives from the earliest pagan times, when a Beltane cake was baked in the ashes of a bonfire to mark the advent of summer and the person receiving the most charred piece had to jump three times through the fire, to the Scripture cakes popular in Victorian times, which obliged you to look up bible references to decipher the ingredients. It presents a picture of weddings celebrated with cakes, from the early sweetened breads broken over the couple's heads through enormous flat round 'bride cakes' to rich plum cakes greased with protective lard (scraped off at the last moment). This coating gradually evolved into sugary white icing, so hard that it took both bride and groom together to cut into it (a custom initially born out of necessity rather than symbolism).

Social commentators see the first white tiered wedding cakes, adorned with cupids, as symbolizing the idea of marriage for love rather than the kind of arrangement based on money or politics that was prevalent in British society. And British baking has other social connotations. For example, in the eighteenth century the Tory gentry doggedly championed the good old British pudding in the face of the elaborate pastries constructed by French chefs brought over to Britain by the new Whig peers. The advent of teashops in the nineteenth century gave the women who mostly ran them a chance to turn their domestic skills into small businesses, selling the cakes they had been baking for their families at the same time as offering a respectable haven for women to be seen unchaperoned, striking a small but important double blow for women's independence. And the 'National Loaf' introduced during the Second World War, to make the most of British grain, has come to symbolize the resilience of wartime families, still baking in the face of rationing.

Our vast and varied repertoire of breads and cakes also owes much to the fact that before the railways made it possible to transport food around the country, recipes grew up based on whatever local ingredients were available. In the Cotswolds, for example, wool was traded for spices such as ginger and exotic fruits, which were used in the likes of Banbury buns and Holywake Bakes (gingerbreads). Such regional cakes were not just baked at home but sold at local fairs and markets, even public executions. Conversely, with the advent of industrialization and easier transport, many local specialities such as Melton Mowbray pork pies and digestive biscuits became national institutions – and remain so today.

Sometimes seminal recipes were born out of circumstance or error. For example, the Dundee cake is thought to have originated at Keiller's marmalade factory in the city during the nineteenth century as a way of using up leftover orange peel, while the Bakewell tart or pudding is rumoured to be the result of a mix-up in the kitchen at a local inn.

Baking, like all things, changes and evolves, bowing to fleeting fashions and absorbing more tangible ideas. Over the centuries, as Britain has become more of a multicultural society and the interest in food from different parts of the world has grown, we have embraced breads, cakes and biscuits from around the world, from brownies and bagels to focaccia and naan. However, everything comes full circle, and alongside our experiments with the new and exotic we are once again in the grip of a fascination with traditional, artisan and old-fashioned home baking.

For all the contemporary twists and unusual ideas or ingredients that the current generation of British bakers brings to our heritage of bread, cakes, biscuits, pies and puddings, we should remember that we have the old wisdom of our great-great-grandmothers, those early domestic scientists, to thank for their experimentation with ingredients, proportions and methods. Their gradual understanding of the wonderful alchemy of baking has bequeathed to us the rich and varied baking repertoire that we are able to enjoy and build upon today.

BONNIE PRINCE CHARLIE AND FLORA MACDONALD

from SCOTLAND

Biscuits and Tea Time Treats

Teatime.

A word that is indelibly woven into the British way of life. Of course, 'teatime' means different things to different people on different occasions. It could be as simple as a cup of tea and a biscuit, our national obsession – no one eats biscuits like the British! Perhaps crumpets toasted over the fire, oozing with yellow melting butter. It might be fat scones served with clotted cream in Devon or Cornwall – just make sure you 'dress' the scones in the right way, since these two counties have long been at war over whether to spread the cream first (Devon) or the jam (Cornwall) – oh, and the Cornish like butter too, Devonians don't. How about some less contentious toasted teacakes, or an altogether more glamorous and decadent extravaganza of designer cupcakes and cutting-edge pastries in a smart restaurant? Then there is the classic English cricket tea, evoking CinemaScope images of sunny afternoons on impossibly pretty village greens, with cricketing wives and girlfriends buttering bread and arranging cakes to the gentle thwack of leather on willow and the tinkle of teaspoons on china. Or Lewis Carroll's 'Mad Tea-Party' (he never actually called it the Mad Hatter's Tea Party), which Alice thought the stupidest she had ever been to in her life!

Whatever your take on teatime, the idea of tea and something sweet represents so much more than just food and drink. However brief or languorous, simple or indulgent, it offers a moment to stop for a quiet interlude in an increasingly fast world, or an opportunity to get together and gossip with friends. And in times of crisis, what do the British famously do? Put on the kettle and get out the biscuit tin, of course.

So entwined in our culture is the idea of teatime that even now, the last lines of Rupert Brooke's haunting, homesick poem 'The Old Vicarage, Grantchester', written while he was in Berlin in 1912 and yearning for his bohemian literary life centred around the Orchard Tea Garden next door to the Grantchester vicarage, touch a universal chord:

> *Stands the Church clock at ten to three?*
> *And is there honey still for tea?*

The whole idea of tea, not just as a homely affair but as a full-blown social event, has been enjoying a huge renaissance over the last decade or so, shaking off its rather quaint and chintzy tourist image of silver trays and trolleys in grand hotel rooms and faded seaside resorts. Afternoon tea is chic again, with innovative chefs in smart restaurants creating complex cakes, and of course the knock-on effect is that afternoon tea at home, as opposed to 'out', is also enjoying a revival.

Just as our contemporary media reports on teatime fashions and recipes, so did the society magazines of the Victorian era, when afternoon tea as an 'event' first took off in Britain. Imagine the excitement of a whole new style of eating and drinking. Of course, simple small cakes and biscuits had been baked all around the country since the earliest times, with recipes varying from region to region. The West Country claim to scone fame is challenged by many a Scot who will say that the first scones were broken bannocks (the round barley cakes that Robert the Bruce and his warriors baked on their shields). Some also link them with the Stone of Scone, where ancient Scottish kings were crowned. Since the seventeenth century, tea as a drink had also become popular (ironically served in coffee houses). However, the idea of taking tea and cakes together mid-afternoon had not yet been considered. In most houses in the early part of the nineteenth century, there were only two meals a day. In poorer households the main fare for workers was usually eaten at midday, with a small supper in the evening; while in well-to-do houses there would be breakfast and then nothing until dinner, usually a long, multi-course affair at the end of the day. The story goes that one afternoon Anna Russell, 7th Duchess of Bedford, felt a 'sinking feeling' of hunger while staying at Belvoir Castle in Rutland and began inviting a select group of ladies to join her for an extra meal in her rooms, involving small cakes and sandwiches, elegant conversation and, naturally, tea, served in fine porcelain. The idea was such a hit that when the duchess returned to London she would send cards to friends, asking them to join her for 'tea and a walking in the fields'.

As was society's wont, the idea was quickly picked up on by fashionable hostesses in town, and a whole new etiquette grew up around the serving of tea that involved much exquisite crockery and silverware, and the wearing of special dainty, flowing tea gowns. The social importance of the occasion was reflected in the literary works of the time. The novelist Henry James, in the opening scene of *The Portrait of a Lady*, set on the lawn of an English country house in the height of summer, observed: 'Under certain circumstances there are few hours in life more agreeable than the hour dedicated to the ceremony known as afternoon tea.'

Of course, this elegant and leisurely ritual could only be enjoyed by the few. In most working households, once the industrial revolution ushered in long shifts in factories and the mines, the traditional lunchtime meal also began to give way to 'tea'. However, this was usually a much more substantial affair, featuring the likes of meat and potatoes or salads as well as sweet things.

Since Victorian times the British have rarely needed much of an excuse to stop for a breather or invite friends and neighbours in for a chat over a cup of tea and a cake or biscuit.

Biscuits. How we love these little luxuries that keep us going at work or in those moments when we need comfort or a treat – we even have a Biscuit Appreciation Society in the UK! The word comes from the Latin *biscoctus*, meaning twice-cooked, as the very earliest versions – sometimes written as 'biskits' – were little more than grain and water paste, baked, then cut up and dried out further so that they were hard and travelled well. More to do with sustenance than pleasure, these biscuits became basic fodder for marching armies and sailors (if the weevils didn't get them first) and were so hard (ship's biscuits were known as 'hardtack') that they had to be dipped in liquid and rehydrated before you could eat them – perhaps that is where our love of dunking biscuits comes from.

Over the centuries, beaten egg, sugar and other ingredients such as dried fruit, even chocolate, began to be used, and biscuits evolved from essentials into treats made for bonfire night, New Year, or to be sold at the village fair. In Scotland especially, butter, sugar and flour had been transformed into shortbread, sometimes cut into voguish triangular petticoat tails. Gingerbread was another favourite, with the biscuits often pressed on to wooden moulds to make biscuits in the form of pigs, cows, Punch and Judy or royal coats of arms. In Edinburgh, ginger biscuits were known as 'parlys' because they were baked for the Scottish parliament. And in the eighteenth century James Boswell, diarist and biographer of Samuel Johnson, was already mentioning almond biscuits – known as macaroons in London.

However, it was the march of the industrial revolution with its large-scale bakeries and, above all, the advent of the railways that elevated regional biscuit recipes into national treasures. In Reading, local baker Thomas Huntley went into partnership with his cousin George Palmer and soon first-class railway passengers to London were enjoying little packets of Huntley & Palmers biscuits. So famous did the biscuits become that Captain Scott even took them on his fated expedition to the South Pole in 1911. And in Edinburgh in 1892 a young employee of the McVitie & Price bakery, Alexander Grant, created one of the most famous of British biscuits, the digestive, so called because it was believed to have antacid properties and aid the digestion, thanks to its high content of baking soda.

Whatever your idea of teatime, whether you see it as traditional or contemporary, a quick break with a biscuit or buttered scone, or a tower of different treats, the ritual of stopping for tea and a little baked delight still has a therapeutic effect in a busy world. So why not get out the baking trays and celebrate this most genial of British traditions?

Stem Gingernuts

MAKES 24

A very easy, old-fashioned biscuit made by the melting and mixing method. As well as ground or powdered ginger, this mixture includes stem ginger, sold preserved in syrup, a combination popular since the eighteenth century.

350g self-raising flour
1 tablespoon ground ginger
1 teaspoon bicarbonate of soda
200g caster sugar
115g unsalted butter

85g golden syrup
1 medium free-range egg, beaten
35g (2 pieces) stem ginger, drained and finely chopped

3 baking trays, greased with butter

Preheat the oven to 170°C/325°F/gas 3.

Sift the flour, ground ginger, bicarbonate of soda and sugar into a mixing bowl. Gently melt the butter with the syrup in a pan over a low heat and set aside until barely warm. Pour this mixture into the mixing bowl, add the beaten egg and the stem ginger and mix with a wooden spoon. When thoroughly combined, roll the mixture into 24 walnut-sized balls, using your hands.

Arrange on the prepared baking trays, spacing them well apart to allow for spreading. Bake in the preheated oven for 15 to 20 minutes, until a good golden brown. Keep an eye on them and, if necessary, turn the trays around halfway through the cooking period so that the biscuits brown evenly.

Leave the biscuits to cool on the trays for a couple of minutes, then transfer to a wire rack and leave to cool completely.

Store in an airtight container.

Somerset Easter Biscuits

MAKES 16

This butter-rich short dough is flavoured with those ingredients associated with Easter: warm, fragrant spices, dried fruit and candied peel. To make a good crunchy topping, brush the biscuits with egg white and sprinkle with sugar towards the end of the baking time.

125g unsalted butter, softened
75g caster sugar
1 medium free-range egg, separated
200g plain flour
a good pinch of salt
a good pinch of baking powder
½ teaspoon ground mixed spice

½ teaspoon ground cinnamon
50g raisins
1 teaspoon finely chopped mixed peel
extra sugar, for sprinkling

a 6.5cm fluted round biscuit cutter
2 baking trays, greased with butter

Preheat the oven to 200°C/400°F/gas 6.

In a large bowl, beat the butter until creamy, using a wooden spoon or an electric whisk or mixer. Gradually beat in the sugar and continue beating for a couple of minutes, until the mixture is light and fluffy. Add the egg yolk (save the egg white for the topping) and beat for a further minute. Sift the flour, salt, baking powder, mixed spice and cinnamon into the bowl and stir until thoroughly combined. Work in the raisins and chopped peel with your hands to make a firm dough.

Turn out on to a lightly floured work surface and roll out to about 5mm thick. Cut into rounds using the fluted cutter. Re-roll the trimmings and cut out more rounds.

Arrange the biscuits, slightly apart, on the greased baking trays. Bake in the preheated oven for about 10 minutes, until firm and pale golden.

Remove from the oven and lightly brush each biscuit with the gently whisked egg white, then sprinkle with a little caster sugar. Return the biscuits to the oven and cook for a further 3 to 5 minutes, until the tops are golden and crunchy. Leave to cool on the trays for a minute, then carefully transfer to a wire rack and leave to cool completely.

Store in an airtight container.

Cornish Fairings

MAKES 18

These traditional West Country biscuits were sold at country fairs (where workers were hired and livestock bought and sold) as edible souvenirs. They are flavoured with chopped candied lemon and orange peel as well as spice. The golden syrup gives them a lovely, slightly chewy texture, but measure it carefully and don't put too much in if you want a nice cracked surface.

100g plain flour	1 tablespoon mixed peel, finely chopped
1 teaspoon baking powder	
½ teaspoon bicarbonate of soda	3 tablespoons golden syrup (flat, not rounded), gently warmed
½ teaspoon ground mixed spice	
40g caster sugar	*3 baking trays, well greased with butter*
50g unsalted butter, chilled and diced	

Preheat the oven to 190°C/375°F/gas 5.

Sift the flour, baking powder, bicarbonate of soda, mixed spice and sugar into a mixing bowl. Add the butter and rub into the flour mixture, using the tips of your fingers, until it looks like fine crumbs. Mix in the peel, followed by the syrup, to make a stiff dough.

Using your hands, roll the mixture into 18 marble-sized balls. Set them on the prepared baking trays, spacing them well apart to allow for spreading. Bake in the preheated oven for 7 to 8 minutes, until a rich golden brown – it's a good idea to turn the trays round in the oven halfway through baking so the biscuits cook evenly.

Leave to cool on the trays for a minute until firm, then lift on to a wire rack and leave to cool completely.

Store in an airtight container.

Murray's bakery in Perth, Scotland, is doing well at keeping the strong tradition of 'little bakes' going. Everything they sell is baked on-site. Now in its third generation, there are still queues outside the door every day.

Chocolate Shortbread

MAKES 12 PIECES

This modern recipe follows the '1, 2, 3' rule of shortbread, that is, one part sugar to two parts butter (unsalted works best) and three parts flour, with the flour a mixture of fine plain flour and either rice flour (for texture) or cornflour (for lightness). Here cocoa powder is added to make up the flour.

As the mixture is rich in cocoa, watch it carefully as it bakes so that it doesn't scorch. However, undercooked shortbread doesn't taste good either, so reduce the oven temperature if it begins to turn too brown before it is fully cooked.

260g plain flour
100g caster sugar
40g cocoa powder
a pinch of sea salt
200g unsalted butter, chilled and diced
extra sugar, for sprinkling

a 20.5cm loose-based sandwich or round cake tin, well greased with butter

Preheat the oven to 180°C/350°F/gas 4.

To make the shortbread in a food processor, put the flour, sugar, cocoa and salt into the bowl and pulse for a few seconds, just to combine the ingredients. Add the butter and run the machine for about 30 seconds – the mixture will look like fine sand. Turn off the machine, remove the blade and tip the dough into the prepared tin.

To make the shortbread by hand, put the flour, sugar, cocoa and salt into a mixing bowl and stir well to thoroughly combine. Add the butter and rub into the dry ingredients, using the tips of your fingers. When the mixture looks like fine sandy crumbs, tip it into the prepared tin. Press the mixture into an even layer, using the back of a spoon. Prick the dough well and lightly score into 12 sections with a round-bladed knife.

Bake in the preheated oven for about 25 minutes, until just firm.

Remove from the oven, sprinkle with sugar, and cut into sections along the marked lines with a very sharp knife. Leave to cool before removing from the tin.

Store in an airtight container.

LEMON SHORTBREAD

Follow the recipe above, replacing the cocoa powder with 40g of rice flour or cornflour and adding the finely grated zest of 1 unwaxed lemon.

Ruth's Shortcake Biscuits

MAKES ABOUT 24

Crisp rich shortbread, with a hint of peanuts, is sandwiched with a rich creamy caramel flavoured with sea salt and more peanuts – a wonderful explosion of tastes and textures.

FOR THE SHORTCAKE MIXTURE:
440g unsalted butter, softened
220g caster sugar
4 tablespoons good-quality crunchy peanut butter
680g plain flour

FOR THE SALTED CARAMEL FILLING:
300g caster sugar
5 tablespoons cold water
100ml double cream
100g unsalted butter, diced
½ teaspoon sea salt flakes, or to taste

2 tablespoons salted roasted peanuts, chopped

FOR THE CARAMEL PEANUTS:
100g caster sugar
2 tablespoons cold water
2 tablespoons salted roasted peanut halves

a 6.5cm round biscuit cutter
3 baking trays, lined with greaseproof paper
a baking tray, oiled
a greaseproof paper icing bag

Put the butter and sugar into a large mixing bowl or the bowl of a large food mixer and beat with an electric whisk or mixer until creamy. Beat in the peanut butter. When thoroughly combined, sift in the flour and mix with a wooden spoon. Using your hands, bring the mixture together into a ball. Flatten into a disc, wrap in clingfilm and chill for about 15 minutes, until firm.

Roll out the dough on a floured work surface to a thickness of about 5mm. Cut out discs using the cutter, then gather up the trimmings, briefly knead, re-roll and cut more discs – you will need an equal number. Arrange the shortcake discs on the lined baking trays, spacing them slightly apart to allow for spreading. Chill for 15 minutes. Meanwhile preheat the oven to 180°C/350°F/gas 4. Bake the shortcakes for 10 to 12 minutes, or until firm and golden. Leave on the trays for 5 minutes to firm up, then transfer to a wire rack and leave to cool completely.

Meanwhile make the caramel filling. Put the sugar and water into a deep pan and heat gently until the sugar has completely dissolved. Brush down the insides of the pan with a damp pastry brush to prevent sugar crystals forming. Once the sugar has dissolved, bring the syrup to the boil and leave to bubble for several minutes, until it turns a rich caramel colour. Remove the pan from the heat, and carefully add the cream and the butter – take care, as the mixture will boil up and splutter. Once the mixture has subsided, return the pan to a low heat, stir gently, and simmer for a minute to make a smooth, thick caramel sauce. Remove from the heat and stir in the salt and chopped peanuts. Transfer to a heatproof bowl and leave to cool.

To make the caramel peanuts, heat the sugar and water in a small pan until the sugar has completely dissolved. Bring to the boil, then leave to bubble for several minutes until it turns to a deep caramel. Remove from the heat. Scatter the peanut halves on the oiled baking tray and pour over the hot caramel to coat completely. Leave to cool and set.

When ready to assemble, sandwich the biscuits in pairs with the salted caramel filling. Break up the caramel peanut mixture and crumble over the top.

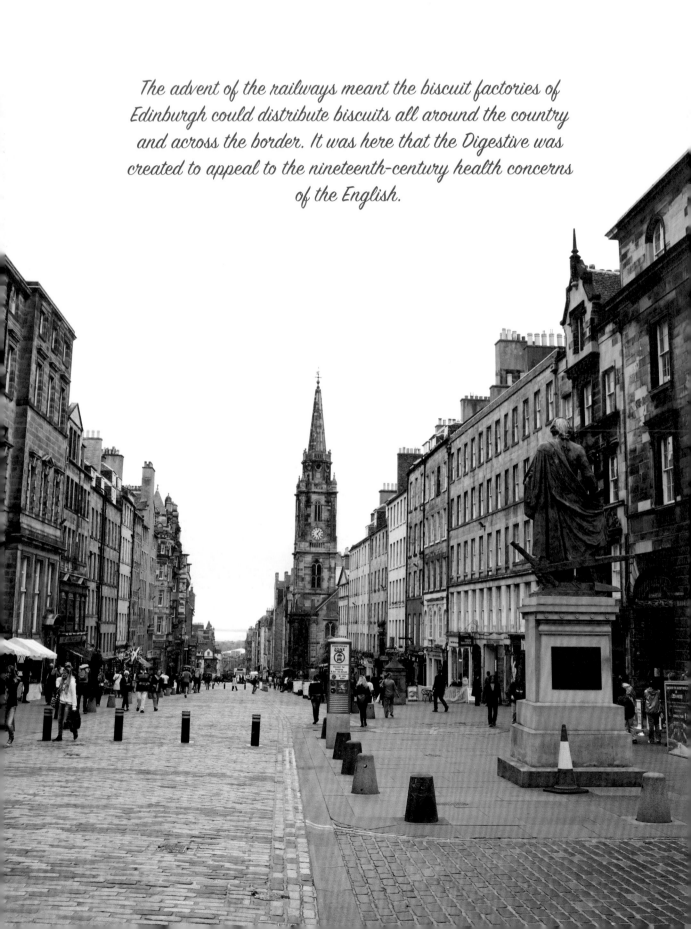

The advent of the railways meant the biscuit factories of Edinburgh could distribute biscuits all around the country and across the border. It was here that the Digestive was created to appeal to the nineteenth-century health concerns of the English.

Petticoat Tails

These thin, triangular, crisp, rich biscuits are thought to date from twelfth-century Edinburgh, and later on to have been a favourite of Mary, Queen of Scots. There is some dispute over the name and the recipe: it could derive from the French for little cakes, *'petites gatelles'*, or from 'tally', the word for a cut-out pattern. Writing in 1826 in her book *The Cook and Housewife's Manual*, Meg Dodds says, '. . . we rather think the name petticoat tails has its origin in the shape of the cakes, which is exactly that of the bell-hoop petticoats of our ancient court ladies', 'petty cotes' being a wide panelled skirt. The traditional pattern is made by cutting a disc in the centre of the shortbread round, then cutting the surrounding dough into segments.

The recipe is butter-rich and crisp. Caster sugar can be used instead of icing sugar, and you can use either cornflour or rice flour. The mixture can be left plain, or flavoured with caraway seeds or a few drops of almond extract.

150g unsalted butter, very soft
40g icing sugar
200g plain flour

50g cornflour
caster sugar, for sprinkling

2 baking trays, greased with butter
a 5cm round cutter

Preheat the oven to 180°C/350°F/gas 4.

Beat the butter and sugar until light and creamy, using a wooden spoon or an electric whisk or mixer. Sift the flour and cornflour on to the mixture and work it in with your hands to make a firm dough. Knead gently to bring it together (some cooks add a very little milk in cold weather). Divide the dough in half, and shape each portion into a ball. Set each one in the middle of a greased baking tray, and gently roll with a rolling pin, or press out with your hands, to an even circle 18cm across and 5mm thick. Press in any stray crumbs or cracks, to give an even surface.

Pinch the outside edge of each circle to decorate. Press the round cutter into the centre of each disc, but do not remove the circle of dough. With a sharp knife cut the dough around the centre circle into 8 segments, without cutting into the centre circle.

Bake in the preheated oven for about 18 to 20 minutes, until lightly golden and crisp all over. If necessary, rotate the trays halfway through the baking time so that the shortbreads cook evenly.

Sprinkle with caster sugar and gently cut along the marked lines, but leave to cool completely before removing from the tray. Traditionally, the triangular segments would be served arranged in a ring, with the centre circle set in the middle.

Store in an airtight container.

Annetha's Moulded Shortbread Biscuits

MAKES ABOUT 20, DEPENDING ON SIZE OF MOULD

200g unsalted butter, very soft	wooden shortbread moulds
110g caster sugar	or biscuit cutters, about 5cm
330g plain flour	2 baking trays, lined with
½ teaspoon ground mixed spice	greaseproof paper
or crushed dried rose petals	

Put the butter and sugar into a mixing bowl and beat with a wooden spoon, electric mixer or whisk until light and fluffy. Sieve the flour and spice, if using, into the bowl (or add the rose petals) and mix in with a wooden spoon. Work the mixture together with your hands to make a ball of dough. Wrap in clingfilm and chill for about 15 minutes.

Turn out on to a lightly floured work surface and roll out about 8mm thick. Using a wooden shortbread mould, dusted with flour, or a biscuit cutter, cut out shapes and arrange slightly apart on the prepared trays. Re-roll the trimmings and cut more shapes.

Chill for 15 minutes. Meanwhile preheat the oven to 180°C/350°F/gas 4.

Bake the shortbread biscuits for 12 to 18 minutes (depending on size/thickness), until firm and a pale gold colour. Leave to cool on the trays for 5 minutes to firm up, then transfer to a wire rack and leave to cool completely.

Coffee Kisses

These rich, melt-in-the-mouth biscuits are flavoured with coffee (instant coffee works best) and can be quickly whipped up using a food processor. They work well as individual biscuits, but are even better with a buttercream filling!

175g self-raising flour
100g caster sugar
100g unsalted butter, chilled and diced
2 teaspoons instant coffee granulesor powder
1 medium free-range egg

FOR THE BUTTERCREAM:
75g very soft unsalted butter
150g icing sugar
4 teaspoons cocoa powder (optional)

2 baking trays, greased with butter

Preheat the oven to 170°C/325°F/gas 3.

To make the dough in a food processor, put the flour and sugar into the bowl and pulse a couple of times to just combine. Add the butter and process until the mixture looks like fine crumbs. Dissolve the coffee in 1 teaspoon of boiling water. Beat the egg until frothy and mix in the coffee. Pour into the processor and run the machine until the dough just comes together.

To make the dough by hand, combine the flour and sugar in a mixing bowl. Add the butter and rub into the flour mixture using the tips of your fingers, until the mixture looks like fine crumbs. Dissolve the coffee in 1 teaspoon of boiling water. Beat the egg until frothy and mix in the coffee. Add to the bowl and stir into the mixture with a wooden spoon to make a firm dough.

Tip the dough on to a work surface and divide into 16 pieces. Flour your hands well, then shape each piece into a neat ball. Arrange them well apart on the prepared baking trays (to allow for spreading) and bake in the heated oven for 12 to 15 minutes, until light golden and firm to the touch.

Leave to cool for a couple of minutes, then transfer to a wire rack and leave to cool completely.

Make a simple buttercream by beating the butter with the icing sugar and cocoa powder, if using. When very light and smooth, use to sandwich the biscuits in pairs.

Jumbles

MAKES 16

These are a childhood favourite – the biscuits made at home after school. Everything is mixed in a saucepan and you can pick and mix the flavourings: chunks or chips of chocolate with pecan or walnut pieces, white chocolate with dried cranberries, chopped apricots and pine nuts, toffee pieces, golden raisins, toasted hazelnuts . . .

125g unsalted butter
100g caster sugar
50g light muscovado sugar
1 medium free-range egg
½ teaspoon vanilla extract

175g plain flour
½ teaspoon baking powder
flavourings: up to 100g in total of chopped chocolate, nuts, dried fruit, etc.

2 baking trays, well greased with butter

Preheat the oven to 190°C/375°F/gas 5.

Gently melt the butter in a pan large enough to hold all the ingredients. Remove from the heat and stir in both sugars. Using a fork, beat the egg with the vanilla in a small bowl until thoroughly combined, then stir into the butter and sugar. Sift the flour and baking powder into the pan and stir in. When thoroughly combined, add your chosen flavourings.

Using a tablespoon, scoop the mixture on to the greased baking trays, setting the biscuits well apart to allow for spreading.

Bake in the preheated oven for about 10 to 12 minutes, until the jumbles are a light golden brown and just firm.

Remove the trays from the oven and leave to cool for 3 minutes before transferring to a wire rack to cool completely.

Store in an airtight container.

Miranda's Decorated Vanilla Biscuits MAKES 24 – 30

Seeds from a vanilla pod flavour and scent these pretty biscuits. You can decorate them as simply or as elaborately as you wish, using the icing below or ready-made writing icing.

FOR THE BISCUIT MIXTURE:	FOR THE DECORATIONS:
200g unsalted butter, softened	500g icing sugar
200g caster sugar	1 tablespoon lemon juice
1 vanilla pod	colouring pastes or food colours
1 medium free-range egg, beaten to mix	biscuit cutters
400g plain flour	*2–3 baking trays, lined with greaseproof paper*
	greaseproof paper or nylon icing bags
	no. 1 icing nozzles (optional)

Put the butter and sugar into a mixing bowl or the bowl of a large free-standing mixer. Split the vanilla pod in half along its length and with the tip of a small knife scrape out the seeds, into the bowl. The vanilla pod can be used to make vanilla sugar (just add it to a jar filled with caster sugar) or wrapped and saved to infuse a custard (see page 290). Beat with an electric whisk or mixer until very light and creamy. Gradually add the egg, beating well after each addition. Sift the flour into the bowl and work in, using a very low speed. Use your hand to bring the mixture together and make a soft dough. Divide the dough in half and form each portion into a thick disc. Wrap in clingfilm and chill until firm – about 30 minutes.

Roll out the dough, a portion at a time, on a floured work surface to a thickness of 5mm. To make this more precise, you can use ready-made guide sticks (available from specialist shops or home-made from strips of wood). Cut out shapes using the cutters. Gather up the trimmings, knead gently, then re-roll and cut out more biscuits. Arrange the biscuits slightly apart on the lined baking trays to allow for spreading, then chill for 15 minutes. Meanwhile preheat the oven to 180°C/350°F/gas 4.

Bake the biscuits in the heated oven for 9 to 12 minutes, until just starting to turn golden brown around the edges and firm to touch. If necessary, rotate the trays in the oven halfway through baking so the biscuits cook evenly. Remove from the oven, leave to firm up for a minute, then transfer the biscuits to a wire rack and leave to cool completely.

When ready to decorate, mix 250g of the icing sugar (half the box) with 2 teaspoons of lemon juice and about 2 tablespoons of cold water to make a stiff icing that can be piped. Divide between separate bowls and colour each as you fancy. Spoon a small amount into a piping bag fitted with a tube, or a greaseproof bag, snipping off the tip, and pipe the outlines of your designs on to the biscuits. Slacken each icing with a few more drops of water so it is like a slightly runny glacé icing, and use to fill in, or colour in, the designs. Depending on the designs, you can do this using a greaseproof paper icing bag with the tip snipped off, or a small palette knife. If necessary make up more icing using the rest of the box. Leave to dry completely before serving.

Macaroons

A well-loved staple of cake shops and tearooms around the country, these round, flattish almond confections fall somewhere between a biscuit (though made without wheat flour), a meringue and a cake. The outsides are crisp, yet the centre is slightly gooey, and they are traditionally baked on edible rice paper because they are notoriously difficult to remove from the baking tray!

125g ground almonds
175g caster sugar
1 tablespoon cornflour
2 medium free-range egg whites
½ teaspoon vanilla extract

10 split almonds or 1 tablespoon flaked almonds, to decorate

1 or 2 baking trays, lined with rice paper
a piping bag fitted with a 1.5cm plain tube (optional)

Preheat the oven to 160°C/325°F/gas 3.

Mix the ground almonds with the sugar and cornflour in a large bowl. In another bowl, whisk the egg whites with the vanilla extract, using a fork, until just frothy. Add the whites to the almond mixture and stir together with a wooden spoon until thoroughly combined, to make a stiff dough.

Spoon the mixture on to the lined baking trays in 10 mounds, spacing them very well apart. Gently spread out each mound to make a disc about 5cm across and 1.5cm high – they will spread in the oven. If you like, you can also pipe the mixture, using a piping bag fitted with a plain 1.5cm tube. Set a split almond in the centre of each round or scatter over the flaked almonds.

Bake the macaroons in the preheated oven for 20 to 25 minutes, until golden.

Leave to cool on the trays, then carefully remove and store in an airtight container.

Jam Thumb-prints

MAKES 16

It's hard to find a more homely and comforting recipe: along with jam tarts, these little raspberry-jam-filled buns are childhood treats. You can use almost any jam as long as it is firm set – the slightly runny 'conserves' available these days taste excellent but they make the buns look messy.

225g self-raising flour
100g caster sugar
125g unsalted butter, chilled and diced
1 medium free-range egg
1 tablespoon cold milk

½ teaspoon vanilla extract
about 1 tablespoon raspberry jam
extra sugar, for sprinkling

2 baking trays, greased with butter

Preheat the oven to 200°C/400°F/gas 6.

To make the dough in a food processor, put the flour and sugar into the bowl and pulse a couple of times until the ingredients are just combined. Add the butter and process until the mixture looks like fine crumbs. Beat the egg with the milk and vanilla in a small bowl until thoroughly mixed and pour into the processor. Run the machine until the ingredients just come together to make a soft dough. If the mixture seems very sticky, work in a little more flour, but if there are dry crumbs and the dough feels stiff and dry, add extra milk.

To make the dough by hand, combine the flour and sugar in a mixing bowl. Add the butter and rub into the dry ingredients, using the tips of your fingers, until the mixture looks like fine crumbs. Beat the egg with the milk and vanilla in a small bowl and stir into the flour mixture, using a round-bladed knife, to make a soft dough. If the mixture is very sticky, work in a little more flour, but if there are dry crumbs at the bottom of the bowl and the dough is crumbly and dry, work in a little more milk.

Divide the dough into 16 equal pieces and shape each one into a ball. Arrange them well apart on the greased baking trays, to allow for spreading. Flour your thumb and press it gently into the middle of each bun to make a small well (don't go all the way through the dough). With a teaspoon, put a marble-sized amount of jam into the centre of each bun.

Bake in the preheated oven for 10 minutes, then reduce the oven temperature to 180°C/350°F/gas 4 and bake for another 5 minutes, until golden.

Remove the tray from the oven and sprinkle the buns with a little sugar. Leave them to cool for 5 minutes before transferring to a wire rack to cool completely.

Store in an airtight container.

Louise's Mini Macaroons

MAKES 12 PAIRED MACAROONS

FOR THE LEMON MACAROONS:
1 medium free-range egg white,
at room temperature
75g caster sugar
pale yellow food colouring paste
60g ground almonds
60g icing sugar, sieved

FOR THE RASPBERRY MACAROONS:
1 medium free-range egg white,
at room temperature
75g caster sugar
deep pink food colouring paste
60g ground almonds
60g icing sugar, sieved

TO ASSEMBLE:
150ml double or whipping cream,
well chilled
1 tablespoon lemon curd
1 tablespoon sieved raspberry jam

*2 baking trays, lined with non-stick
baking parchment*
a piping bag, fitted with a 2cm plain tube
a greaseproof paper icing bag

Preheat the oven to 140°C/275°F/gas 1. Draw 12 even circles each 5cm across on the lining paper on each tray.

To make the lemon macaroons, put the egg white, caster sugar and a very little colouring paste (use the tip of a knife) into a mixing bowl or the bowl of a large food mixer, and whisk with an electric whisk or mixer until the mixture is very thick and mousse-like. Combine the almonds and icing sugar and gradually whisk in, then continue whisking for 1 minute after the last addition to make a shiny, smooth and thick mixture. Spoon into the piping bag and pipe inside the drawn circles to make 12 small macaroons.

Make the raspberry macaroon mixture in the same way, using the red colouring paste instead of the yellow. Clean the piping bag and tube. Bake both trays of macaroons in the heated oven for about 25 minutes, until firm. Remove from the oven and leave to cool on the trays.

When ready to assemble, whip the cream until stiff, then divide in half. Swirl the lemon curd through one portion of cream so that there are still visible streaks of lemon. Add the raspberry jam to the other portion of cream and swirl together in the same way. Spoon the lemon cream into the clean piping bag and pipe a blob of cream on to the underside of 6 lemon macaroons. Then sandwich with the other 6. Clean the bag and tube again and repeat, using the raspberry cream to sandwich the raspberry macaroons. Chill until ready to serve.

Burn O'Vat Rock Cakes

MAKES 10

Burn O'Vat is a beauty spot near Ballater in Aberdeenshire. For many years the tiny tea shop there, now long gone, was well known for its moist, crumbly, lightly spiced rock cakes. For a richer rock cake use the 'luxury' type of dried fruit mix, with cherries and apricots as well as raisins, currants, sultanas and chopped candied lemon and orange peel.

225g self-raising flour
½ teaspoon ground mixed spice
85g unsalted butter, chilled and diced
85g golden granulated sugar
100g mixed dried fruit and peel

1 medium free-range egg
2 tablespoons milk
1 tablespoon demerara sugar, for sprinkling

a baking tray, greased with butter

Heat the oven to 200°C/400°F/gas 6.

Sift the flour and mixed spice into a mixing bowl. Add the diced butter and rub into the flour until the mixture resembles fine crumbs. Stir in the sugar and dried fruit with a wooden spoon. In a separate bowl, lightly beat the egg with the milk until combined, then stir just enough into the fruit mixture to bind to a very firm, stiff dough – it's important that the dough holds its shape, but if there are dry crumbs at the bottom of the bowl and the dough won't stick together, add more milk, a teaspoon at a time.

Divide the dough into 10 and spoon on to the prepared baking tray in heaped peaky mounds (to look like rocks), spaced well apart. Sprinkle with the demerara sugar.

Bake in the preheated oven for 12 to 15 minutes, or until the cakes are a good golden brown and firm to the touch.

Transfer to a wire rack and leave to cool. Eat warm or at room temperature, the same day.

Chocolate Brownies

CUTS INTO 16

We've taken these irresistible chocolate squares, originally from Boston, to our hearts. Not just for teatime, brownies are perfect warmed through for dessert with a scoop of ice cream and some hot chocolate sauce. This recipe is easy to follow and uses both cocoa and dark chocolate for a rich, deep taste. Like most chocolate recipes, brownies are best eaten the day after baking.

225g unsalted butter, diced
100g dark chocolate, broken up
200g caster sugar
4 large free-range eggs, at room temperature
½ teaspoon vanilla extract
50g plain flour

50g cocoa powder
a good pinch of salt
75g walnut pieces
icing sugar, for dusting

a 20.5cm square tin, greased with butter and the base lined with greaseproof paper

Heat the oven to 180°C/350°F/gas 4.

Put the butter and chocolate into a small, heavy-based pan. Set over the lowest possible heat and leave to melt gently, stirring frequently, until smooth but not hot. Remove the pan from the heat and leave to one side until needed.

Put the sugar, eggs and vanilla extract into a mixing bowl large enough to hold all the ingredients. Mix thoroughly with a wire whisk or wooden spoon. Whisk in the melted chocolate mixture. Sift the flour, cocoa and salt into the bowl and mix thoroughly. Stir in the nuts, then transfer the mixture to the prepared tin and spread evenly. Bang the tin on a work surface to expel any air bubbles.

Bake in the heated oven for about 25 minutes, until a skewer inserted into the centre of the mixture comes out with moist crumbs – the mixture will continue cooking after it comes out of the oven and it's vital not to overcook it. Note that the mixture will puff up in the oven but sink on cooling.

Stand the tin on a wire cooling rack and leave to cool completely before cutting into squares. Dust with icing sugar just before serving.

Store in an airtight container and eat within a week.

Jonathan's Meringues with a Whisky Cream

MAKES ABOUT 36 PAIRS OF MERINGUES

This is a lovely idea for a party treat; the meringues can be made well in advance, then sandwiched with the whipped whisky cream mixture shortly before serving. For the best flavour, use a really good-quality dark chocolate with 70% cocoa solids plus a single malt whisky.

FOR THE MERINGUE MIXTURE:
3 medium free-range egg whites, at room temperature
200g caster sugar

FOR THE FILLING:
200ml double cream, well chilled
1 tablespoon whisky
40g icing sugar

TO DECORATE:
200g good-quality dark chocolate, chopped or broken up
a couple of good pinches of ground ginger

a piping bag fitted with a 2cm plain tube
baking trays lined with greaseproof paper

Heat the oven to 110°C/225°F/gas ¼.

Put the egg whites into a spotlessly clean and grease-free mixing bowl or the bowl of a large food mixer (it's a good idea to rub the inside of the bowl with a cut lemon). Using an electric whisk or mixer, whisk the egg whites until they form soft peaks. Gradually add the sugar, a large spoonful at a time, whisking for about a minute after each addition to make a very stiff and glossy meringue. Transfer the meringue mixture to a piping bag fitted with a plain tube and pipe small meringues (about 3cm across and 2.5cm high) on to the lined trays.

Bake in the heated oven for about 1 hour, until firm and dry but not coloured. Remove and leave to cool.

Put the broken-up chocolate into a heatproof bowl and set over a pan of steaming water. Leave to melt gently, stirring frequently, until smooth. Remove the bowl from the pan and stir in the ginger.

To assemble, put the cream, whisky and icing sugar into a mixing bowl or the bowl of a food mixer and whisk until firm. Use the cream to sandwich the meringues in pairs and drizzle over the melted chocolate mixture. Keep cool until ready to serve. Best eaten the same day.

Hopetoun Delight

MAKES 6

This traditional recipe, a twist on cranachan, or cream crowdie, comes from Hopetoun House, Edinburgh, home of the Marquess of Linlithgow. Here, the shortbread is baked into cup shapes, filled just before serving with the toasted oatmeal, whisky and cream mixture and finally topped with locally grown raspberries. A fine treat!

FOR THE SHORTBREAD CUPS:	FOR THE FILLING:
100g unsalted butter, at room temperature	225ml double cream
50g caster sugar	40g medium oatmeal
130g plain flour	30g caster sugar or vanilla sugar
20g ground rice	2 tablespoons whisky
	200g fresh raspberries
	a bun tin or mince pie tray, or tartlet tins, preferably non-stick but greased with butter, if not

To make the shortbread, beat the soft butter with the sugar, using a wooden spoon or electric whisk, until pale and fluffy. Sift the flour and ground rice on to the creamed mixture and gradually work in, using a wooden spoon at first, then your hands, to make a firm dough. Divide the mixture into 6 and shape each piece into a ball. Put each ball into a hole in the bun or mince pie tray and gently press out, using your thumbs, to line the hole and make a cup shape. Neaten the rims and prick the bases with a fork. Chill for 20 minutes. Meanwhile, heat the oven to 170°C/325°F/gas 3.

Bake the shortbread cups for 20 to 25 minutes, until a pale gold colour around the edges. Halfway through the cooking time, remove the tray from the oven, gently press down the centre of each shortbread cup using the back of a teaspoon – they will have risen very slightly. Then return the tray to the oven for the rest of the cooking time.

Leave to cool for 5 minutes, until firm enough to handle, then carefully turn out and leave to cool completely on a wire rack.

To make the filling, whip the cream in a bowl until it forms stiff peaks. Cover and chill for 30 minutes. Meanwhile, put the oatmeal and sugar into a non-stick frying pan, set over a low heat, and stir until the oatmeal is lightly coloured and the sugar just starts to melt – about 5 minutes. Tip on to a plate and leave to cool.

To assemble, gently stir the cooled oatmeal and the whisky into the whipped cream. Set the shortbread cups on individual serving plates and spoon in the cream mixture. Top with the raspberries and serve immediately.

Sticky Nutty Flapjacks

CUTS INTO 12

The golden syrup in these makes them such a treat. The recipe is old and basic – just porridge oats (the jumbo ones are good here), butter, muscovado sugar and syrup, mixed in a pan – and the nuts can be left out or replaced with raisins, chopped dried apricots or even chocolate chips.

150g unsalted butter
125g light brown muscovado sugar
2 tablespoons golden syrup
200g jumbo porridge oats
a good pinch of salt

75g unsalted mixed nuts (almonds, Brazils, hazelnuts, pistachios and cashews), roughly chopped

a 20cm square tin, greased with butter

Heat the oven to 150°C/300°F/gas 2.

Put the butter, sugar and golden syrup into a pan large enough to hold all the ingredients. Heat gently, stirring from time to time, until the butter has melted. Remove the pan from the heat and stir in the oats and salt. Add the roughly chopped nuts. When the ingredients are thoroughly combined, transfer the mixture to the prepared tin and spread it out evenly. Use the back of a spoon to gently press down the mixture.

Bake in the heated oven for 25 to 30 minutes, until golden brown. Remove from the oven and leave to cool for 10 minutes.

Run a round-bladed knife around the inside of the tin to loosen the flapjack, then score into 12. Leave to cool before cutting into bars.

Store in an airtight container.

Grasmere Gingerbread

CUTS INTO 12

Grasmere, in the Lake District, has been associated with gingerbread, or ginger shortbread (there are many versions) since the mid-eighteenth century. It is thought that the recipe arrived with the Jamaican sugars, spices and slaves that came through the nearby port of Whitehaven, and was passed on to local servants. Sarah Nelson, who worked as a domestic servant, established her now famous Grasmere Gingerbread Shop in the former village schoolroom. Her 1854 recipe, a crunchy, chewy, spicy cross between a flapjack and shortbread, is kept in a bank vault – you have to visit Grasmere to enjoy it.

125g light brown plain flour
125g oatmeal
125g light brown muscovado sugar
1 teaspoon ground ginger
½ teaspoon baking powder

150g unsalted butter, chilled and diced
25g (1 large piece) stem ginger, drained and finely chopped

a 20cm square tin, well greased with butter

Heat the oven to 180°C/350°F/gas 4.

Put the flour, oatmeal, sugar, ground ginger and baking powder into a food processor. Pulse a few times until the ingredients are just combined, then add the diced butter. Run the machine just until the mixture looks like fine sand – don't overwork the ingredients and let them form a dough. Remove 4 tablespoons of the sandy crumbs and set aside, then add the diced stem ginger to the bowl. Run the machine very briefly until the ingredients are mixed, then tip into the prepared tin. Press into an even layer with the back of a spoon and sprinkle the reserved sandy crumbs on top.

Bake in the heated oven for about 25 minutes, until lightly golden.

Remove from the oven and carefully run a round-bladed knife around the inside of the tin to loosen, then gently cut into squares or rectangles. Leave to cool completely before removing from the tin.

Store in an air-tight container.

Chocolate Banana Bread

MAKES 1 MEDIUM LOAF CAKE – CUTS INTO 12

Homely and a delicious treat, banana bread is simple to make – a good recipe to do with children. Use really ripe bananas, not too finely mashed, plus some good dark chocolate chopped into thumbnail-sized chunks. Eat plain the same day, or the next day with cream cheese, butter or, if you're feeling really decadent, chocolate spread.

250g self-raising flour	250g peeled ripe bananas – about 2 large or 3 medium
a good pinch of salt	
150g caster sugar	75g dark chocolate, chopped
100g unsalted butter, melted and cooled	100g walnut pieces
2 medium free-range eggs, beaten	a 900g loaf tin, about 26 x 12.5 x 7.5cm, greased with butter and the base lined with greaseproof paper

Preheat the oven to 180°C/350°F/gas 4.

Mix the flour with the salt and sugar in a mixing bowl. Add the melted, cooled butter and the beaten eggs. Roughly mash the bananas with a fork – there should still be some lumpy bits – and add to the bowl. Add the chocolate and walnut pieces and mix all the ingredients together with a wooden spoon until thoroughly combined.

Transfer the mixture to the prepared tin and spread evenly. Bake in the preheated oven for 55 minutes, until the loaf is a good golden brown and a cocktail stick inserted into the centre comes out clean.

Leave to cool for 5 minutes, then turn out on to a wire rack and leave to cool before slicing. Store in an airtight container.

Jewish Honey Cake

Otherwise known as *lekach*, these are traditionally baked for Rosh Hashanah, the Jewish New Year. There is no one definitive recipe, as different communities have their own traditions. However, this moist, well-flavoured cake is always based on honey, for the hope that the New Year will be sweet. Nuts – chopped walnuts, slivered almonds, pistachios or pine nuts – add texture, and apples – diced, grated, as juice or purée – are often considered essential (apples are dipped in honey at this autumn festival). Here, the flavouring is strong coffee, but other bakers use rum or brandy and/or lemon and orange zest. It is vital to bake this cake several days in advance, since the flavours develop as it matures.

275g plain flour
1 teaspoon ground cinnamon
1 teaspoon ground ginger
1 teaspoon ground mixed spice
1 teaspoon baking powder
½ teaspoon bicarbonate of soda
2 medium free-range eggs, at room temperature
150g dark muscovado sugar

250g runny honey
125ml good-quality vegetable or sunflower oil
125ml hot coffee (made with 2 tablespoons instant coffee dissolved in boiling water)
100g walnut pieces

a 900g loaf tin, about 26 x 12.5 x 7.5cm, greased with butter and lined with greaseproof paper

Preheat the oven to 180°C/350°F/gas 4.

Remove a tablespoon of the weighed flour and set aside. Sift the rest of the flour into a bowl with the cinnamon, ginger, mixed spice, baking powder and bicarbonate of soda.

In another bowl, large enough to hold all the ingredients, whisk the eggs with the sugar until well blended. Whisk in the honey, followed by the oil and then the coffee. Gradually whisk in the flour to make a thick, smooth batter. Toss the chopped nuts in the reserved flour then stir into the cake mixture. Pour into the prepared tin and bake in the preheated oven for about 1 hour, or until a cocktail stick inserted into the centre comes out clean.

Leave to cool in the tin for 15 minutes, then carefully remove and cool completely on a wire rack. Wrap in foil and keep for at least 3 days (some bakers insist on a week) before cutting.

Apple Scone Round

CUTS INTO 8

Made with Bramley apple, this old-fashioned scone round is at its best served warm with a piece of Wensleydale cheese. Clotted cream comes a close second, though.

225g self-raising flour
a good pinch of salt
½ teaspoon bicarbonate of soda
½ teaspoon ground cinnamon
60g unsalted butter, chilled and diced

60g demerara sugar, plus extra for sprinkling
1 large Bramley cooking apple
(or tart dessert apple), weighing 250–275g
about 150ml full fat creamy milk

a baking tray, greased with butter

Preheat the oven to 220°C/425°F/gas 7.

Sift the flour, salt, bicarbonate of soda and cinnamon into a mixing bowl. Add the diced butter and rub into the flour, using the tips of your fingers. (Lifting your hands up to the rim of the bowl so that the flour falls back down will give the scones a lighter texture.) When the mixture resembles fine crumbs, stir in the sugar.

Peel, core and dice the apple and add to the bowl. Add about 125ml of the milk and mix in using a round-bladed knife, gradually working in more milk, a teaspoon at a time, to make a soft but not sticky dough (how much milk is needed will depend upon the juiciness of the apple). Using floured hands, lightly shape the dough into a ball and place on the prepared baking tray. Gently pat out to a round about 20cm across. Brush with any remaining milk, then sprinkle with demerara sugar. Using a sharp knife, score the round into 8 wedges but do not pull them apart or move them.

Bake in the preheated oven for about 15 minutes, until a good golden brown.

Leave to cool on the baking tray for 5 minutes, then cut into wedges and eat warm.

Scone Palace, home of the Stone of Destiny, where the kings of Scotland were crowned and whose name, some say, may be linked to the earliest forms of scone.

Scones

Warm floury scones, split in half and spread with good raspberry or strawberry jam and thick clotted cream, are at the centre of a traditional West Country cream tea. Buttermilk, the slightly tart liquid whey left after milk is churned to make butter, adds extra lift and flavour. There's much discussion over which way round to layer the cream and jam. Traditionally, a Devon cream tea sees the jam spread on top of the cream, whereas a Cornish scone is spread with butter, then jam and finally topped with the cream.

250g self-raising flour	about 100ml buttermilk
a good pinch of salt	or milk (not fat-free)
50g caster sugar	*a 6cm round cutter*
50g unsalted butter, chilled and diced	*a baking tray, greased with butter*
1 medium free-range egg	

Preheat the oven to 220°C/425°F/gas 7.

To make the dough in a food processor, put the flour, salt and sugar into the bowl and pulse briefly to just combine. Add the butter to the bowl and process until the mixture looks like fine crumbs. Beat the egg with 100ml of buttermilk or milk. With the machine running, pour the egg mixture into the processor, stopping the machine as soon as the mixture comes together to make a ball of slightly soft dough. If there are dry crumbs, add a little extra milk.

To make the dough by hand, sift the flour, salt and sugar into a mixing bowl. Add the butter and rub into the flour using the tips of your fingers. For a light texture raise your hands just above the rim of the bowl so that the mixture falls back through your fingers. When the mixture looks like fine crumbs, beat the egg with 100ml of buttermilk or milk and stir in using a round-bladed knife. Use your hands to bring the mixture together to make a ball of slightly soft dough. If there are dry crumbs in the bottom of the bowl, work in a little more liquid.

Turn the dough out on to a lightly floured work surface and knead gently for a couple of seconds, just to bring it together. Flour your hands, then pat out the dough about 3cm thick and stamp out rounds with the cutter. Press the trimmings together, pat out and cut more rounds.

Set the rounds slightly apart on the prepared baking tray and bake in the preheated oven for 10 to 12 minutes, until a good golden brown. Transfer to a wire rack and leave to cool slightly. The scones are best eaten while still warm, though any left over are good split, toasted and spread with butter.

SOME OTHER IDEAS

For sultana scones (see picture opposite), make the dough, then gently work in 50g of sultanas before cutting into rounds. For blueberry scones, make the dough, then gently work in 75g of fresh blueberries and the finely grated zest of ½ a lemon before cutting into rounds.

Welsh Cakes

MAKES 15

These lovely little warm snacks are baked on top of the stove or fire, on a bakestone or heavy griddle, rather than in the oven. They can be made, cooked and eaten within moments. Some people like to split them and fill them with jam when they're hot off the griddle, but they are perfect just dusted with sugar.

225g self-raising flour
a pinch of salt
100g unsalted butter, chilled and diced
75g caster sugar, plus extra for sprinkling
25g currants or sultanas (or a mix)

1 medium free-range egg yolk, mixed with 3 tablespoons milk

a 6cm round cutter
a griddle or heavy-based frying pan,

Sift the flour and salt into a mixing bowl. Add the butter and rub in using the tips of your fingers until the mixture looks like fine crumbs. Stir in the sugar and fruit. Add the egg yolk and milk and stir the ingredients together using a round-bladed knife, to make a soft but not sticky dough. If the dough is dry and won't come together, add a little more milk.

Turn the dough out on to a lightly floured work surface and roll out about 1cm thick. Cut into rounds using the cutter, re-rolling the trimmings as necessary.

Heat the griddle or frying pan – grease it very lightly only if necessary, as the Welsh cakes should not be 'fried'. Cook the cakes in batches, until puffed up, a good golden brown and just firm on each side, adjusting the heat so they cook evenly. Allow about 2 minutes on each side. Remove from the pan, dust with sugar and eat straight away.

Pitcaithly Bannock

CUTS INTO 12

Originally, the bannock was a flattish round cake of dough made from oatmeal or barley flour, cooked on a griddle over an open fire, or in a pan among the embers. Later came the Selkirk bannock, much loved by Queen Victoria, a flat, round, dinner-plate-sized bread made from a yeast dough enriched with butter and lard (not unlike lardy cake), mixed dried fruit and peel. Pitcaithly, a beauty spot in Perthshire, was popular with tourists and tea rooms were built to accommodate their visits. It soon became known for its own style of bannock. It is a round, rich shortbread, flavoured with chopped almonds and candied mixed lemon and orange peel.

100g very soft unsalted butter
50g caster sugar, plus extra for sprinkling
200g plain flour
25g blanched almonds, finely chopped

25g mixed peel, very finely chopped
extra split almonds, to decorate (optional)

a baking tray, greased with butter

Preheat the oven to 170°C/325°F/gas 3.

Put the butter and sugar into a mixing bowl and work them together with your hands until thoroughly combined and very creamy. Sift the flour into the bowl and mix in, still using your hand. When thoroughly combined, but not yet formed into a dough, work in the chopped nuts and peel. Press and knead the mixture until it comes together – don't worry if it seems quite crumbly.

Tip the dough out on to the prepared tray and firmly press it into a round about 20cm across. Make sure it is of even thickness, and squeeze and press together any cracks or loose crumbs. Prick well with a fork, decorate with the split almonds, if you are using them, and score into 12 segments with a sharp knife.

Bake in the preheated oven until firm and barely coloured – about 35 minutes. Remove the tray from the oven, sprinkle with a little sugar, then gently cut along the scored lines. Leave to cool completely before removing from the tray. Store in an airtight container.

Wheaten Biscuits for Cheese

MAKES 14

These crisp and slightly crumbly biscuits are made with light brown flour, which has the flavour but not the heaviness of 100% wholemeal, plus a little oatmeal and some poppy seeds. Perfect with cheese!

175g light brown plain flour
4 tablespoons medium oatmeal
1 teaspoon baking powder
½ teaspoon sea salt flakes
2 tablespoons caster sugar
2 teaspoons poppy seeds

100g unsalted butter, chilled and diced
3 tablespoons milk

a 7cm round cutter
2 baking trays, greased with butter

Preheat the oven to 200°C/400°F/gas 6.

Put the flour, oatmeal, baking powder, salt, sugar and poppy seeds into the bowl of a food processor. Pulse a few times to combine the ingredients. Add the butter and run the machine until the mixture looks like coarse sand. Add the milk and run the machine again until the mixture comes together into a ball of soft but not sticky dough.

Turn the dough out on to a lightly floured work surface and roll out about 5mm thick. Cut into rounds, using the cutter, and arrange on the prepared baking trays, setting them slightly apart.

Bake in the preheated oven for 10 to 12 minutes, until the edges of the biscuits turn a light brown. Remove the trays from the oven and leave the biscuits to cool for a couple of minutes before transferring to a wire rack to cool completely. Store in an airtight container.

Cheddars

MAKES 50

Rich with mature cheese and warm with red chilli, these little savoury biscuits are great served with drinks or eaten with tomato soup. The mixture becomes very difficult to handle because it is so dense, so it is best made in a food processor.

200g plain flour
½ teaspoon sea salt flakes
½ teaspoon dried red chilli flakes, or to taste
150g extra mature Cheddar cheese, grated
150g unsalted butter, chilled and diced

1 whole medium free-range egg, plus 1 egg yolk

3 baking trays, greased with butter and lined with greaseproof paper

Put the flour, salt, chilli flakes and cheese into the bowl of a food processor and pulse a few times until just combined. Add the diced butter and run the machine until the ingredients look like coarse sand. Add the whole egg and the yolk and run the machine again until the ingredients come together to make a firm dough.

Turn out on to a lightly floured work surface and form into a log shape with your hands. Bang the roll down on to the work surface a few times to eliminate any pockets of air. With your hands, roll the dough until it forms an even cylinder 50cm long. Cut into 3, then wrap in greaseproof paper and chill for 30 minutes. The dough can be kept, well wrapped, in the fridge for 3 days or frozen for up to a month.

When ready to bake, heat the oven to 200°C/400°F/gas 6.

Cut the dough into slices 1cm thick and arrange slightly apart on the prepared baking trays. Bake in the heated oven for 10 to 12 minutes, until lightly golden. Remove the trays from the oven and leave to cool for a couple of minutes before transferring to a wire rack to cool completely. Store in an airtight container.

Oatcakes

Not so long ago, a sack of oatmeal was part of the wages for many farm workers, keepers and crofters in Scotland, wheat flour being an expensive treat. Oatmeal formed the basis for most meals, from porridge to skirlie, puddings to coating fish. Oatcakes were eaten for breakfast with a bowl of broth or spread with marmalade; today they are popular for health reasons and are eaten with raspberry jam or honey at teatime or to accompany soft cheeses.

The recipe may seem simple but it does need practice to learn the knack, for the mixture is likely to crumble as you roll it out and crack in the oven. Here, the lightness comes from the steam produced during baking, and the flavour and shortness come from the fat – dripping, bacon fat and lard are traditional, though now butter is often used.

225g medium oatmeal
½ teaspoon sea salt flakes
a good pinch of baking powder (optional)
25g dripping, bacon fat, lard or butter, melted

85–125ml boiling water
extra oatmeal, for rolling out

a 6.5cm round cutter
a baking tray, greased with butter

Heat the oven to 180°C/350°F/gas 4.

Combine the oatmeal, salt and baking powder, if using, in a mixing bowl. Stir in the melted fat with a round-bladed knife. Work in enough boiling water to bind the mixture together – it should not be too sticky (though it will firm up as you work it) and neither should it be dry or crumbly. Gently knead the dough in the bowl for about 30 seconds – you may need to work in more water if it falls apart.

Lightly dust a work surface with oatmeal and roll out the dough about 0.5cm thick. Cut into rounds using the cutter and place on the prepared baking tray. Gather up the trimmings into a ball (you may need to add a bit more water to bring it together again), then roll out and cut more rounds.

Bake in the heated oven for about 20 minutes, until firm and crisp.

Leave the oatcakes to cool before lifting them off the tray.

Store in an airtight container.

WHEAT HEART BRAND

Bread

FINEST QUALITY SINCE 1843

Our daily bread, the 'staff of life' . . . Since biblical times,

bread has been one of the world's most fundamental foods, and nowhere more so than in Britain, where most of us eat it every day, toasted and spread with butter and marmalade for breakfast – the British are famous as lovers of buttered toast – or filled with everything from cheese to Caesar salad for a lunchtime sandwich. We have taken to heart the aristocratic snack apparently 'invented' by the 4th Earl of Sandwich as a way of continuing his card game without having to stop to eat. So heavily have we always relied on bread that we even use the word as slang for money, and we work to 'make some dough' or 'earn a crust'.

We may eat less bread than we did fifty years ago, but we revel in a greater diversity. No longer is the British bread basket confined to traditional loaves, for in bakeries, farmers' markets and supermarkets a cornucopia of styles are on offer, from Italian focaccia to Indian naan and Irish soda bread. Bagels are as popular in London as New York, while breads are flavoured with seeds, nuts, olives, herbs, spices and fruit, and made with every kind of flour, from spelt to rye, reflecting not only a surge of interest in food from around the world, but mirroring our multicultural society and the fact that wherever people have settled they have brought their native breads with them.

Of course, the loaf as we know it today bears little resemblance to the first flatbreads, little more than whole grain mixed with water and baked on a stone – hard and pretty unpalatable by today's standards. Ever since we began baking bread, we have been looking for ways to make it lighter and easier to eat. Probably by accident, the earliest bread-makers discovered that the natural fermentation of wild yeasts that exist all around us could help their dough to puff up. Over time, bakers developed their own 'leavens', 'cultures' or 'starters' by mixing warm water with bread flour and leaving it in a warm place so that it would start to ferment. If they added honey or fruit, this would feed the wild yeasts and boost the process. They could then mix this with more flour and water and let it rise and ferment some more before baking. This process produces what we now call sourdough bread, once the only kind of bread we could make and now one of the most fashionable.

The Romans in Britain were skilled bakers who used barm, the wild yeasts that form during the making of beer, in their bread-making (developing a relationship between bread and brewing that has traditionally been a strong characteristic of British and northern European breads). They transformed Kent, in particular, into prime wheat-growing country, and formed the first guilds, attempting to set minimum weights and maximum prices for loaves.

Such early bread-makers would have been unable to explain the miracles performed by yeast and gluten. It was only in the nineteenth century that the science of bread-making began to be properly understood and commercial yeasts developed. The Anglo-Saxons, being hunters rather than farmers, were so terrified of the wheat they saw magically appearing from the ground and being made into dough that seemed to come alive that they cast spells at every stage of bread-making.

As with all British foods, over the centuries regional breads grew up around the country, involving knots, plaits and crusty round cobs, and local names from Chelsea buns to Kentish Huffkins, the staple diet of the Kentish hop-pickers. In Ireland, with the advent of sodium bicarbonate, a raising agent which in Britain was used mainly for cakes, the culture of soda bread grew up: bread made using the softer local flours, together with buttermilk and baking soda.

Before the industrial revolution, most breads in Britain were still made with whole grain, roughly crushed using grindstones in small mills powered by wind or water, so that although the dough rose up, its texture was still heavy and dense. However, it had also been discovered that if you sieved out the coarser part of the bran, a new whiter, softer loaf could be made, and 'white' bread became the fashionable loaf to be seen eating. Of course, it was expensive to make, so only relatively affluent folk could afford it. What colour bread you ate defined your place in society. This is evident as far back as the thirteenth century. At that time, bakers' guilds, in another attempt to build on the Roman idea of standardizing weights and prices, issued the Assize of Bread; however, the difficulty of comparing the heavy 'wheaten' loaf the masses ate with the softer white loaf that the rich could afford eventually led to the foundation of separate 'brown' and 'white' bakers' guilds.

All this changed with the industrial revolution, when for the first time bakers began making bread on a large scale. In order to give more people the white bread they craved at a price they could afford, they often adulterated it with the likes of chalk or alum, which whitened the dough.

In the 1870s, Britain also began importing high-protein wheat grown in Canada which was cheaper and stronger than the native strains of wheat that often suffered from our damp, misty island climate and rarely contained enough protein to develop the elasticity in the gluten needed to make a springy loaf. This, combined with mechanical mixers, large-scale bread ovens, commercial yeasts and a new way of milling, using big rollers rather than stones so that the grains separated more easily into bran and flour, meant that light, white bread was now available to everyone. The wheat germ, which we now consider so valuable, was discarded as fodder for animals. Towards the end of the nineteenth century, against the fashionable tide, a few pioneers such as Richard 'Stoney' Smith, who began baking Hovis bread, and Dr Thomas Allinson, believing that the germ was nutritionally important, began putting it back into bread. They created a niche product focusing on roughage as much as flavour – again aimed at wealthy but nutritionally concerned sectors of society.

During the Second World War, due to shortages of imported grain, the government was forced to galvanize British farmers into growing more wheat again, and it was after the war that the biggest sea change in British baking occurred. Once rationing finished, Britain was again clamouring for soft white bread, so in the late fifties the British Baking Industries Research Association at Chorleywood in Hertfordshire began investigating ways to help the British baker make the best use of home-grown wheat. In 1961 they came up with the 'Chorleywood Process', which replaced the traditional long, slow fermentation process of bread-making with a new, all-singing-and-dancing 'no-time dough' which could be whizzed up by high-speed industrial mixers. They could use lower-protein flour and, thanks to the addition of a cocktail of fats, 'improvers', emulsifiers, 'conditioners' (and latterly enzymes), produce masses of loaves that were not only voluminous and cheap but also kept the appearance of freshness for a long time. Shelves and shelves of soft white loaves, pre-sliced and wrapped in plastic bags, were celebrated in iconic TV ads with catchy jingles. How exciting it all must have seemed; what a welcome luxury, after years of wartime deprivation.

Half a century later, however, we are querying the equation of speed and quality, and a groundswell of campaigning artisan bakers, food writers and high-profile chefs and restaurateurs argue that it is time to return to old-fashioned, slower traditions of bread-making, in which time and patience are the real key. Time and patience to let the natural chemistry of the baking process work its miracle as the dough ferments slowly, developing flavour and texture.

And with the renaissance of the small artisan baker we are seeing a resurgence in traditional methods: a return to stone milling, crushing the grains more gently and slowly, to produce more characterful flours that haven't been stripped of the nutritious germ. There are now several commercially worked windmills and watermills around the country producing breads by the old traditional methods.

Above all, a new, committed community of millers, bakers and campaigners is encouraging us all to take up home baking again, to rediscover the real pleasure of working with a living, changing and continually surprising dough, making not only loaves but all the spin-off buns and tea breads that will bring a smile to your family's faces. It might sound like a cliché, but there really is little to beat the comforting smell of home-made bread baking in the oven – not least because when you bake your own bread, you know exactly what goes into it.

BREAD

SARRE

FLOUR MILL
QUALITY STONEGROUND FLOUR

Produced in a genuine Kent Windmill

SARRE
MILL
BUILT
1820

Kent is historically Britain's first and finest wheat-growing county and was once the source of flour for the bread that fed the Romans. The windmill at Sarre is one of the few remaining commercial windmills left in the country.

ABOUT FLOUR: Bags of flour are usually ground from wheat unless otherwise labelled; good ranges of flours from other grains are now available from larger supermarkets and whole-food stores.

- *Stoneground flour* means that the cereal grains (wheat, rye, oats, etc.) are milled between two large stones instead of the steel rollers used for mass-produced flours. Stoneground flour has a different texture and often a fuller flavour.

- *Wheat flours* are our staple cereal. They are defined by their rate of extraction – how much of the whole cleaned wheat grain or kernel is used to make the flour. White flour usually contains about 75% of the kernel and has most of the bran and wheat germ removed. Wholemeal flour has 100% extraction, which means the complete wheat kernel is ground. The high proportion of bran in the flour – those coarse golden specks – means that the loaf will rise less well than one made with all white flour, as the bran hinders the gluten, but the flavour and health benefits will be greater.

Wheat flour for bread-making is labelled as bread flour or strong flour, as it contains flour milled from wheat with a higher proportion of protein to starch than the flour used for pastry and cakes. As the dough is kneaded, the protein develops into strands of gluten, which help the dough to rise by expanding around the carbon dioxide gases produced by the yeast. Some flours are labelled as being extra strong or very strong, and these are usually made from 100% Canadian wheat; they are excellent for making most loaves but not so good for many European breads like baguettes, ciabattas, croissants and brioches.

- *Barley flour* was a staple in Scotland and northern England long before wheat was grown there. The flour is low in gluten, so the loaves tend to be dense, but a little added to a dough made with wheat or rye flour adds flavour.

- *Oat flour* is not as widely available as oatmeal, oatflakes or porridge oats, but can be quickly made from oatflakes in a food processor. Mixed with wheat flour, it makes a well-textured, tasty loaf.

- *Rye flour* used to be a staple in places where the soil was too poor or too cold for wheat to thrive – mainly northern, eastern and central Europe – but it is now popular for its deep flavour and dark, chewy crumb, and it works best when used in a sourdough mixture. It has a low gluten content, which makes it harder to work than wheat flours, but some people find it easier to digest.

- *Spelt flour* has been grown throughout Europe for centuries. It comes from the same family as common wheat but has a slightly different genetic make-up, so it is more nutritious and higher in protein. It is popular with organic farmers looking for disease-resistant crops, and makes a really good, well-flavoured loaf.

Some wheat flours have malted wheat grains added to give a sweeter taste and slightly crunchy texture, and some millers now sell blends of flour as well as speciality flours for making pizzas, ciabatta, baguettes and gluten-free breads.

Store flour in a cool, dry spot and check the use-by date, especially with wholemeal flours and flours with added grains. Don't use flour that smells slightly rancid or has developed weevils or small mites.

Yeast is the living organism that makes bread rise. It requires moisture, gentle warmth and flour or sugar to stimulate its growth. As it grows, it produces a gas, carbon dioxide, which pushes up and expands the dough.

The recipes in this chapter use dried powdered yeast, sold as easy-blend, easy-bake or instant dried yeast, in 7g sachets. The powder must be added to the flour and the dry ingredients (never added to the liquid) and thoroughly combined.

Fresh yeast, sold at wholefood stores and the bakery counters of larger supermarkets with in-store bakeries, feels a bit like clay; it is greyish brown with a distinct aroma. It can be stored, tightly wrapped and in a sealed plastic box in the fridge, for a good week. If the yeast becomes stale, dark brown or a dry, powdery grey, throw it away – it will be useless.

Use 15g of fresh yeast instead of a 7g sachet of dried yeast. Crumble the yeast between your fingers into a small bowl, cream to a smooth liquid with about 7 tablespoons of your measured liquid (water or milk), then work in a little of the measured flour and leave for about 15 minutes. When the mixture is frothy and bubbly, it is ready to use – just add it to the flour and dry ingredients with the rest of the lukewarm liquid. If the mixture doesn't look frothy, your yeast may not be in good health and you need to replace it.

The temperature of the liquid you use to make the dough is crucial to its success; too hot and the yeast will be killed, too cool and its growth will be slowed right down.

The ideal temperature is about 38°C or 98.6°F – it should feel very comfortable if you dip your finger in it. Some recipes want the yeast to grow at a fairly slow rate and state cold water in the ingredients list, or say the dough should be left to rise in the fridge overnight.

Sourdoughs are breads usually made with a 'starter' rather than fresh or dried yeast. A starter is made from a mixture of flour and water left to ferment at room temperature for three to four days. The batter absorbs natural yeasts from the air, as well as 'good' bacteria that develop the flavour. Starters need to feed and be nurtured, but once vigorous they can be added to the flour, salt and water mixture instead of (or as well as) commercial yeasts.

Thorough kneading is vital to success. It ensures that the yeast is evenly distributed so the dough rises evenly. But its main function is to develop the gluten in the flour – the stronger the flour (that is, the more protein it contains – this is stated on the pack), the more gluten there is and the more the dough is able to rise. Kneading works on the gluten so that it stretches as the yeast produces bubbles of carbon dioxide, then sets in the oven – rather like scaffolding supports a building.

---

if you have a large free-standing electric mixer with a dough hook, make good use of it. You will need to reduce the kneading time – 4 to 5 minutes is best – and use the lowest possible speed. Don't overwork the dough or use a food processor, or you may have a loaf with large holes or one that collapses in the oven. Under-kneading the dough may result in a soggy, flat or dense loaf.

HOW TO KNEAD: Gather the dough mixture into a ball. If necessary, work in a little extra flour if the dough is sticky, or a little more liquid if there are dry crumbs. Set the timer for 10 minutes. First stretch the dough away from you by holding one end down with your hand and using the other hand to pull and stretch out the dough as if it were an elastic band. Gather the dough back into a ball. Give the ball a quarter-turn, then keep repeating these three movements. As the dough is kneaded in this way, it gradually changes in texture and appearance and will start to feel and look smooth, glossy and very pliable. Shape the dough into a neat ball and leave to rise as instructed in the recipe.

HOW TO SHAPE AND MAKE AN OVAL LOAF: Punch down the risen dough to deflate it, then gently knead on a lightly floured work surface to redistribute the gas bubbles. Form into an oval, then make a good crease in the dough lengthways along the centre of the oval using the edge of your hand. Roll the dough over to make a sausage shape (crease in the centre), then roll the dough on to the prepared baking tray so that the seam is underneath, the top is smooth and the loaf is evenly shaped. Slash the top with a sharp knife, then cover and leave to rise as instructed in the recipe before baking.

HOW TO MAKE A TIN LOAF: Punch down the dough, turn out, gently knead, then pat out the dough to a rectangle the length of your tin. Roll up the dough from one short end, like a Swiss roll, pinch the seam together with your fingers, then put the dough into the tin, seam side down and with the ends tucked underneath. The tin should be half-filled. Slash the dough lengthways along the centre with a sharp knife, then cover and leave to rise before baking.

HOW TO MAKE A ROUND LOAF: Punch down the dough, then gently knead it into a ball shape. Roll the ball around under your cupped hand until smooth and neatly shaped. Set on the prepared baking tray. Snip the top with kitchen scissors or score with a sharp knife, then cover and leave to rise before baking.

A Plain White Loaf of Bread

MAKES 1 LARGE LOAF OR 2 MEDIUM LOAVES

This is how to make an excellent loaf with plenty of flavour and a soft crumb that's popular with all the family and is as good for sandwiches as it is for toast. It also freezes well. The method is simple and the dough can be used to make a tin-shaped loaf or a round or oval loaf or rolls. You can experiment by replacing some of the white flour with wholemeal flour, rye flour or flour with added malted grains, as well as seeds, nuts and dried fruit.

675g strong white bread flour	about 425ml lukewarm water
1½ teaspoons salt	*a 900g loaf tin, about 26 x 12.5 x 7.5cm*
1 x 7g sachet of easy-blend/	*or 2 x 450g tins, about 19 x 12.5 x 7.5cm*
easy-bake dried yeast	*or a large baking tray, greased with butter*

Combine the flour, salt and yeast in a large mixing bowl or the bowl of a food mixer. Make a well in the centre and add the lukewarm water. Using your hand or the dough hook attachment of the mixer, mix the flour into the water to make a soft but not sticky dough – if there are dry crumbs and the dough feels stiff and dry, work in a little more lukewarm water; if it is very sticky and sticks to your fingers, add a little more flour.

Turn the dough out on to a lightly floured work surface and knead thoroughly for 10 minutes, or knead it for 4 minutes in the mixer using the dough hook on the lowest possible speed. Return the dough to the bowl, cover with a damp tea towel or a snap-on lid and leave to rise until doubled in size – this will take about 1 hour in a warm place, 2 hours at normal room temperature, or 3 hours in a cool larder.

Punch down the dough to deflate, and turn it out on to the lightly floured work surface. To make 2 medium loaves, divide the dough into 2 equal pieces and pat each into a rectangle roughly the length of the loaf tin. Roll up the dough from one short end like a Swiss roll, then tuck the ends under and set the loaf in the tin seam side down (see page 95). Repeat for the other piece of dough. Slip the tins into a large plastic bag and slightly inflate so that the plastic doesn't stick to the dough, or cover lightly with a damp tea towel. Leave to rise as before until doubled in size – about 1 hour at normal room temperature. Don't let the dough over-rise and become too big or it may collapse in the oven. The dough can also be shaped into one large loaf to fit the larger tin or into a neat ball or oval shape, set on a well-greased baking tray and left to rise in the same way.

Towards the end of the rising time, heat the oven to 230°C/450°F/gas 8. Uncover the loaf and sprinkle a little flour on top; alternatively brush it with a little milk or beaten egg and sprinkle with seeds (poppy, sesame, sunflower, pumpkin, cumin, caraway, linseeds), cracked wheat, rye, oat or wheat flakes. Using a sharp knife, make a deep slash along the length of the loaf. Bake for 15 minutes, then lower the oven temperature to 200°C/400°F/gas 6 and bake for 15 to 20 minutes longer (20 to 30 minutes if you're making one larger loaf), or until the top is a good golden brown and the turned-out loaf sounds hollow when tapped underneath. If there is a dull thud, return the loaf to the oven, straight on the oven shelf without the tin, for another 5 minutes and test again. Leave to cool on a wire rack.

Cottage Loaf

This attractive loaf, which is actually one smaller loaf on top of another, used to be hugely popular in England. Its shape may have evolved from joining two loaves together to make more floor space in the old-fashioned bread ovens. It is a test of the baker's skill to achieve a crisp golden crust and fine-textured, well-flavoured crumb as well as a good shape. To achieve this shape the dough must be quite firm, so be ready to work in a little extra flour if necessary and keep the final rising (before baking) at a fairly cool temperature to avoid over-proving. Although now most often made with white bread flour, you could use a mixture of white and wholemeal.

675g strong white bread flour | 400ml water, at room temperature
1½ teaspoons sea salt | 1 medium free-range egg, beaten
1 x 7g sachet of easy-blend/ | with a pinch of salt, for brushing
easy-bake dried yeast | *a large baking tray, greased with butter*

Combine the flour, salt and yeast in a large mixing bowl or the bowl of a food mixer. Make a well in the middle and pour in the water. Gradually work the flour into the water to make a fairly firm dough, using your hand or the dough hook attachment of the mixer. Add a little more water if there are dry crumbs and the dough won't come together.

Turn the dough out on to a lightly floured work surface and knead thoroughly for 10 minutes, or knead it for 4 minutes in the mixer using the dough hook on the lowest possible speed. The dough should be silky smooth and very pliable, but if it sticks to your fingers work in more flour because it needs to be quite firm. (See pages 92–95).

Return the dough to the bowl and either cover with a damp tea towel or a snap-on lid or slip the bowl into a large plastic bag. Leave to rise at normal room temperature until doubled in size, about 1½ hours.

Punch down the risen dough and turn out on to a lightly floured work surface. Knead for a minute to expel any pockets of gas, then cut off one-third of the dough. Shape each piece of dough into a neat ball and place well apart on the prepared baking tray. Slip the tray into a large plastic bag and leave to rise at cool room temperature until almost doubled in size, about 30 to 40 minutes. Meanwhile preheat the oven to 230°C/450°F/gas 8 and put a metal baking dish or roasting tin into the oven to heat.

Uncover the dough and gently flatten each piece with your fingers. Put the smaller ball on top of the larger one. Dip your fingers in flour, then push 2 fingers and a thumb joined together into the middle of the loaf to join both pieces. Leave for 10 minutes longer, then brush with the beaten egg to glaze. Using a small sharp knife or razor blade, score all around the edge of both balls of dough.

Put the tray with the loaf on it into the oven, then pour some cold water into the hot metal dish to create plenty of steam (this will help give a good, crisp crust). Quickly close the door and bake for 15 minutes, then reduce the oven temperature to 200°C/400°F/gas 6 and bake for about 20 to 25 minutes more, or until the loaf sounds hollow when tapped underneath. Cool on a wire rack.

The Grant Loaf

This excellent, quick and easy loaf is named after Doris Grant, who first published the recipe in *Your Daily Bread* in 1944. She claimed it was the result of an accidental success – the mixture is mixed rather than kneaded, then given just one rising in the tin – but it has inspired at least a couple of generations of breadmakers. It has a lovely flavour and makes superb toast.

A few tips: Use good-quality stoneground wholemeal flour (the extra strong Canadian type works best), and make sure the mixture doesn't rise too quickly. This will help avoid any holes developing in the centre of the loaf. In hot weather use water straight from the cold tap, and avoid leaving the loaf to rise in too warm a place (such as the airing cupboard or over the stove). Once you have made the loaf a few times you can add your own touches, such as sesame seeds or medium oatmeal, generously sprinkled inside the tin and on top of the loaf mixture before rising. A rounded teaspoon of well-flavoured honey (added with the water) is nice, or try a good spelt flour for a wonderfully nutty wheat taste.

750g strong stoneground wholemeal bread flour
1½ teaspoons sea salt
1 x 7g sachet of easy-blend/ easy-bake dried yeast

15g unsalted butter, diced
650ml lukewarm water

a 900g loaf tin, about 26 x 12.5 x 7.5cm, greased with butter

Put the flour, salt and yeast into a large mixing bowl and mix thoroughly with your hand. In really cold weather, or if your flour has been stored in an unheated larder, it is a good idea to gently warm the flour or at least bring it up to room temperature. Add the diced butter and rub into the flour with the tips of your fingers until it disappears. Make a well in the centre and pour in the lukewarm water.

Using your hand, gradually work the flour into the water to make a very soft and really sticky dough. It will feel totally unlike any regular bread dough. Using your hand, mix and beat the dough vigorously in the bowl, working from the sides into the middle, until it feels elastic and slippery (rather than wet) and starts to leave the sides of the bowl clean – about 5 minutes. Tip the dough into the prepared loaf tin. Wet your fingers and gently ease the dough into the corners so it fills the tin evenly.

Cover the tin with a damp tea towel or slip it inside a large plastic bag. Slightly inflate the bag so it doesn't stick to the dough, then fasten the ends to make a mini-greenhouse. Leave to rise in a warm (not hot) spot until the dough has almost reached the top of the tin – 45 to 60 minutes, depending on the temperature. Meanwhile, heat the oven to 200°C/400°F/gas 6.

Uncover the dough and bake in the heated oven for 45 minutes. Remove the tin from the oven, turn out the loaf and tap it underneath – if it sounds hollow like a drum, it is fully baked. If there is a dull thud, return the loaf to the oven, straight on the oven shelf without the tin, for another 5 minutes and test again. Leave to cool completely on a wire rack before slicing.

Edward's Cumin and Fennel Loaf

MAKES 1 LARGE LOAF

A delicious combination of flavours come together here, merging a taste of overseas with traditional British bread-making skills.

500g strong white bread flour
1 teaspoon salt
2 teaspoons cumin seeds
1 teaspoon fennel seeds
10g fresh yeast, or 1 x 7g sachet of easy-blend/easy-bake dried yeast
350ml lukewarm water

olive oil, for kneading
wholemeal flour, for sprinkling

a baking tray, lined with greaseproof paper and sprinkled with cornmeal
a baking stone, pizza stone or unlined baking tray

Mix the flour and salt with the cumin and fennel seeds in a large mixing bowl. Crumble the fresh yeast into the lukewarm water and mix well – if using dried yeast, mix 1½ teaspoons from the sachet into the flour mixture (save the rest of the sachet for another recipe, or discard).

Add the water to the flour mixture and mix with your hand to make a slightly soft, shaggy-looking dough. Cover the bowl with a tea towel and leave for 10 minutes.

Pour about a teaspoon of oil on to a work surface, and lightly oil your hands. Tip the dough on to the work surface and flip it over so it too is coated in oil. Fold the dough in half, press down where the edges meet, then stretch out the dough with the other hand. Repeat this kneading movement 10 times, then return the dough to the lightly oiled mixing bowl, cover with clingfilm or a snap-on lid and leave to rest for 10 minutes. Repeat this kneading and resting process twice more – after the dough has been kneaded for a total of 3 times, return it to the bowl, cover as before and leave for 30 minutes. Turn out and repeat the kneading process one last time. Shape the dough into a ball and set on the prepared baking tray. Cover with a slightly damp tea towel and leave to rise until doubled in size – about 1 hour at room temperature.

Meanwhile put the baking stone, pizza stone or baking tray into the oven. Turn on the oven and heat to 220°C/425°F/gas 7. Spray the dough with water, then sprinkle with wholemeal flour. Slide the loaf, on its sheet of baking parchment, off the tray and on to the hot baking stone, pizza stone or baking tray. Bake in the hot oven for 15 minutes, then reduce the oven to 190°C/375°F/gas 5 and bake for a further 25 to 30 minutes, or until the loaf sounds hollow when tapped underneath. Transfer to a wire rack and leave to cool completely.

Farmhouse Soda Bread

MAKES 1 MEDIUM LOAF

The traditional bread of Ireland gets its lovely light texture and superb flavour from mixing good-quality, creamy white unbleached flour with buttermilk and bicarbonate of soda. This farmhouse loaf was usually cooked in a heavy cast-iron pan, covered with a lid, on top of the stove or suspended over the embers of an open fire.

450g plain white flour, organic or best-quality
1 teaspoon bicarbonate of soda

1 teaspoon salt
about 350ml buttermilk

a non-stick baking tray, lightly dusted with flour

Heat the oven to 220°C/425°F/gas 7.

Sieve the flour, bicarbonate of soda and salt into a bowl and make a well in the centre. Pour the buttermilk into the well and mix it into the dry ingredients with a round-bladed knife, or your hands, to make a soft, slightly sticky, rough-looking dough.

Turn the dough out on to a lightly floured work surface and shape it into a ball. Set it on the baking tray and gently flatten it so it is 3 to 4cm high. Using a table knife, score the dough with a cross. Dust with flour and bake for about 35 minutes, until a golden brown. To test if the loaf is cooked, tap it underneath with your knuckles. If it sounds hollow, it is ready; if it gives a dull thud, bake it for a few minutes longer and test again. Transfer to a wire rack to cool. Best eaten warm the same day.

FRUIT SODA BREAD (TOP LOAF, OPPOSITE)

For a sweet, speckled bread, add 1 tablespoon of sugar with the flour and rub in 30g of diced unsalted butter. Mix in 100g of dried fruit, then finish as in the recipe. You could also substitute the chopped chocolate for dried fruit.

BROWN SODA BREAD

In a bowl, mix 200g of light brown plain flour or wholemeal plain flour, with 200g of plain white flour. Mix in 25g of wheat germ, 25g of wheat bran, a teaspoon of salt and 1½ teaspoons of bicarbonate of soda. Add 350ml of buttermilk and mix it in with a round-bladed knife, or your hands, to make a soft, slightly sticky, but rough-looking dough. Turn out the dough and cook as the farmhouse soda bread.

Jasminder's Focaccia

MAKES 1 LARGE LOAF

A stunningly attractive loaf with a vibrant Mediterranean topping that's almost a meal in itself.

FOR THE DOUGH:
500g strong white bread flour
½ teaspoon salt
1 x 7g sachet of easy-blend/
easy-bake dried yeast
1–2 tablespoons fresh rosemary sprigs,
finely chopped
6 tablespoons extra virgin olive oil
300ml lukewarm water

FOR THE TOPPING:
1 medium red pepper
1 medium orange pepper
1 medium green pepper
4 tablespoons extra virgin olive oil
1 clove of garlic, crushed
8 sun-dried tomato halves, from a jar,
drained of oil
sea salt flakes and freshly ground
black pepper
a few sprigs of fresh rosemary

a large baking tray, oiled

In a large mixing bowl or the bowl of a large food mixer, combine the flour with the salt and 1½ teaspoons of dried yeast from the sachet (save the rest for another recipe, or discard). Stir in the chopped rosemary, then add the oil. Using your hand or the dough hook attachment of the mixer on the lowest possible speed, work in enough of the lukewarm water to make a soft and just slightly sticky dough. Turn out the dough on to a lightly floured work surface and knead until very smooth and pliable – about 10 minutes by hand or 5 minutes with the mixer. Return the dough to the lightly oiled bowl, turn it over so it is coated in oil, then cover the bowl with clingfilm or a snap-on lid and leave to rise until doubled in size – about 1 hour at room temperature.

Meanwhile, halve and deseed the peppers, then cut into 2cm chunks. Put into a mixing bowl with 2 tablespoons of the olive oil and toss until thoroughly coated. Heat a heavy grill or griddle pan and chargrill the peppers over a high heat until speckled with dark brown patches – don't allow the peppers to blacken, as they will be cooked again in the oven. Tip them back into the mixing bowl, add the crushed garlic and a little salt and pepper, and mix thoroughly. Roughly chop the sun-dried tomatoes.

Punch down the risen dough to deflate, then turn out of the bowl. Set the dough in the centre of the oiled tray and press and shape with your hands to make a rough square with sides about 26cm. Press your fingers into the dough to make dimples, then poke fresh rosemary sprigs into them. Scatter the chopped tomatoes over the dough and top with the pepper mixture. Leave to rise for 20 minutes. Meanwhile heat the oven to 220°C/425°F/gas 7.

Drizzle the rest of the olive oil over the top of the bread, and season with salt and pepper. Bake in the heated oven for 10 minutes, then reduce the oven temperature to 190°C/375°F/gas 5 and bake for a further 15 minutes, until the edges and base are a good golden brown – if necessary, slip the bread off the tray and bake straight on the oven shelf for a few extra minutes. Cool for a few minutes on a wire rack, and eat warm.

Four-plait Challah MAKES 1 LARGE LOAF

Challah, the elaborately plaited Sabbath loaf made from a soft sweet dough containing eggs, honey and fat, was first made by the Jews of central Europe in the Middle Ages. It travelled with them on their migrations, first to eastern Europe, then to the West. Very accomplished bakers make impressive 12-strand plaits; this recipe is for a very achievable 4-strand version. It can be finished with poppy seeds or sesame seeds, or just left plain with its lovely rich glossy egg glaze. This non-dairy version uses sunflower or safflower oil, but if you would rather use butter, replace the oil with 85g of unsalted butter, melted and cooled to lukewarm.

700g strong white bread flour
2 teaspoons salt
1 x 7g sachet of easy-blend/
easy-bake dried yeast
250ml lukewarm water
3 medium free-range eggs, at room
temperature, beaten
3 tablespoons runny honey

100ml sunflower oil

TO FINISH:
1 medium free-range egg,
beaten with a pinch of salt, to glaze
1 tablespoon poppy seeds
and/or sesame seeds

a large baking tray, well greased with butter

Mix the flour with the salt and yeast in a large mixing bowl or the bowl of a free-standing mixer. Make a well in the centre and pour in the water, beaten eggs, honey and oil. Gradually work the flour into the liquids, using your hand or the dough hook attachment of the mixer on the lowest possible speed. Work the mixture until it comes together to make a soft but not sticky dough: if there are dry crumbs at the bottom of the bowl or the dough feels tough and dry, work in a little more water; if it feels very sticky, work in a little more flour.

Turn the dough out on to a lightly floured work surface and knead for 10 minutes, or knead for 4 minutes in a mixer using the dough hook, until it feels firmer and very smooth and elastic. It is important that the dough is fairly firm and able to keep its shape when plaited, so be prepared to work in a little more flour if it still feels soft after thorough kneading. Return the dough to the bowl, cover with a damp tea towel and leave at room temperature until doubled in size – about 1 ½ hours. If the dough gets too hot or rises too fast it will be harder to shape.

Punch down the risen dough to deflate, then turn out on to a lightly floured work surface and cut into 4 equal portions. With your hands roll each one into a sausage about 40cm long. Pinch the rolls firmly together at one end, then arrange vertically in front of you with the join at the top and the rolls side by side and slightly apart. Run the far-left roll under the 2 middle ones, then run it back over the last one it went under. Run the far-right roll under the twisted 2 in the middle, then back over the last one it went under. Repeat until all the dough is plaited and pinch the ends together at the base of the plait. Transfer to the prepared baking tray and slip the tray into a large plastic bag, slightly inflated. Leave to rise at normal room temperature, as before, until almost but not quite doubled in size – about 40 to 50 minutes. Meanwhile heat the oven to 220°C/425°F/gas 7.

Uncover the plait and brush with 2 thin coats of the beaten egg glaze, making sure you don't 'glue' the dough to the baking tray. Decorate with seeds, if using. Bake in the heated oven for 10 minutes, then reduce the oven temperature to 190°C/375°F/gas 5 and bake for a further 30 minutes, or until the loaf is a deep golden brown and sounds hollow when tapped underneath.If necessary, rotate the tray during baking so the loaf colours evenly. Cool on a wire rack.

Stilton and Walnut Rolls

MAKES 12 ROLLS

The flavour of these depends on the cheese; too much will make the rolls greasy and heavy, too little and they will lack taste. Many blue cheeses are too salty, while others are too bland, but Stilton, with its complex, creamy strength, works very well – especially with the walnuts. Or try extra mature Cheddar cheese, seasoned with dried red chilli flakes and a few chopped sun-dried tomatoes instead of the walnuts. The dough can also be made into a large loaf.

350g strong white bread flour	250ml lukewarm water
350g strong stoneground wholemeal flour	200g Stilton cheese, crumbled
1¼ teaspoons salt	100g walnut pieces, toasted
1 x 7g sachet of easy-blend/easy-bake yeast	
200ml lukewarm milk	2 x 22cm round cake tins,
	or 2 baking trays, well greased with butter

Combine the flours, salt and yeast in a large mixing bowl, using your hand, or the bowl of a food mixer, using a dough hook attachment. Make a well in the centre and pour in the milk and water. Mix, with your hand or the dough hook, to make a soft but not sticky dough. If the dough feels dry and hard, work in a little more water; if it feels very sticky, work in a little more white or wholemeal flour.

Turn the dough out on to a lightly floured work surface and knead thoroughly for 10 minutes, or knead for 4 minutes in the mixer using the dough hook on the lowest possible speed. Gently work in the crumbled cheese and the nuts, and return the dough to the bowl. Cover with a damp tea towel or a snap-on lid and leave in a warm place until doubled in size – about 1 to 1¼ hours.

Punch down the risen dough to deflate, then turn out on to a lightly floured work surface. Divide the dough into 12 equal pieces, and shape into neat balls. Arrange 6 balls in each tin or on each tray, slightly apart, to make a ring. Cover with a damp tea towel and leave to rise until doubled in size – 45 minutes to 1 hour. Towards the end of the rising time, heat the oven to 230°C/450°F/gas 8. Uncover the rolls and bake in the heated oven for 20 minutes, until a good golden brown. Remove from the tins or trays and leave to cool on a wire rack.

TO MAKE A LOAF:

To make the dough into a loaf, gently knead the punched-down dough for a few seconds, then shape the dough into a neat ball and set on the prepared baking tray. The dough can also be shaped to fit into a greased 900g (about 26 x 12.5 x 7.5cm) loaf tin. Cover and leave to rise until doubled in size, then slash the top of the loaf several times with a sharp knife. Bake in the heated oven as above for 20 minutes, then reduce the oven temperature to 400°C/200°F/gas 6 and bake for a further 15 to 20 minutes, or until the turned-out loaf sounds hollow when tapped underneath. Turn out on to a wire rack and leave to cool completely before slicing.

# Bagels MAKES 12

Bagels – bangles, the rolls-with-the-holes – with their spongy crumb and chewy, glossy crust originally come from southern Germany and travelled to the Polish *shtetl*, where they were sold by street hawkers. Jewish bakers took their highly popular bagels with them on their migration west; in the late nineteenth century Brick Lane in east London was the centre of the newly arrived Jewish community and became (it is said) the best place, other than New York, for bagels.

500g extra-strong white bread flour
1½ teaspoons salt
3 tablespoons sugar
1 x 7g sachet of easy-blend/ easy-bake dried yeast
250ml lukewarm water
2 teaspoons malt extract
1 medium free-range egg, at room temperature, beaten
2 tablespoons melted butter or sunflower oil

To finish:
1 tablespoon malt extract, for the poaching water
1 egg white, lightly beaten
poppy seeds, sesame seeds, sunflower seeds or onion flakes, for sprinkling (optional)

3 baking trays, greased with butter

Put the flour, salt, sugar and yeast into a large mixing bowl or the bowl of a food mixer. Mix well with your hand or the dough hook attachment, then make a well in the centre.

Mix the water with the malt extract, beaten egg and melted butter or oil. Pour into the well and mix into the flour, using your hand or the mixer on the lowest possible speed to make a soft but sticky dough. If the dough feels tough and dry, work in a little more water; if it feels very wet and sticky, work in a little more flour. Cover the bowl with a damp tea towel or a snap-on lid and leave for 10 minutes.

Turn the dough out on to a lightly floured work surface and knead thoroughly for 10 minutes, or knead it in the mixer for 4 minutes using the dough hook, until very smooth and pliable. Return the dough to the bowl, cover as before and leave to rise at normal room temperature, rather than in a hot spot, until doubled in size – about 1½ hours. Punch down the risen dough to deflate, then turn it out on to the lightly floured work surface. Divide the dough into a dozen equal pieces and roll into neat balls. Cover them with a dry tea towel and leave for 10 minutes. Slightly flatten the balls with your hands, then push a floured forefinger through the centre of each ball to form a ring. Gently rotate or twirl the ring on your finger to make the hole larger, stretching it to a diameter of about 3cm – it will close up as it cooks.

Arrange the bagels, spaced well apart, on a floured baking tray. Cover with a dry tea towel and leave for 15 minutes. Heat the oven to 200°C/400°F/gas 6. Bring a large pan of water to the boil and stir in a tablespoon of malt extract. Gently drop the bagels, 2 at a time, into the boiling water and poach for 30 seconds. Using a slotted spoon, flip them over and poach for a further 30 seconds. Lift out the bagels with the slotted spoon, drain thoroughly and arrange well apart on the prepared baking trays. When all the bagels have been poached, brush them lightly with egg white, making sure you don't 'glue' the dough to the tray. Sprinkle with seeds, if using, and bake in the heated oven for 20 to 25 minutes, until a glossy golden brown. Remove from the oven, transfer to a wire rack and leave to cool completely.

David's Thyme and Sun-dried Tomato Rolls

MAKES 9

These crunchy rolls with a moist and well-flavoured crumb are good with soups and salads or filled.

350g strong white bread flour
1 teaspoon caster sugar
1 teaspoon salt
1 x 7g sachet of easy-blend/
easy-bake dried yeast
4 tablespoons olive oil

200ml lukewarm water
2 teaspoons fresh thyme leaves, chopped
6 sun-dried tomato halves, from a jar,
drained of oil and chopped

a large baking tray, greased with butter

Combine the flour, sugar, salt and yeast in a mixing bowl or the bowl of a large food mixer. Add the oil and, using your hand or the dough hook attachment of the mixer on a low speed, work in enough lukewarm water to make a soft but sticky dough. Knead until smooth and pliable – about 10 minutes by hand or 5 minutes in the mixer. Knead in the thyme leaves and the sun-dried tomatoes, then cover the bowl with a snap-on lid or clingfilm and leave to rise until doubled in size – about 1 hour at room temperature.

Punch down the risen dough to deflate, then turn out on to a lightly floured work surface. Knead gently for a few seconds, then divide the dough into 9 pieces. Shape each portion into a neat ball and arrange well apart on the baking tray. Cover the tray lightly with a sheet of clingfilm or a clean, dry tea towel and leave to rise until doubled in size – about 20 minutes.

Meanwhile heat the oven to 190°C/375°F/gas 5. Uncover the rolls and bake in the heated oven for 15 to 20 minutes, until a good golden brown.

Transfer to a wire rack and leave to cool.

Naan

Naan, the very popular bread introduced to Britain by migrants from the Punjab, is made with fine white flour plus yoghurt, which ferments the dough and adds flavour as well as leavening. The dough is rapidly made, there's no kneading, and it is quickly shaped by hand. Although traditionally baked in a tandoor, a clay oven sunk into the ground, you can get a very good result at home using a red-hot grill.

250g self-raising flour	TO FINISH:
½ teaspoon salt	40g unsalted butter
3 rounded tablespoons plain live yoghurt	1 clove of garlic, peeled and crushed
115ml lukewarm water	2 tablespoons chopped fresh coriander

Combine the flour and salt in a mixing bowl. Add the yoghurt and the lukewarm water, a little at a time, working the ingredients together with your fingers. Bring the flakes of dough together, adding just enough water to make a soft, slightly sticky and rough, shaggy-looking dough. Cover the bowl and leave in a warm spot for an hour to ferment (as it's a yeast-free dough it won't rise).

When ready to cook, thoroughly heat the grill and wire grill rack, using the highest setting. Flour your fingers and a work surface, then divide the dough into 8 equal portions. Shape each into a neat ball, then flatten and stretch out each one to make an oval roughly 20cm long. Cook the naans in batches under the heated grill until they puff up and are speckled with brown spots – about 1 to 1½ minutes each side. Meanwhile, gently melt the butter with the garlic and stir in the chopped coriander. As soon as the naans are cooked, remove them from the grill with kitchen tongs, quickly brush with the warm melted butter mixture and serve immediately.

Barm Brack

This is an Irish loaf – the name comes from 'barm', meaning dough made from liquid ale yeast (left over from beer-making). It was originally baked for Hallowe'en in a cast-iron pot suspended over the fire, and eaten after dark to accompany ghost stories. Inside the loaf were baked several 'fortunes', wrapped in greaseproof paper. A thimble or dried pea meant the recipient would remain single, a piece of cloth meant being reduced to rags, while a silver sixpence signified coming into money. If your piece contained a ring, you would marry within a year, but a religious medallion indicated that you would go into a convent or the priesthood. This loaf has been given a modern twist by covering the surface in an icing-sugar-and-water mix, but it is also good toasted and makes the finest bread and butter pudding.

250g mixed currants and sultanas
450g strong white bread flour
1 teaspoon salt
1 teaspoon ground cinnamon
1 teaspoon ground mixed spice
75g butter, diced
75g light brown muscovado sugar

1 x 7g sachet of dried easy-blend/easy-bake yeast
125ml lukewarm milk
2 medium free-range eggs
1 tablespoon sugar, dissolved in
2 tablespoons boiling water, for glazing
icing sugar, to coat (optional)

a 20cm round deep cake tin
or spring-clip tin, greased with butter

Put the dried fruit into a bowl, cover with warm water (or leftover tea from the pot) and leave to soak while making the dough. Mix the flour with the salt, cinnamon and mixed spice in a large bowl or the bowl of a large food mixer. Add the butter and rub into the flour, using your fingertips, until the mixture looks like fine crumbs. Mix in the sugar and yeast. Combine the milk and eggs, and add to the flour mixture. Work the ingredients together with your hand, or using the dough hook attachment of the mixer on the lowest speed, to make a soft but not sticky dough.

Turn the dough out on to a lightly floured surface and knead thoroughly for 10 minutes, or knead in the mixer for 4 minutes, using the dough hook, until it feels very smooth and elastic. Thoroughly drain the soaked fruit and gently knead into the dough, working the mixture until the fruit is evenly distributed. Return the dough to the bowl, cover with a damp tea towel or a snap-on lid, and leave to rise in a warm spot until doubled in size – about 1 hour.

Punch down the risen dough to deflate, then turn out on to a lightly floured work surface and shape into a ball. Flatten into a round to fit and gently place in the prepared tin. Cover with a damp tea towel, or put the tin inside a large plastic bag, gently inflate, then close securely. Leave to rise in a warm place until doubled in size – about 1 hour, depending on the temperature. Meanwhile heat the oven to 200°C/400°F/gas 6.

Uncover the tin and bake the loaf for 50 to 60 minutes, or until the turned-out loaf sounds hollow when tapped underneath. Cover with greaseproof paper if it seems to be browning too quickly during baking. When you've made sure the loaf is fully baked, quickly brush it with the hot sweet glaze and return it to the oven shelf (don't put it back into the tin) for 2 minutes. Remove from the oven and cool on a wire rack before slicing or coating with icing sugar mixed with water.

Lardy Cake

An utterly delicious British treat from the days when this was a luxury baked for feasts, harvest suppers and farm celebrations. Many recipes from northern England insist on adding a really generous amount of mixed spice, while those from the west like plenty of good pork lard. Lardy cakes are best eaten warm from the oven. This recipe comes from West Camel, Somerset.

500g strong white bread flour
1 teaspoon salt
1 x 7g sachet easy-blend/easy-bake dried yeast
250ml lukewarm milk
1 medium free-range egg
100g lard or white fat (such as Trex), at room temperature, in small pieces

100g unsalted butter, at room temperature, finely diced
200g caster sugar
200g mixed sultanas and currants

2 x 20–21cm sandwich tins, lightly greased with butter

Mix the flour with the salt and yeast in a mixing bowl or the bowl of a large food mixer. Make a well in the centre. Lightly beat the warm milk and the egg and pour into the well. Gradually mix the flour into the liquid using your hand, or the dough hook attachment of the mixer on the lowest speed, to make a soft but not sticky dough. Turn the dough out on to a lightly floured work surface and knead for 10 minutes until smooth and very elastic, or knead in the mixer for 4 minutes using the dough hook attachment. Return the dough to the bowl, cover with a damp tea towel and leave in a warm place to rise until doubled in size – about 1 hour.

Punch down the risen dough to deflate, then turn it out on to a lightly floured surface and cut it in half. Cover one piece with a damp tea towel and set aside. Set aside half the lard (or white fat), butter, sugar and fruit with the covered portion of dough. Roll out the uncovered portion into a rectangle about 30 x 15cm. Dot the top two-thirds of the rectangle with one third of the remaining lard and butter, then sprinkle over a third of the remaining sugar and a third of the remaining fruit. Fold the uncovered bottom third of the dough up over half the filled portion of dough, then fold down the top third of the dough to make a 3-layer dough sandwich. Seal the open edges by pressing down with the rolling pin. Give the dough a quarter turn so that the completely enclosed side is to your left. Repeat the whole procedure twice more to make a total of 3 rollings, fillings and foldings, always giving the dough a quarter turn to the left before you begin rolling. Leave the dough to rest uncovered while you roll, fill and fold the second piece of dough in the same way. Leave this dough to rest too, for 10 minutes.

Gently roll out each piece of filled dough into a 20cm-square. Put a piece of dough into each tin, tucking the corners under so the dough roughly fits the tins. Cover with a damp tea towel and leave to rise at room temperature, until the dough has almost doubled in size and expanded to fit the tins – about 1 hour. If you leave them in too warm a temperature the fat will ooze out and the cooked cakes will be heavy. Once the dough has risen, place in the fridge for 30 minutes. Meanwhile heat the oven to 220°C/425°F/gas 7.

Lightly score the tops of the cakes with a knife and bake for 25 minutes, until golden. Remove the cakes from the tins, turn them upside down and put them back into the tins, so the fat and caramel seep downwards. Bake for 5 minutes more, then turn out and cool on a wire rack.

Yorkshire Teacakes

At one time, no high tea went without teacakes the size of saucers, plain or studded with dried fruit, split and toasted. The 'right' way to serve them is to toast first the bottoms, then the tops, then split the teacakes and toast the insides. Finally, lay shards of butter on the bottom layer, cover with the top and invert. Wrap and keep warm for 2 minutes, then turn right side up.

450g strong white bread flour	50g unsalted butter, chilled and diced
1 teaspoon salt	100g dried mixed fruit and peel
1 x 7g sachet of easy-blend/	250ml lukewarm milk,
easy-bake dried yeast	plus a little extra for brushing
2 tablespoons caster sugar	2 baking trays, greased with butter

Combine the flour with the salt, yeast and sugar in a large mixing bowl or the bowl of a food mixer. Add the diced butter and rub into the flour, using your fingertips, until the pieces of butter disappear. Mix in the dried fruit, then make a well in the flour and pour in the milk. Mix with your hand, or the dough hook attachment of the mixer, to make a soft but not sticky dough. If there are dry crumbs at the bottom of the bowl or the dough feels dry and tough to work, mix in a little more milk a tablespoon at a time. If the dough feels wet and sticky, work in extra flour a tablespoon at a time.

Turn the dough out on to a lightly floured work surface and knead thoroughly for 10 minutes, or knead in the mixer for 4 minutes on the lowest possible speed, until it feels very stretchy and elastic.

Return the dough to the bowl, cover with a damp tea towel or a snap-on lid and leave in a warm place until doubled in size – about 1 hour.

Punch down the risen dough to deflate, then turn out on to a lightly floured work surface and divide into 8 equal portions. Shape each portion into a neat ball, then gently flatten to make a cake about 10cm across and 2cm high. Arrange the cakes spaced well apart on the prepared baking trays. Cover loosely with damp tea towels and leave to rise as before until doubled in size – about 45 minutes. Towards the end of the rising time, heat the oven to 200°C/400°F/gas 6.

Uncover the teacakes and lightly brush with milk. Bake in the heated oven for 20 minutes, until a good golden brown. Transfer to a wire rack to cool.

Hot Cross Buns

MAKES 12

These extra-spicy buns marked with a dough cross are traditionally eaten warm from the oven on Good Friday. There is evidence that the ancient Egyptians offered similar small round yeast cakes to the goddess of the moon, while the Greeks and Romans made them for the goddess of light, a custom taken up by the Saxons, who added the cross. This recipe is made from both white and wholemeal flours to give plenty of flavour and a light texture; you can use all white flour or all wholemeal if you prefer. The buns freeze well.

350g strong white bread flour
100g strong wholemeal bread flour
50g caster sugar
1 teaspoon sea salt
2 teaspoons ground mixed spice
½ teaspoon freshly grated nutmeg
1 x 7g sachet of easy-blend/
easy-bake dried yeast
50g unsalted butter, diced
125g mixed dried fruit and peel

200ml lukewarm milk
2 medium free-range eggs, lightly beaten

FOR THE CROSS:
4 tablespoons strong white bread flour
2 tablespoons cold water

FOR THE GLAZE:
4 tablespoons milk
2 tablespoons caster sugar

a large baking tray, greased with butter

Put both flours, the sugar, salt, mixed spice, nutmeg and yeast into a large bowl, or the bowl of a large food mixer, and mix well. Add the diced butter and rub in using the tips of your fingers, until the mixture looks like fine crumbs. Stir in the dried fruit. Make a well in the centre and pour in the lukewarm milk and the beaten eggs. Gradually draw the flour into the liquid to make a very soft dough, using your hand or the dough hook attachment of the mixer. Turn the dough out on to a lightly floured work surface and knead thoroughly for 10 minutes, or knead in the mixer for 4 minutes using the dough hook on the lowest possible speed, until silky smooth and very elastic – if the dough is very sticky and hard to work, knead in a little extra strong white flour so it no longer sticks to your fingers, but you don't want a tough, dry and hard dough.

Return the dough to the bowl, cover with a damp tea towel or a snap-on lid and leave in a warm spot until doubled in size – about 1 hour.

Punch down the risen dough to deflate and turn out on to a lightly floured work surface. Divide the dough into 12 equal pieces and shape them into neat balls. Set well apart on the prepared baking tray, then slip the tray into a large plastic bag, slightly inflated so the buns don't come into contact with the plastic, and leave to rise as before until doubled in size – about 45 minutes (or overnight in the fridge). Towards the end of the rising time, heat the oven to 200°C/400°F/gas 6.

To make the cross, mix the flour with enough cold water to make a smooth thick paste that can be piped. Spoon into a greaseproof paper piping bag (or a small plastic bag) and snip off the tip. Uncover the buns and pipe a paste cross on to each one. Bake in the heated oven for about 15 minutes, until golden brown. Meanwhile, make the sticky glaze by heating the milk with the sugar until dissolved. Boil for 1 minute, then brush over the buns as soon as they emerge from the oven. Transfer to a wire rack and leave to cool.

Cornish Saffron Buns MAKES 16

Today most of our saffron comes from Spain, but until 100 years ago it was grown extensively at Stratton in Cornwall and around Saffron Walden in Essex, and has been part of our cooking heritage since medieval times. Saffron comes from the saffron crocus, and each one produces just three stamens, with 4,000 stamens weighing only 30g. When soaked in water, the stamens turn the liquid a brilliant golden orange and it was this vivid colour that was highly prized.

1 teaspoon saffron strands (half a 0.4g sachet)
3 tablespoons lukewarm water
500g strong white bread flour
1 teaspoon salt
175g unsalted butter, chilled and firm
75g caster sugar
1 x 7g sachet easy-blend/easy-bake dried yeast

225g dried mixed fruit and peel
175ml lukewarm milk

TO FINISH:
25g unsalted butter, melted
2 tablespoons demerara sugar

2 baking trays, well greased with butter

Heat the oven to 180°C/350°F/gas 4. Put the saffron on to a heatproof saucer and toast in the oven for about 10 minutes, until the strands turn a slightly darker reddish-brown. Soak the strands in the lukewarm water for at least an hour, overnight if possible.

Sift the flour and salt into a large mixing bowl or the bowl of a food mixer. Add the diced butter and rub into the flour, using the tips of your fingers, until the mixture looks like fine crumbs. Stir in the sugar, yeast and the dried fruit. When thoroughly combined, make a well in the centre and pour in the lukewarm milk and the soaked saffron with its golden liquid. Mix with your hand, or the dough hook attachment of the mixer, to make a very soft but not sticky dough. If necessary add more milk or water, a tablespoon at a time.

Turn the dough out on to a lightly floured work surface and knead thoroughly for 10 minutes, or knead for 4 minutes in the mixer on the lowest speed, until it is very elastic, silky and smooth. Return the dough to the bowl, cover with a damp tea towel and leave in a warm spot until doubled in size – about 3 hours (the dough can also be left to rise overnight in a cool larder or in the fridge). This very rich mixture takes longer to rise than a plain dough.

Punch down the risen dough to deflate. Flour your fingers, then pull off 16 pieces of dough and roll each one between your palms to make a neat bun. Arrange well apart on the prepared trays and cover with a damp tea towel. Leave to rise in a warm spot until doubled in size – about 1½ to 2 hours. Towards the end of the rising time, heat the oven to 190°C/375°F/gas 5.

Bake the buns for 12 minutes, then reduce the temperature to 180°C/350°F/gas 4 and bake for another 5 minutes, or until the buns have puffed up, look a good golden brown colour and sound hollow when tapped underneath. Lightly brush with melted butter and sprinkle with sugar, then bake for 2 minutes more. Cool on a wire rack and eat warm with unsalted butter.

TO MAKE A LOAF:

To make a loaf, punch down the risen dough and shape to fit a 900g loaf tin (about 26 x 12.5 x 7.5cm), well greased. Leave to rise as above, then bake for 40 minutes before lowering the temperature to 180°C/350°F/gas 4 and baking for 15 minutes longer. Brush with melted butter, sprinkle with sugar and bake for 2 minutes. Turn out and cool on a wire rack.

Mark's Sticky Marmalade Tea Loaf MAKES 1 LARGE LOAF

Incredibly quick and easy but so delicious! All the better for using chunky home-made Seville orange marmalade.

225g self-raising flour
1 teaspoon baking powder
2 teaspoons ground ginger
1 teaspoon ground mixed spice
175g soft light brown muscovado sugar
100g chopped mixed nuts

175g unsalted butter, very soft
3 medium free-range eggs, beaten
140g marmalade (preferably home-made)

a 900g loaf tin, about 26 x 12.5 x 7.5cm, greased with butter and the base lined with greaseproof paper

Preheat the oven to 180°C/350°F/gas 4.

Sift the flour, baking powder, ginger and mixed spice into a mixing bowl. Stir in the sugar and the chopped nuts. Add the soft butter and eggs to the bowl. Add all but 1 tablespoon of the marmalade to the bowl (reserve the last one for finishing the loaf) and mix well with a wooden spoon. When thoroughly combined, spoon the mixture into the prepared tin and spread evenly.

Bake in the heated oven for 1 to 1¼ hours, or until a skewer inserted into the centre comes out clean. If necessary, cover with foil or greaseproof paper after about 40 minutes to prevent the loaf becoming too brown.

Carefully remove the loaf from the tin and leave to cool on a wire rack for 5 minutes. Meanwhile, gently warm the marmalade with a couple of teaspoons of water and brush over the warm loaf.

Leave to cool completely, then serve thickly sliced.

Welsh Bara Brith

The name means 'speckled bread', as this is a moist, slightly spicy tea bread speckled with fruit. It is usually made with mixed dried vine fruits – currants, sultanas and raisins – and at one time only fresh blackcurrants were used. Here, the rich flavour comes from soaking the dried fruit overnight in strong tea (no milk), with a little ground cinnamon and grated nutmeg added later. Although bara brith was traditionally made with yeasted bread dough by commercial bakers, this easy soak-and-stir recipe for a teatime loaf is now popular with home bakers. Serve thickly sliced and buttered.

250g mixed dried fruit
100g dark brown muscovado sugar
225ml strong hot tea (no milk)
a good pinch of salt
¼ teaspoon ground cinnamon
¼ teaspoon grated nutmeg

1 large free-range egg, beaten
250g self-raising white or light brown flour

a 450g loaf tin, about 19 x12.5 x7.5cm greased with butter and lined with a long strip of greaseproof paper to cover the base and 2 short sides

Put the dried fruit and sugar into a large heatproof mixing bowl. Pour over the hot tea and stir well. Cover the bowl with a clean dry tea towel and leave to soak for at least 6 hours (preferably overnight).

When ready to bake, heat the oven to 160°C/325°F/gas 3. Add the salt, cinnamon, nutmeg and beaten egg to the soaked fruit (pour away any extra tea) and stir well with a wooden spoon. Mix in the flour, then transfer the mixture into the prepared tin and spread evenly. Bake in the heated oven for about 1 hour, until a skewer inserted in the centre comes out clean. Stand the tin on a wire cooling rack and leave for about 15 minutes to firm up before turning out. Leave to cool completely before slicing.

Chelsea Buns

MAKES 16

For almost a century, until its demise in 1839, the Chelsea Bun House in Bunhouse Place, just off Pimlico Road in London, was famous for its spicy, sugary buns. The owners also claimed to have invented the hot cross bun, and one Good Friday tens of thousands of people, including King George III, thronged down Ebury Street, keen to be seen in the fashionable queue to buy sticky buns.

175ml milk
50g unsalted butter
450g strong white bread flour
1 teaspoon salt
3 tablespoons caster sugar
1 x 7g sachet of easy-blend/
easy-bake dried yeast
1 medium free-range egg

FOR THE FILLING:
50g unsalted butter, melted
75g dark muscovado sugar
150g dried mixed vine fruits
(raisins, sultanas and currants)

FOR THE STICKY GLAZE:
2 tablespoons milk
2 tablespoons caster sugar
2 tablespoons runny honey

a 21 x 25cm cake tin, brownie tin
or roasting tin, greased with butter

Gently heat the milk and butter so the butter just melts, then remove from the heat and cool until lukewarm. Meanwhile, mix the flour with the salt, sugar and yeast in a large mixing bowl or the bowl of a large free-standing mixer. Make a well in the centre.

Beat the egg into the milk and butter mixture and pour into the well in the flour. Using your hand, or the dough hook attachment of the mixer on the lowest possible speed, work the flour into the liquid to make a soft but not sticky dough. Turn the dough out on to a lightly floured work surface and knead thoroughly for 10 minutes, or knead for 4 minutes using the mixer.

Return the dough to the bowl, cover with a damp tea towel or a snap-on lid, and leave to rise in a warm place until doubled in size – about 1 hour. Punch down the dough to deflate, then turn out on to a floured work surface. Divide the dough into 2 and roll out each piece to a rectangle about 38 x 13cm.

Brush the melted butter over both pieces of dough, then sprinkle with the sugar followed by the dried fruit. Starting from one long side, lightly roll up each piece of dough like a Swiss roll. Using a sharp knife, cut each roll into 8 even slices and arrange, cut side up, in the tin so they are barely touching – they will join together as they rise. Cover and leave to rise in a warm place until almost doubled in size – 30 to 40 minutes. Meanwhile, heat the oven to 200°C/400°F/gas 6.

Uncover the dough and bake for 20 to 25 minutes until a good golden colour. Meanwhile, make the glaze by very gently warming the milk, sugar and honey – but don't let the mixture come anywhere near boiling. Brush the sticky glaze over the buns and return them to the oven for another 5 minutes. Remove the tin from the oven and leave to cool for 10 minutes. Run a round-bladed knife around the inside of the tin and carefully turn the buns on to a wire rack. When cool, gently pull them apart. Store in an airtight container.

Butteries

Delicious eaten warm for breakfast with plenty of dark, chunky Seville orange marmalade. To get the layers and flake-like crumb, the bread dough is rolled out into a rectangle, dotted with fat, then folded up a total of three times, as if making rough puff pastry (see page 187). It's important to be quite rough with the pastry so the butteries don't rise too neatly. Make sure the dough is well chilled and rested to avoid a tough or cake-like result, or the fat oozing out.

675g strong white bread flour
1½ teaspoons salt
1 x 7g sachet of easy-blend/ easy-bake dried yeast
1 tablespoon caster sugar
about 350ml water from the cold tap

150g unsalted butter, at room temperature
150g lard or white vegetable fat, at room temperature

3–4 baking trays, lightly floured

Mix the flour with the salt, yeast and sugar in a large mixing bowl or the bowl of a free-standing food mixer. Make a well in the centre and pour in the cold water. Mix with your hand, or the dough hook attachment of the mixer on the lowest possible speed, to make a soft but not sticky dough. If there are dry crumbs in the bowl or the dough feels hard and dry, work in a little more water a teaspoon at a time. Turn the dough out on to a floured surface and knead thoroughly for 10 minutes, or knead in the mixer for about 4 minutes, until very smooth and pliable. Return the dough to the bowl, cover with a damp tea towel or a snap-on lid and leave to rise at normal room temperature until doubled in size – 1½ to 2 hours.

Mash the butter and lard until fairly evenly mixed, then divide into 3 equal portions. Punch down the risen dough to deflate, then turn out on to a lightly floured work surface and roll out into a rectangle about 45 x 15cm. Dot the top two-thirds of the rectangle with one portion of the fat mixture. Fold the uncovered bottom third of the rectangle up over half the fat-covered dough, then fold the top third of the dough down to make a 3-layer dough sandwich. Seal the open edges by pressing down with a rolling pin. Wrap the dough in clingfilm and chill for 30 minutes. Repeat the rolling, fat-dotting, folding and chilling routine twice more; each time roll out the dough with the completely enclosed side on your left, chilling for 30 minutes after the final roll and fold.

Roll the dough into a large brick shape and cut into 20 equal pieces. Shape each piece into a ball and slightly flatten. Don't be too precious with the dough. Arrange well apart on the prepared baking trays. Then chill in the fridge for 20 minutes. Cover and leave until slightly risen and puffy – 20 to 30 minutes. Meanwhile heat the oven to 200°C/400°F/gas 6. Bake the butteries for 20 to 25 minutes, until golden brown and crisp on top. Transfer to a wire rack to cool slightly. Eat warm the same day, or freeze – they'll keep for up to a month.

English Muffins

MAKES 8

Master Baker John Kirkland's *The Modern Baker and Confectioner*, published in 1907, gives the definitive recipe: 'Muffins are thick, extremely light fermented dough cakes, not holey or tough, three inches across and almost two inches thick.' He recommends a soft dough made from not too strong flour, and three risings for lightness. Not actually baked, muffins are cooked on top of the stove using a griddle or heavy-based frying pan – but they're too good a classic to miss! Toppings are optional, but as well as jam and honey, anchovy spread (Gentleman's Relish) is excellent, with or without scrambled eggs.

350g strong white bread flour
100g plain white flour
1 teaspoon salt
1 x 7g sachet of easy-blend/ easy-bake dried yeast
225ml lukewarm water

150ml lukewarm milk
rice flour or cornmeal, for dusting

2 baking trays, a griddle or very heavy-based frying pan

Mix the flours with the salt and yeast in a large mixing bowl or the bowl of a free-standing food mixer. Make a well in the flour and pour in the lukewarm water and milk. Mix with your hand, or the dough hook attachment of the mixer on the slowest possible speed, to a very soft, slightly sticky dough. Work and knead the dough in the bowl until soft, elastic, smooth and no longer sticky – about 10 minutes, or 4 minutes using the mixer.

Cover the bowl with a damp tea towel or a snap-on lid and leave to rise in a warm place until doubled in size – about 1 hour. Turn the dough out on to a lightly floured work surface. Dip your hands in lukewarm water and knead it for 5 minutes (or knead in the mixer for 3 minutes). Return the dough to the bowl, cover and leave as before for another 30 minutes.

Divide the dough into 8 pieces. John Kirkland says: 'The usual method is to squeeze the dough through a ring made by the thumb and forefinger of one hand.' Squeeze off this ball of dough and drop it on to a baking tray well dusted with rice flour or cornmeal. Sprinkle the dough with more rice flour or cornmeal. Once you have a tray of muffins, spaced well apart and liberally sprinkled with rice flour or cornmeal, cover them with another light baking tray or plastic kitchen tray and leave to rise in a warm place for 30 minutes. This gives the muffins their traditional flat tops.

Heat an ungreased griddle or frying pan until moderately hot. Put the muffins, a few at a time, on to the griddle, turning them upside down so that the side that was uppermost on the baking tray is now downwards on the griddle. Cook the muffins slowly, allowing 10 to 12 minutes for each side, until a good golden brown. They are ready when the sides spring back when pressed.

As soon as they are cooked, remove them from the griddle and wrap them in a clean, dry cloth to keep warm while cooking the remainder. Once cold, the muffins freeze well.

Crumpets

MAKES 8

Another old-fashioned griddle recipe from Master Baker John Kirkland. Here, a thick yeast batter is cooked on a hot griddle in special heavy rings to make crumpets that are crisp on the outside and light inside, ready to toast by the fire and spread with plenty of butter. Not technically 'baked', but these are a nationwide favourite at teatime.

225g strong white bread flour	1 teaspoon salt
225g plain white flour	½ teaspoon bicarbonate of soda
¾ teaspoon cream of tartar	150ml lukewarm milk
1 x 7g sachet of easy-blend/ easy-bake dried yeast	*a griddle or heavy-based frying pan*
500ml lukewarm water	*3–4 x 9cm crumpet rings, non-stick or well greased with butter*

Sift the flours and the cream of tartar into a large mixing bowl and stir in the yeast. Add the lukewarm water and mix with your hand to make a smooth batter, beating well for a couple of minutes. Cover the bowl with clingfilm and leave it to stand in a warm place for an hour – the batter will rise, then fall back.

Uncover the bowl and sprinkle the salt over the batter. Beat well for a minute, then cover the bowl again and leave for 20 minutes. Stir the bicarbonate of soda into the warm milk and gently stir into the batter.

Heat the ungreased griddle or frying pan and when it is very hot put in a greased crumpet ring. Spoon or pour in enough of the batter, about 3 tablespoons, to half-fill the ring: this will be your 'test' crumpet – if holes do not form, the batter is slightly too thick and you need to add a little more water. But if the batter is too thin and runs out of the ring gently, stir in a little more flour. As soon as the surface is set and covered with holes (7 to 8 minutes), carefully ease off the ring, using a dry tea towel so you don't burn your fingers. Turn the crumpet over and cook the holey side for a couple of minutes until lightly speckled – the side first cooked should be deep golden brown. Adjust the temperature as necessary. Continue to cook the rest of the batter in batches and either eat straight from the griddle, spread with butter, or leave to cool, wrapped in a clean tea towel, then toast and butter.

PIKELETS (OPPOSITE, BOTTOM)

Distant relations to crumpets, pikelets come from Derbyshire, Yorkshire and Lancashire, and are known as *bara pyglyd* in Wales. They are more like a thick, holey pancake than the 3cm deep crumpet, and less doughy, as they are cooked on the griddle but without the crumpet ring to contain the batter.

Make up the batter as for crumpets but increase the amount of milk to 275ml. When ready to cook, drop 2 tablespoons at a time in circles on to the hot, ungreased griddle or into a small frying pan and cook for about 3 minutes on each side; they will be larger, thinner and crisper than crumpets and you should make 30 from the batter. They freeze well and can be toasted from frozen.

TARTS AND
FLANS

A bacon and cheese tart for lunch;

a glistening crimson berry tart on a summer's day; a comforting treacle tart when the evenings draw in . . . The British heritage of tarts and flans is rich and varied, stretching back over centuries, charting the popular foods of different eras and highlighting regional variations. Some of our most famous tart recipes are specific to a village, town or region, and many have hotly disputed origins – take Bakewell tart, or should it be Bakewell pudding? The whole debate about its origins and the authentic recipe begins with what to call it.

Historians believe that as far back as Neolithic times, as well as baking rounds of paste made from grain and water on hot stones to make flatbreads and biscuits, people were also shaping such paste around stones before baking it to form rough cases that could be filled with wild fruits and honey: the first fruit tarts. And although these days we tend to associate more contemporary fruit tarts with French *pâtisseries* rather than English bakeries, it is worth remembering that recipes have survived from the seventeenth century for the likes of Taffety tarts, featuring pastry topped with that favourite old English fruit the quince, as well as apple and even orange.

Long before the seventies craze for quiche, a savoury tart – being an open pie – was considered the perfect way to showcase ingredients. In a flan you could show off your prizewinning vegetables or herbs from the garden, a local cheese or ham, combining them in as visually stunning a way as possible inside a pastry case to make a very impressive meal.

Until the industrial revolution, and the beginning of food production and transportation on a large scale, cooking was all about such fresh local ingredients. The recent rise of farmers' markets around the country has not only given more people access to local food once again, but bakers, farmers and cheese-makers are creating home-made tarts packed full of their own produce and bringing them to market, reviving our interest in this kind of baking and reminding us that it is the quality of ingredients that raises the simplest tart from mundane to special.

Even the humble jam tart is a real treat when made with buttery pastry and home-made fruit jam. The jam tart was a favourite of Victorian housewives, who loved to make them in complicated designs, the most elaborate version being the Epiphany tart for Twelfth Night, with pastry latticework and different coloured jams, resembling a stained-glass window. And it is a treat that has found its way on to many a famous table. Maria Floris, Soho baker/*pâtissier* to the rich and famous in the 1950s and cake-maker to Winston Churchill, noted in her book *Baking* that one of the PM's secretaries had told her the jam tart was his favourite pastry.

When chef Marcus Wareing cooked for the Queen's eightieth birthday banquet, what did he serve for dessert? A deep custard tart made to his grandmother's recipe. However ingrained the custard tart has become in British slapstick humour – how many comic characters and pantomime dames have had one thrown in their faces? – a carefully made pastry case filled with rich egg custard is a sumptuous and delicious thing whose history stretches back in time.

The very name reflects the influence of the Romans and the French, by way of the Normans, on our cooking, since it is derived from the Anglo-Norman *crustarde*, or *crustade*, from the French *crouste* (crust), which in turn comes from the Latin *crusta*. The Romans understood the binding qualities of eggs, using them in savoury dishes containing cheese or meat, or sweet 'custards' with honey, nuts and spices, as recorded in the writings of Apicius. However, custard baked inside hand-raised pastry cases, rather grimly known as coffins (which may have been designed to be eaten or may have been merely brittle receptacles), really became popular during the Middle Ages, when tarts would be baked after the bread, when the ovens had cooled down.

In her book *English Food*, Jane Grigson gives a recipe for a Coronation doucet or custard tart ('*doucet*' refers to something sweet, from the French *douce*). Apparently such a doucet was served as part of the third course at Henry IV's coronation banquet, along with candied quince and fritters, curlews, partridges, quails and rabbits. The recipe is for a pastry case filled with a custard flavoured with saffron and honey. Often doucets would contain minced pork or beef as well as fruit and herbs, since in medieval times there was no appreciable difference between savoury and sweet courses and a mixture of such ingredients made the tart more colourful. Sometimes in richer households almond milk, made from boiling up ground almonds and syrup or water, sometimes with wine added, was used instead of cow's milk, as this could be eaten on certain religious 'fast days' when meat and dairy produce were forbidden.

The famous Bakewell pudding or tart is one of the recipes that most likely evolved from these medieval custards, though its very name (or names) sparks a fury of controversy. The most recounted story is that Bakewell tart first emerged following a mistake at the White Horse Inn, which later became the Rutland Arms, the inn at Bakewell where Jane Austen stayed in the 1860s. One version of the yarn has this mistake occurring in 1820, another in 1859. The first story goes that a guest at the inn ordered a strawberry tart, but a hapless cook, instead of adding the egg and almond mixture to the pastry, poured it over the strawberry jam by mistake before baking it. The other version is that the landlady of the inn, one Mrs Greaves, was entertaining guests and asked her cook to make a particular pudding which involved an egg mixture spread over the base of a pastry case, topped with strawberry jam – perhaps a version of the kind of custard tarts topped with fruit that were being made as early as the mid-eighteenth century. However, the cook got it the wrong way round. Truth or myth, such was the success of this sweet pastry dessert that three bakeries in Bakewell still claim to have been the first to get hold of the new recipe and sell the puddings or tarts commercially.

What we do know is that in 1845 the cookery writer Eliza Acton gave a recipe for Bakewell pudding that she explained was famous not only in Derbyshire but in 'several of our northern counties, where it is usually served on all holiday occasions'. This was a recipe for a rich custard flavoured with almonds, poured over a layer of mixed jams and baked – but there was no pastry. By 1861, Isabella Beeton was giving a recipe for a similar pudding encased in puff pastry in her *Book of Household Management*. Over the years, a slightly different version has evolved using shortcrust pastry and more almonds to create a sponge closer to the French frangipane, sometimes topped with icing, and the name 'pudding' has often given way to 'tart'. Jane Grigson, however, is adamant that a true Bakewell tart should be made with jam and custard and no ground almonds, the addition of which, she insists, is 'quite wrong'.

What is certain is that other similar custard-based tarts existed around the same time, such as Manchester tart – a pastry case filled with a layer of jam, followed by custard and finished with desiccated coconut, a version of which is also included by Mrs Beeton. Buxton puddings featured breadcrumbs instead of almonds in the custard; while further south, Duke of Cambridge tarts had a layer of candied peel, rather than jam, beneath the custard. Another similar dish was Chester pudding (not to be confused with the Irish Chester cake, which involves pastry and a bread-pudding-like filling). This was a pastry case filled with a custard flavoured with almonds and sometimes lemon, but topped with meringue – possibly the precursor of lemon meringue pie or tart.

So much controversy, so much history, so much variety – and so much that can be done with a simple casing of pastry and your favourite sweet or savoury ingredients.

Bakewell, in the beautiful Peak District, is where the famous Bakewell pudding — or tart — originates. Legend claims it evolved following a mix-up by a cook at the local inn, now the Rutland Arms.

SHORTCRUST PASTRY: This is the easiest pastry to make by hand, and if you have a food processor it really only takes a couple of minutes from start to finish. Shortcrust has a 'short' – that is, a crumbly, light – texture. At its simplest it is a dough made from plain flour (labelled for use in cakes and pastry, rather than bread-making), fat (butter tastes best, but older recipes go for equal amounts of butter and lard, or white or vegetable cooking fat), a little salt and cold water to bind it all. The shortness of the pastry, and that important melt-in-the-mouth quality, depends on the quantity and type of fat and the way it is incorporated into the flour. Most cooks use 1 part fat to 2 parts flour (say, 50g fat to 100g flour). Cold unsalted butter gives a better taste and texture than highly salted butter. To make the pastry richer, more fat is used (up to three-quarters fat to flour in the some recipes). Extra sugar and an egg yolk or two is also often added. Save the egg whites for meringues – they freeze well.

HOW TO MAKE SHORTCRUST PASTRY BY HAND: Sift the flour and salt into a large mixing bowl – this helps aerate the flour and removes lumps. Cut the cold fat into small dice and add to the flour. Toss lightly so the lumps of fat are coated in flour, then, using a round-bladed knife, cut them into much smaller pieces. Now put both hands into the bowl and pick up a small quantity of the mixture between the fingertips and thumb of each hand. Lift your hands up to the rim of the bowl, rub the flour and pieces of fat together between your fingertips and let them fall back down on to the rest of the mixture. Do this until the whole mixture looks like fine crumbs, with no clumps of fat.

Gradually pour in the ice-cold water while stirring with a round-bladed knife. Keep stirring until the dough comes together – you only need enough to bind the mixture together. If there are dry crumbs at the bottom of the bowl, add more water a teaspoon at a time. The dough should hold together and be firm rather than soft. If it feels sticky, work in a little more flour. Gather it together with your hands and knead it very briefly so it forms a ball. Try not to handle or work the dough too much, as you don't want the fat to start to melt and make the pastry oily. Wrap the pastry in clingfilm and chill for 15 to 20 minutes, until firm but not hard.

HOW TO MAKE SHORTCRUST PASTRY IN A FOOD PROCESSOR: Put the flour and salt into the processor bowl and pulse a couple of times to combine, and to aerate the flour. Dice the fat and add to the bowl, then process just until the mixture looks like fine crumbs. Pour the ice-cold water into the machine through the feed tube, while the machine is running; the dough should come together in a clump. If this doesn't happen, add a little more water a teaspoon at a time through the feed tube. Remove the ball of dough from the machine, then wrap in clingfilm and chill for 15 to 20 minutes, until firm but not hard.

HOW TO LINE A FLAN TIN: It is much easier to line a flan tin if the pastry is cold and firm but not hard, rather than soft and sticky, so once you have made the pastry wrap it in clingfilm and chill it for as long as possible until you are ready to bake.

Roll out the pastry on a lightly floured surface to the diameter of your flan tin plus twice its height.

Flour the rolling pin, then gently roll the dough around the pin and lift it over the top of the tin. Carefully unroll the dough so it drapes over the tin. Flour your fingers and delicately press the dough on to the base of the tin, then up the sides, so there are no air pockets. Roll the pin over the top of the tin to cut off the excess dough (if you have any holes, use this to patch them). The sides of the pastry case should stand just slightly higher than the sides of the tin in case the pastry shrinks during baking, so use your thumbs to ease the pastry upwards and make a neat rim about 5mm higher than the rim of the tin. Curve your forefinger inside this new rim and gently press the pastry over your finger so it curves slightly inwards – this makes it easier to unmould after baking. For the best results, chill the flan case well before baking; this gives the pastry time to relax after it has been rolled and stretched, and reduces the risk of it shrinking in the oven.

- -

HOW TO BAKE 'BLIND': The aim is a crisp, well-baked pastry case ready for filling.

Make sure the pastry case is well chilled and firm. Prick the base of the pastry-lined flan tin with a fork – this helps to stop it bubbling up during baking. Cut a round of non-stick baking paper about 10cm larger than the diameter of the tin. Crumple the paper to make it flexible, then open it out and gently press it into the pastry case to cover the base and sides. It is important to press the paper into the angle where the sides meet the base. Fill the paper-lined case with ceramic baking beans, dried beans, uncooked rice or stale bread crusts to weight it down.

Bake in an oven preheated to 190°C/375°F/gas 5 for about 15 minutes, or until the pastry is just firm and lightly golden. Carefully remove the paper and beans – the pastry is still very fragile – and return the flan tin to the oven. Reduce the oven temperature to 180°C/350°F/gas 4 and bake the empty pastry case for a further 5 to 7 minutes, or until the pastry base is crisp and lightly golden. Make sure the pastry is thoroughly cooked before removing it from the oven – there should be no damp-looking pale patches.

- -

Bacon and Egg Tart MAKES 1 MEDIUM TART

Preserving has been an important skill in Britain for well over 1,000 years, used in order to help food last over the winter months. Methods of salting, curing and smoking meats vary from area to area but bacon appears to be a wonderfully British speciality, cured by most farms and cottagers up and down the country until the start of the First World War. This is a luxuriously rich, creamy tart, made with thick-cut smoked bacon, eggs and cream.

FOR THE RICH SHORTCRUST PASTRY:
175g plain flour
a pinch of salt and a grind of pepper
110g unsalted butter, chilled and diced
1 medium free-range egg yolk, mixed with
2 tablespoons ice-cold water

FOR THE FILLING:
225g thick-cut smoked back bacon
2 tablespoons chopped parsley
salt and pepper
4 medium free-range eggs
400ml single cream
3 tablespoons milk

a 22cm loose-based deep flan tin
a baking tray

To make the pastry by hand, sift the flour, salt and pepper into a mixing bowl. Add the diced butter and rub in with the tips of your fingers until the mixture looks like fine crumbs. Using a round-bladed knife, mix in the egg yolk mixture to make a firm dough. If the mixture seems dry and crumbly, stir in a little water a teaspoon at a time. (See also page 148.)

To make the pastry in a food processor, put the flour, salt and pepper into the bowl of the processor and pulse a couple of times to combine. Add the diced cold butter and run the machine until the mixture looks like fine crumbs. With the machine running, add the yolk mixture and process just until the dough comes together. If there are dry crumbs in the bottom of the bowl, add more water a teaspoon at a time just until you have a firm dough. (See also page 148.)

Wrap the dough in clingfilm and chill for 20 minutes. Roll out on a lightly floured surface to a circle about 28cm across, and use to line the flan tin (see page 151). Prick the base with a fork, then chill.

Heat the oven to 190°C/375°F/gas 5. Line the pastry case with a piece of greaseproof paper, fill with baking beans, and bake 'blind' (see page 151) for 15 minutes, or until the pastry is set and firm. Remove the paper and beans and bake for a further 5 to 7 minutes, or until the pastry base is cooked and lightly coloured. Remove from the oven and leave to cool while preparing the filling. Put a baking tray into the oven to heat, and reduce the oven temperature to 180°C/350°F/gas 4.

Snip the bacon into thin strips. Put into a non-stick frying pan (add a little butter if your pan is not non-stick) over a medium heat. Fry, stirring frequently, until crisp and golden brown. Drain thoroughly, then scatter the bacon over the base of the pastry case. Sprinkle over the chopped parsley and season with a little salt and plenty of pepper.

Beat the eggs with the cream and milk in a wide jug. Stand the flan tin on the hot baking tray. Pour in half the egg mixture, then set the tray on the oven shelf, slightly pulled out. Carefully pour in the rest of the egg mixture to fill the pastry case (you may not need all of it). Gently push the shelf into place and bake for about 35 minutes, until puffed, golden brown and just firm. Remove from the oven, cool slightly, then unmould (the filling will sink slightly). Serve warm or at room temperature.

Blue Shropshire and Broccoli Tart

MAKES 1 MEDIUM TART

Blue Shropshire has had an interesting geographical history. It was invented by Scottish cheese-maker Andy Williamson almost 40 years ago and was first known as Inverness-shire Blue. When that dairy closed, the cheese recipe travelled south and has become a speciality of the Skailes family at Cropwell Bishop in Nottingham. It is softer and creamier than Stilton, with a sharper tang, which makes it an excellent candidate for baking as well as for the cheese board.

FOR THE WALNUT PASTRY:
175g plain flour or light brown plain flour
a good pinch of salt
50g walnut pieces
110g unsalted butter, chilled and diced
about 2 tablespoons ice-cold water

FOR THE FILLING:
400g broccoli – to yield 250g trimmed florets
175g Blue Shropshire or Stilton cheese
3 medium free-range eggs
300ml single cream
1 tablespoon snipped fresh chives (optional)
salt and pepper, to taste

a 22cm loose-based flan tin
a baking tray

Make the pastry in a food processor: put the flour, salt and walnuts into the processor bowl and run the machine until the nuts are finely chopped and the mixture looks sandy. Add the pieces of cold butter and process again until the mixture looks like fine crumbs. With the machine running, add 2 tablespoons of ice-cold water through the feed tube and process until the mixture comes together to make a ball of dough. If there are dry crumbs and the mixture won't form a dough, add more ice-cold water a teaspoon at a time. (See also page 148.) Wrap the dough in clingfilm and chill for 20 minutes.

Roll out the pastry on a lightly floured work surface to a circle about 28cm across and use to line the flan tin (see page 151). Chill for 15 minutes, and meanwhile heat the oven to 190°C/375°F/gas 5. Line the pastry case with a piece of greaseproof paper, fill with baking beans and bake 'blind' (see page 151) for 15 minutes. Remove the paper and beans and bake for a further 5 to 7 minutes, or until the pastry is crisp and light brown. Remove the flan tin from the oven, put the baking tray in to heat, and turn down the temperature to 180°C/350°F/gas 4.

While the pastry case is baking, prepare the filling. Bring a pan of water to the boil and add the trimmed broccoli florets. As soon as the water returns to the boil, remove the pan from the heat and drain the broccoli, shaking the colander well. Trim off any rind from the cheese, then crumble, not too finely as it's nice to come across the odd large lump. Lightly whisk the eggs with the cream, stir in the chives (if using) and add a little salt and plenty of ground pepper.

Arrange the florets in the pastry case and scatter over the cheese. Stand the flan tin on the hot baking tray and carefully pour the egg mixture over the broccoli and cheese. Bake in the heated oven for 30 to 35 minutes, until just firm. Remove from the oven, leave to cool for 5 minutes, then unmould. Serve warm or at room temperature the same day

Salmon and Watercress Flan

MAKES 1 MEDIUM FLAN

Watercress is very English – grown in the cool, clear chalky riverbeds of the south. Here, it adds a peppery flavour to the rich flesh of the salmon. This is perfect for a summer picnic.

FOR THE RICH SHORTCRUST PASTRY:
1 tablespoon poppy seeds
225g plain flour
¼ teaspoon salt
150g unsalted butter, chilled and diced
2–3 tablespoons ice-cold water, to bind
a little egg white, for brushing

FOR THE FILLING:
400g salmon fillets
4 tablespoons white wine
25g unsalted butter
2 medium shallots, peeled and finely chopped
100g watercress sprigs, washed
3 medium free-range eggs
300ml single or whipping cream
salt, pepper and nutmeg, to taste

a 23–4cm loose-based deep flan tin
a baking tray

To make the pastry, put the poppy seeds into a small dry frying pan and stir over a low heat for 5 minutes. Remove from the heat, tip into a small bowl and leave to cool. Put the flour, salt and cold poppy seeds into the bowl of a food processor and pulse a couple of times to combine. Add the butter and run the machine until the mixture resembles fine crumbs. With the machine running, add the water, a tablespoon at a time, until the mixture comes together to make a soft but not sticky dough. Wrap the dough in clingfilm and chill for 20 minutes. (See also page 148.)

Roll out the dough on a lightly floured work surface to a circle about 29cm across and use to line the flan tin (see page 151), making sure the rim of the pastry stands slightly above the tin. Prick the base well, then chill for 20 minutes while heating the oven to 190°C/375°F/gas 5.

Line the pastry case with greaseproof paper, fill with baking beans and bake 'blind' (see page 151) for 15 minutes. Remove the paper and beans, reduce the temperature to 180°C/350°F/gas 4 and bake the empty pastry case for a further 5 minutes. Lightly brush the base of the pastry with egg white and return it to the oven for 1 minute. Remove from the oven and put a baking tray in to heat.

Meanwhile, cook the fish: put the salmon fillet into a pan that just fits it and pour over the wine. Bring to the boil, then cover tightly and leave the fish to cook over a low heat in the steam of the wine for 12 to 15 minutes, until the flesh just flakes. Remove and leave to cool, then flake the fish, discarding the skin but saving the cooking liquid. Melt the butter in a medium pan, add the finely chopped shallots and cook very gently over a low heat until soft and tender – about 10 minutes. Roughly chop the watercress and add to the pan with the fish cooking liquid, stirring over medium heat until the watercress wilts and the liquid evaporates. Remove from the heat and leave to cool. Beat the eggs with the cream in a jug and season with a little salt, plenty of pepper and several gratings of nutmeg.

When ready to assemble, put the flaked fish into the pastry case. Scatter the watercress mixture on top, then set the flan tin on the heated baking tray. Pour the egg mixture into the pastry case and carefully put into the oven. Bake until just golden, slightly puffed and just set – about 25 minutes. Remove from the oven, stand for 10 minutes, then carefully unmould. Serve warm the same day.

Westmorland Tart MAKES 1 MEDIUM TART

In the eighteenth century, when boats loaded with goods from the West Indies came back to their home ports on the north-west coast of Britain, dried fruits, sugars, spices, ginger and dark rum soon made their way into local dishes. This tart is similar to the popular, better-known Cumberland rum nicky, a sticky combination of dates, dark sugar, preserved ginger and rum, but is lighter and less sweet thanks to the fresh fruit juice and the crunchy, slightly bitter walnuts.

FOR THE SWEET SHORTCRUST PASTRY:
175g plain flour
a pinch of salt
2 tablespoons caster sugar
110g unsalted butter, chilled and diced
1 medium free-range egg yolk, mixed with 2 tablespoons ice-cold water

FOR THE FILLING:
200g large raisins
85g chopped dates

85g dark brown muscovado sugar
juice of ½ a lemon
juice of ½ an orange
25g unsalted butter, diced
3 tablespoons dark rum
100g walnut halves or large pieces

TO SERVE (OPTIONAL):
Cumberland rum cream (see below)

a 22cm deep loose-based flan tin

To make the sweet shortcrust pastry by hand, sift the flour, salt and sugar into a mixing bowl. Add the diced butter and rub in using the tips of your fingers until the mixture looks like fine crumbs. Using a round-bladed knife, mix in the egg yolk mixture to make a firm dough. If the mixture seems dry and crumbly, stir in a little water a teaspoon at a time. (See also page 148.)

To make the pastry in a food processor, put the flour, salt and sugar into the processor bowl and pulse a couple of times until combined. Add the diced butter and process until the mixture looks like fine crumbs. With the machine running, add the yolk mixture and process until the dough comes together. If there are dry crumbs in the bottom, add a little water a teaspoon at a time until you have a firm dough. (See also page 148.)

Wrap the dough in clingfilm and chill for 20 minutes. Roll out the dough on a floured work surface to a circle about 28cm across, and line the flan tin (see page 151). Prick the base with a fork, then chill for 20 minutes while heating the oven to 190°C/375°F/gas 5.

Line the pastry case with greaseproof paper, fill with baking beans, and bake 'blind' (see page 151) in the heated oven for 15 minutes, or until the pastry is firm. Remove the paper and beans and bake for a further 5 to 7 minutes, or until the pastry is crisp and light golden brown. Remove from the oven. While the pastry case is baking, make the filling. Put the raisins, dates, sugar, lemon and orange juices, butter and rum into a medium pan and heat gently, stirring frequently, until the butter has melted. Bring to the boil, then remove from the heat. Leave to stand until cool, then stir in the walnuts.

Spoon the filling into the pastry case – do not pack or press it down. Return the flan tin to the oven and bake for a further 5 to 10 minutes, until the walnuts have turned golden brown. Remove from the oven. Cool slightly, then unmould. Serve just warm or at room temperature.

CUMBERLAND RUM CREAM

Whip 150ml of chilled double cream with 20g of icing sugar and 2 tablespoons of dark rum until stiff. Cover and chill until ready to serve.

Tudor-Style Baked Cheesecake

MAKES 1 MEDIUM CHEESECAKE

This is a light, well-flavoured cheesecake made from low-fat ricotta, a soft Italian cheese, though it was originally made with fresh soft curd cheese and was often flavoured and coloured with saffron. This style of tart, using curds, became popular in Tudor times and often featured at feast-day celebrations. Later on, in Georgian England, a cheese cake or 'pye' made with puff pastry and with a filling thickened with breadcrumbs was developed.

FOR THE SWEET SHORTCRUST PASTRY:
175g plain flour
a pinch of salt
2 tablespoons caster sugar
1 tablespoon ground almonds
110g unsalted butter, chilled and diced
1 medium free-range egg yolk, mixed with 2 tablespoons ice-cold water

FOR THE FILLING:
500g low-fat ricotta
200ml sour cream
2 medium free-range eggs
2 tablespoons ground almonds
100g icing sugar
grated zest and juice of 1½ medium lemons
1 tablespoon large raisins
2 tablespoons flaked almonds

a 22cm loose-based flan tin
a baking tray

To make the pastry by hand, sift the flour, salt, sugar and ground almonds into a mixing bowl. Add the diced butter and rub in with the tips of your fingers until the mixture looks like fine crumbs. Stir in the yolk mixture, using a round-bladed knife, to make a firm dough. If the mixture seems dry and crumbly, stir in a little water a teaspoon at a time.

To make the pastry in a food processor, put the flour, salt, sugar and ground almonds into the processor bowl and pulse until combined. Add the diced butter and process until the mixture looks like fine crumbs. With the machine running, add the yolk mixture and process just until the dough comes together. If there are dry crumbs in the bottom of the bowl, add a little more water a teaspoon at a time until you have a firm dough. (See also page 148.)

Wrap the dough in clingfilm and chill for 20 minutes. Roll out on a lightly floured work surface to a circle about 28cm across, and use to line the flan tin (see page 151). Prick the base with a fork, then chill for 20 minutes while heating the oven to 190°C/350°F/gas 5.

Line the pastry case with greaseproof paper, fill with baking beans and bake 'blind' (see page 151) for 15 minutes. When the pastry is firm, remove the paper and beans and bake for a further 5 to 7 minutes, until the pastry base is crisp and lightly coloured. Remove from the oven, reduce the temperature to 150°C/300°F/gas 2 and put the baking tray in to heat.

To make the filling, put the ricotta, sour cream, eggs, almonds, icing sugar and lemon zest and juice into the bowl of a food processor. Pulse until thoroughly combined and very smooth. Stand the flan tin on the heated baking tray and pour the filling into the pastry case. Scatter over the raisins, followed by the flaked almonds, and bake in the heated oven for 1 to 1¼ hours, until just firm. Turn off the oven but don't open the oven door, and leave the cheesecake to cool slowly for 1½ hours. Unmould, then cover and chill overnight. Remove from the fridge half an hour before serving.

Yorkshire Pink 'Champagne' Rhubarb Cheesecake

MAKES 1 LARGE CHEESECAKE

This is a modern cheesecake, deep and rich, offset by sweet 'forced' rhubarb. Forced rhubarb from the Yorkshire Triangle has recently been given the sought-after protected-name status by the EU. Rhubarb is thought to have been introduced to Europe by Marco Polo as a medicine, but by the eighteenth century it was a popular, beneficial foodstuff. The sweet-tasting pink variety favoured today is the result of an accidental discovery in the Chelsea Physic Garden in 1817, when a bright pink rhubarb plant was found growing under a mound of soil. This 'blanching', covering the plant with soil so it doesn't get the chance to turn green and fibrous in the light, has now become big business in Yorkshire and tourists flock in the spring to 'see' the rhubarb growing in pitch-dark sheds, where it's harvested by candlelight.

FOR THE BASE:
100g digestive biscuits, crushed
50g unsalted butter, melted

FOR THE FILLING:
900g good-quality cream cheese (not low-fat)
grated zest of 1 unwaxed lemon and 1 unwaxed orange
1 teaspoon vanilla extract
200g caster sugar

4 medium free-range eggs, beaten
450ml sour cream

FOR THE TOPPING:
275g young pink rhubarb
3 tablespoons good strawberry jam or conserve

a 22–23cm springclip tin, greased
a baking tray

Heat the oven to 150°C/300°F/gas 2. To make the base, mix the biscuit crumbs with the melted butter, tip into the prepared tin, then press down with the back of a spoon to make an even layer. Chill while making the filling.

Put the cream cheese, grated lemon and orange zests, vanilla and sugar into a mixing bowl, or the bowl of a food mixer. Beat at low to medium speed with an electric whisk or the mixer until very smooth, scraping down the sides of the bowl from time to time. Gradually beat in the eggs, followed by the sour cream. When thoroughly combined, pour the filling into the tin, set on the baking tray. Carefully transfer to the oven (the tin will be almost full) and bake for 1¾ hours, or until just firm. The mixture will puff up, then sink on cooling (it nearly always cracks too, but the topping disguises this). Turn off the oven but don't open the oven door, and leave the cheesecake to cool slowly for 1½ hours. Remove from the oven and, when completely cold, cover and chill overnight.

The topping can be baked alongside the cheesecake. Rinse the rhubarb, trim off the ends and cut on the diagonal into 2 to 3cm lengths. Spread the jam over the base of a large ovenproof baking dish and arrange the rhubarb on top. Cover tightly with foil, and bake for 20 to 30 minutes until tender. Remove from the oven and leave to cool completely. When ready to finish the cheesecake, remove the rhubarb from its liquid, draining well. Spoon the rhubarb cooking juices into a small pan and simmer over a low heat for a few minutes until syrupy. Unclip the tin and set the cheesecake on a serving plate. Arrange the fruit on top, and brush generously with the hot syrup. Chill until ready to serve.

Nutmeg Custard Tart

It's the nutmeg that lifts this homely dessert out of the bland and ordinary: the rich, creamy, sweet egg custard filling needs the warm flavour and fragrance of the freshly grated nutmeg. Along with mace (its lacy, lighter brown, net-like covering), nutmeg has been a popular spice in Europe since the twelfth century, enlivening green vegetables such as cabbage and spinach as well as milky dishes like rice puddings and white sauces.

FOR THE SWEET SHORTCRUST PASTRY:	FOR THE FILLING:
175g plain flour	400ml single cream
a pinch of salt	200ml milk
2 tablespoons caster sugar	a few blades of mace
110g unsalted butter, chilled and diced	a little freshly grated nutmeg
1 medium free-range egg yolk, mixed with	2 medium free-range eggs, plus 2 yolks
2 tablespoons ice-cold water	75g caster sugar
	a 22cm loose-based deep flan tin
	a baking tray

To make the pastry by hand, sift the flour, salt and sugar into a mixing bowl. Add the diced butter and rub in with the tips of your fingers until the mixture looks like fine crumbs. Using a round-bladed knife, mix in the egg yolk mixture to make a firm dough. If the mixture seems dry and crumbly, stir in a little more water a teaspoon at a time. (See also page 148.)

To make the pastry in a food processor, put the flour, salt and sugar into the processor bowl and pulse a couple of times until combined. Add the diced butter and process until the mixture looks like fine crumbs. With the machine running, add the yolk mixture and process just until the dough comes together. If there are dry crumbs in the bottom of the bowl, add more water a teaspoon at a time to make a firm dough. (See also page 148.)

Wrap the dough in clingfilm and chill for 20 minutes. Roll out on a lightly floured work surface to a circle about 28cm across, then use to line the flan tin (see page 151). Prick the base with a fork, then chill for 15 minutes. Meanwhile, heat the oven to 190°C/375°F/gas 5. Line the pastry case with greaseproof paper, fill with baking beans and bake 'blind' (see page 151) for about 15 minutes, until lightly golden and just firm. Remove the paper and beans and bake for a further 5 to 7 minutes, until the base is thoroughly cooked, firm and lightly browned. Remove from the oven and leave to cool while making the filling. Reduce the oven temperature to 150°C/300°F/gas 2 and put the baking tray into the oven to heat up.

Put the cream and milk into a pan, add the mace and a couple of gratings of nutmeg. Slowly bring to the boil, then remove from the heat and leave to cool for 5 minutes. In a heatproof bowl, thoroughly beat the eggs and yolks with the sugar, using a wooden spoon, until lighter in colour and very smooth. Stand the bowl on a damp cloth so it doesn't wobble, then gradually pour the hot cream into the bowl in a steady stream, stirring constantly. Set the flan tin on the hot baking tray and strain the mixture through a sieve into the pastry case. Grate nutmeg over the surface – you can be quite generous – then carefully transfer the tray to the oven and bake the tart for about 30 minutes, until lightly coloured and just firm – it will continue to cook for a while after it is removed from the oven (if overcooked, the mixture will curdle). Leave to cool, then carefully unmould. Serve at room temperature the same day.

Treacle Tart

MAKES 1 MEDIUM TART

Eaten warm with custard or cream, this very simple pud is an old-fashioned treat. It is one of those 'something good made out of nothing' recipes that has moved from its homely roots and is now found in the smartest restaurants. Whereas you could often find a farmhouse version made with wholemeal crumbs, or the addition of a good pinch of ground ginger or a tablespoon of black treacle, today chefs often add eggs, cream and sea salt. You can also add a Bramley cooking apple, peeled, cored and grated, to the mixture with breadcrumbs for a lighter, more fluffy filling.

FOR THE SHORTCRUST PASTRY:	FOR THE FILLING:
220g plain flour	6 rounded tablespoons golden syrup
a good pinch of salt	75g fresh white breadcrumbs
1 teaspoon caster sugar	grated zest and juice of
160g unsalted butter, chilled and diced	1 large unwaxed lemon
2–3 tablespoons ice-cold water	
	a 26cm deep ovenproof pie plate

To make the pastry by hand, sieve the flour, salt and sugar into a mixing bowl. Add the diced butter and rub into the flour, using the tips of your fingers, until the mixture looks like fine crumbs. Using a round-bladed knife, stir in enough ice-cold water to bind the ingredients together to make a firm dough. (See also page 148.)

To make the pastry in a food processor, put the flour, salt and sugar into the bowl of the processor and pulse for a couple of seconds until just combined. Add the pieces of butter and process until the mixture looks like fine crumbs. With the machine running, add 2 tablespoons of ice-cold water through the feed tube – the mixture should come together to make a ball of firm dough. If the mixture seems dry and crumbly and won't bind, add more water a teaspoon at a time. (See also page 148.)

Wrap the dough in clingfilm and chill for 20 minutes. Roll out the dough on a lightly floured work surface to a circle 3cm larger than your plate. Wrap the pastry around the rolling pin, drape it over the plate, then gently unroll it so it covers the plate. Press the pastry on to the base, pressing out any pockets of air. Trim off the excess with a sharp knife. Chill while making the filling.

Heat the oven to 190°C/375°F/gas 5. Gently warm the syrup in a small pan until it becomes runny, then remove from the heat and stir in the breadcrumbs, lemon zest and juice. Leave to stand for 10 minutes; if the mixture seems very sloppy, add another spoonful of crumbs, but if it seems stiff and dry, add another spoonful of syrup. Spoon the filling into the pastry case without pressing down or compacting the mixture. Bake in the heated oven for about 30 minutes, until the pastry is golden. Serve warm with cream (also good with custard).

Lemon Meringue Tart MAKES 1 MEDIUM TART

The American dessert Chester pudding is a tart with thin, crisp pastry filled with a rich, lemony egg custard then topped with stiffly whipped egg whites sweetened with white sugar and quickly browned. It sounds rather like our much-loved lemon meringue pie. Could it be that English home-bakers took the pudding with them when they emigrated to the New World and it returned a couple of centuries later with an American twist?

FOR THE SWEET SHORTCRUST PASTRY:
175g plain flour
a good pinch of salt
1 tablespoon caster sugar
115g unsalted butter, chilled and diced
1 medium free-range egg yolk,
mixed with 2 tablespoons ice-cold water

FOR THE LEMON FILLING:
3 medium unwaxed lemons
40g cornflour

300ml water
3 medium free-range egg yolks
85g caster sugar
50g unsalted butter, diced

FOR THE MERINGUE TOPPING:
4 medium free-range egg whites
200g caster sugar

a 22cm loose-based deep flan tin
a baking tray

To make the pastry by hand, sift the flour, salt and sugar into a mixing bowl. Add the cold diced butter and rub in with the tips of your fingers until the mixture looks like fine crumbs. Using a round-bladed knife, mix in the egg yolk mixture to make a firm dough. If the mixture seems dry and crumbly, stir in more water a teaspoon at a time. (See also page 148.)

To make the pastry in a food processor, put the flour, salt and sugar into the processor bowl and pulse until just combined. Add the butter and process until the mixture looks like fine crumbs. With the machine running, add the yolk mixture and process until the dough comes together. If there are dry crumbs, add some water a teaspoon at a time until you have a slightly firm dough. (See also page 148.)

Wrap the dough in clingfilm and chill for 20 minutes, then roll out on a lightly floured surface to a circle about 28cm across and use to line the flan tin (see page 151). Prick the base with a fork, then chill for 15 minutes. Heat the oven to 190°C/375°F/gas 5. Line the pastry case with greaseproof paper, fill with baking beans and bake 'blind' (see page 151) for about 15 minutes, until lightly golden and just firm. Remove the paper and beans, lower the oven temperature to 180°C/350°F/gas 4 and bake for a further 5 minutes, or until the base is crisp and lightly golden. Remove from the oven and leave to cool while making the filling. Leave the oven on and put the baking tray in to heat.

Rinse the lemons, then grate the zest into a heatproof bowl. Add the juice and the cornflour and stir to make a smooth paste. Bring the water to the boil in a medium-sized pan and pour it on to the lemon mixture, stirring constantly with a wooden spoon. When thoroughly combined, pour the mixture back into the pan and cook, stirring constantly, until it boils and thickens. Reduce the heat and simmer gently, stirring, for a minute. Remove the pan from the heat and beat in the egg yolks, quickly followed by the sugar and butter. Spoon the filling into the pastry case and spread evenly.

Put the 4 egg whites into a large bowl and whisk until they stand in soft peaks. Gradually whisk in the sugar to make a stiff, glossy meringue. Pile the meringue on top of the lemon filling so it is totally covered. Stand the tart on the hot baking tray and bake for 20 minutes, until the meringue is a golden brown. Leave to cool, then unmould and serve at room temperature.

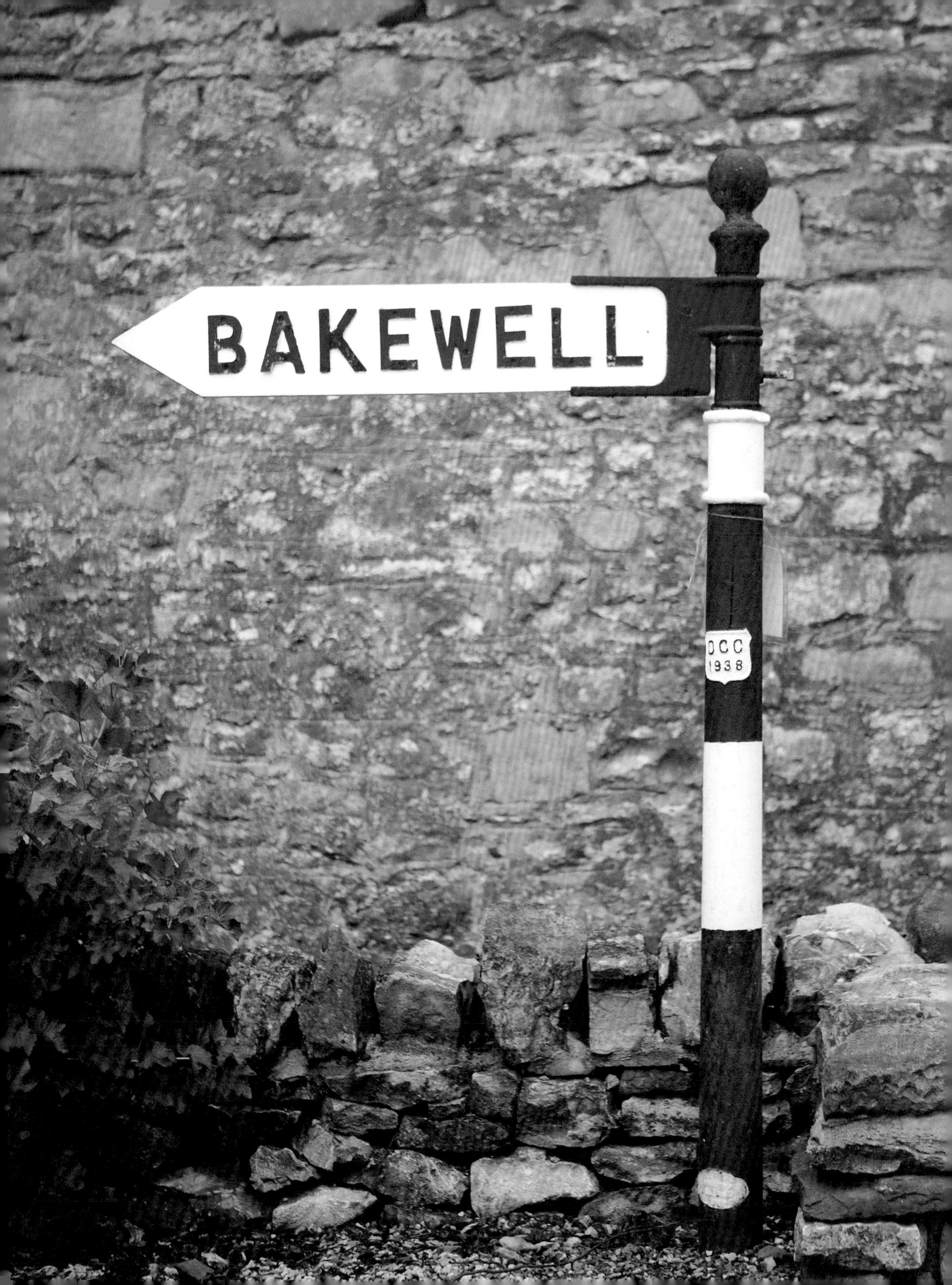
BAKEWELL
DCC
1938

Bakewell Tart MAKES 1 MEDIUM TART

The origins of this famous bake from the small Derbyshire town of Bakewell are hotly disputed. Legend has it created by an Italian pastry cook at the Rutland Arms Hotel. There are also two different types: the pudding has a puff pastry base spread with strawberry jam, and a soft and creamy custard topping. Some local bakers have adapted this with apricot jam and the addition of orange flower water to the custard. The newer tart is made with shortcrust pastry, then a layer of raspberry jam covered with almond sponge, topped with lemon water icing and a sprinkling of flaked almonds.

FOR THE SWEET SHORTCRUST PASTRY:
175g plain flour
a pinch of salt
2 tablespoons caster sugar
115g unsalted butter, chilled and diced
1 medium free-range egg yolk,
mixed with 2 tablespoons ice-cold water
3 tablespoons raspberry jam

FOR THE TOPPING:
60g unsalted butter, soft but not runny
60g caster sugar
1 medium free-range egg,
at room temperature

30g self-raising flour
¼ teaspoon baking powder
50g ground almonds
a few drops of almond essence

FOR THE ICING:
100g icing sugar, sieved
1 teaspoon lemon juice
about 1 tablespoon cold water

flaked almonds, to decorate

a 22cm loose-based flan tin
a baking tray

To make the pastry by hand, sift the flour, salt and sugar into a mixing bowl. Add the diced butter and rub in with your fingers until the mixture looks like fine crumbs. Using a round-bladed knife, mix in the egg yolk mixture to make a firm dough. If the mixture seems dry and crumbly, stir in a little water a teaspoon at a time. (See also page 148.)

To make the pastry in a food processor, put the flour, salt and sugar into the processor bowl and pulse a couple of times until combined. Add the diced butter and process until the mixture looks like fine crumbs. With the machine running add the yolk and water, and process just until the dough comes together. If there are dry crumbs in the bottom of the bowl, add a little more water a teaspoon at a time until you have a slightly firm dough. (See also page 148.)

Wrap the dough in clingfilm and chill for 20 minutes. Roll out on a floured work surface to a circle about 28cm across, then use to line the flan tin (see page 151). Prick the base with a fork, spread with the jam and chill while making the topping and heating the oven. Heat the oven to 180°C/350°F/gas 4. Put the baking tray in the oven to heat up.

Put the soft butter, sugar, egg, sieved flour and baking powder, ground almonds and almond essence into a mixing bowl. Beat well with a wooden spoon or an electric whisk until thoroughly combined. Spoon on top of the jam and spread evenly. Bake in the heated oven, on the hot baking tray, for 30 minutes, or until the pastry is a light golden brown and the filling is firm to the touch and golden. Remove from the oven, leave to cool, then unmould.

Mix the icing sugar with the lemon juice and water to make smooth, runny icing – if necessary add more water a teaspoon at a time. Spoon the icing into a greaseproof paper icing bag, or into a corner of a small plastic bag, and snip off the tip. Pipe the icing over the tart in a random or zigzag pattern. Scatter with flaked almonds. Serve gently warmed or at room temperature.

Strawberry Tart MAKES 1 MEDIUM TART

A celebration of our best produce: glorious dark red ripe berries, oozing sweet juice and sunshine, plus a rich and thickly creamy custard and crisp sweet pastry make the perfect dessert for a summer feast. To make this tart even more decadent, completely cover the custard base with 600g strawberries. You can also add a couple of teaspoons of orange liqueur (Cointreau or Grand Marnier) to the custard before you add the whipped cream if you like that kind of thing.

FOR THE RICH SWEET SHORTCRUST PASTRY:
175g plain flour
a pinch of salt
2 tablespoons icing sugar
110g unsalted butter, chilled and diced
2 medium free-range egg yolks,
mixed with 1 tablespoon ice-cold water

FOR THE CUSTARD CREAM:
300ml milk
finely grated zest of 1 medium unwaxed orange

4 medium free-range egg yolks,
at room temperature
60g caster sugar
2 tablespoons cornflour
150ml double or whipping cream, well chilled

FOR THE TOPPING:
200g ripe strawberries
4 tablespoons good strawberry jam

a 22cm loose-based deep flan tin

To make the pastry by hand, sift the flour, salt and icing sugar into a mixing bowl. Add the cold diced butter and rub into the flour using the tips of your fingers until the mixture looks like fine crumbs. Using a round-bladed knife, stir in the egg yolk mixture to make a firm dough; if it seems dry and crumbly, stir in a little water a teaspoon at a time. To make the pastry in a food processor, put the flour, salt and icing sugar into the processor bowl and pulse a couple of times to combine. Add the cold diced butter and process until the mixture looks like fine crumbs. With the machine running, add the yolk mixture and process until the mixture comes together. If there are dry crumbs, add more water a teaspoon at a time. (See page 148.)

Wrap the dough in clingfilm and chill for 20 minutes. Roll out on a lightly floured surface to a circle about 28cm across, then carefully line the flan tin (see page 151) – this rich pastry is less robust than regular shortcrust. Prick the base of the pastry case, then chill for 20 minutes. Meanwhile, heat the oven to 190°C/375°F/gas 5. Line the pastry case with greaseproof paper, fill with baking beans, and bake 'blind' (see page 151) for 15 minutes, until the pastry is firm. Remove the paper and beans and bake for a further 5 to 10 minutes, until the pastry is crisp and golden brown. Remove from the oven and leave to cool completely.

Meanwhile, make the custard filling. Heat the milk with the orange zest in a medium pan. In a heatproof bowl, whisk the egg yolks with the sugar and cornflour with a wire hand-whisk until smooth – about 1 to 2 minutes. Whisk in the hot milk. When thoroughly combined, tip the mixture back into the pan and set over a medium heat. Whisk constantly until the mixture boils and thickens to make a smooth custard. Tip the mixture on to a plate and press a piece of dampened greaseproof paper on to the surface to prevent a skin forming as it cools. Chill for at least 20 minutes.

Wipe the berries with damp kitchen towels, then hull. Heat the jam in a small pan until boiling, then push through a sieve. Return the sieved jam to the pan. Whip the cream until it holds soft peaks. Transfer the custard to a mixing bowl, stir until very smooth, and fold in the whipped cream. Set the pastry case on a serving plate and fill with the custard cream. Arrange the berries on top. Reheat the jam until it starts to bubble, then brush over the berries. Serve immediately.

Jam Tarts

MAKES 12 LITTLE TARTS

'The Queen of Hearts she made some tarts…' Often thought to look like stained-glass windows, to get this traditional effect use several brightly coloured, well-flavoured jams – apricot, strawberry or raspberry, blackberry or hedgerow, gooseberry or greengage. Firm-set jam works better here than a softer fruit conserve. You can also make a large jam tart and decorate with narrow strips of pastry to look like a latticed window.

FOR THE SHORTCRUST PASTRY:	FOR THE FILLING:
200g plain flour	6 tablespoons good-quality jam
a good pinch of salt	
1 teaspoon caster sugar	a round fluted cutter, about 7.5cm,
125g unsalted butter, chilled and diced	and small shaped cutters (optional)
about 2 tablespoons ice-cold water	a 12-hole mince pie or bun tray

To make the pastry by hand, sieve the flour, salt and sugar into a mixing bowl. Add the diced butter and rub into the flour, using the tips of your fingers, until the mixture looks like fine crumbs. Using a round-bladed knife, stir in enough ice-cold water to bind the ingredients together to make a firm dough. (See also page 148.)

To make the pastry in a food processor, put the flour, salt and sugar into the bowl of the processor and pulse for a couple of seconds just to combine. Add the pieces of butter and process until the mixture looks like fine crumbs. With the machine running, add 2 tablespoons of ice-cold water – the mixture should come together to make a ball of firm dough. If the mixture seems dry and crumbly and won't bind, add more water a teaspoon at a time. (See also page 148.)

Wrap the dough in clingfilm and chill for 20 minutes. Heat the oven to 180°C/350°/gas 4. Roll out the pastry on a lightly floured work surface to a rectangle about 3mm thick and roughly the size of your bun tray. Dip the round cutter in flour, then cut out circles of pastry, gathering up the trimmings, re-rolling and cutting more until you have 12. Gently press the pastry into the holes in the bun tray. Put a rounded teaspoon of jam into the middle of each one. If liked, cut decorations from the leftover pastry, using the smaller cutters, and set them on top of the jam.

Bake in the heated oven for 15 to 20 minutes, until the pastry is a light golden brown. Remove from the oven, leave to cool for 5 minutes, then remove the tarts from the tray to a wire cooling rack (take care, as the hot jam will burn). Leave to cool completely before eating.

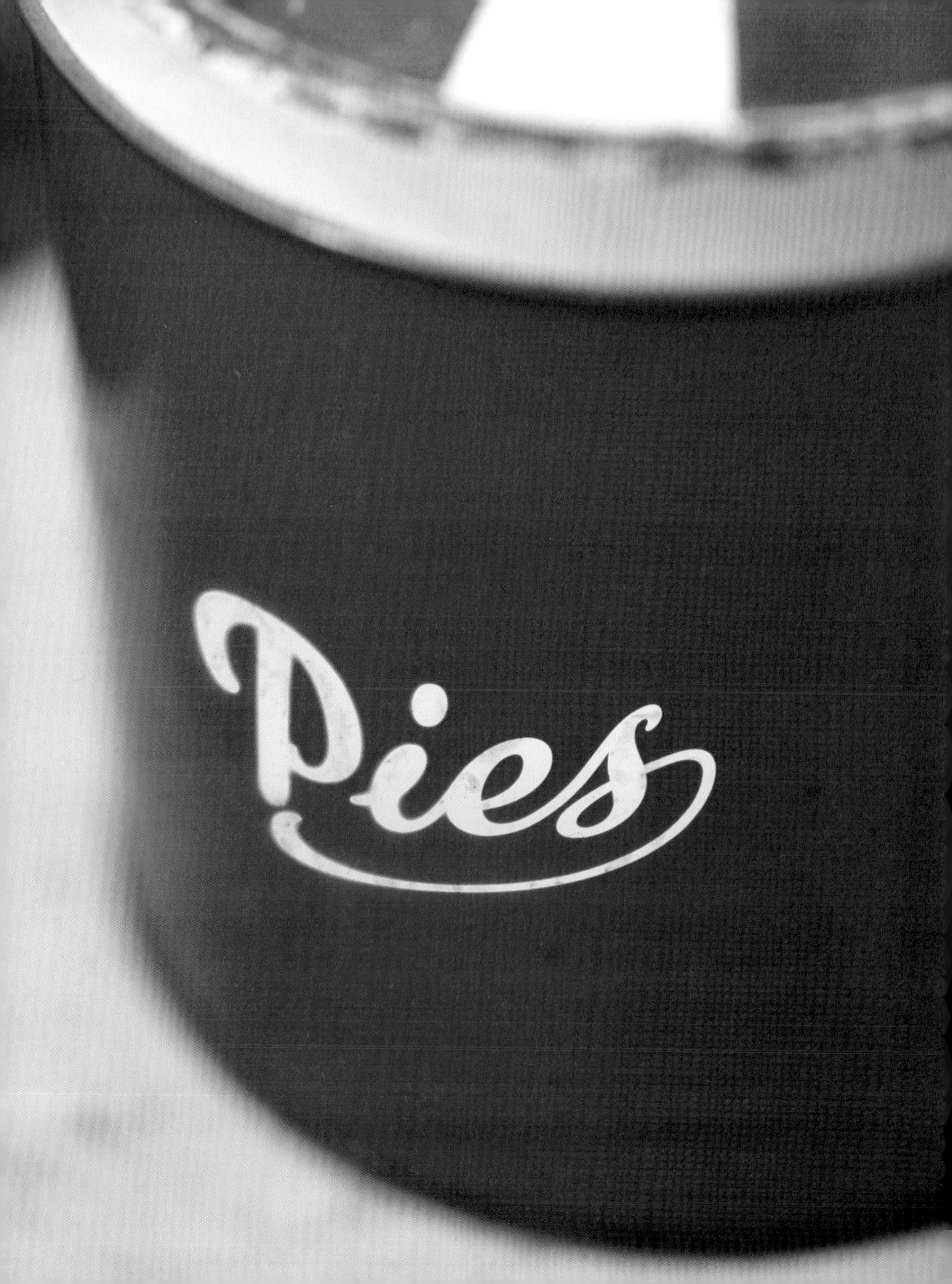
Pies

A pie is quintessentially British.

A proper picnic should always include a pork pie, encased in crisp pastry; a mince pie says Christmas; and half-time at a football match isn't quite right without a meat pie – 'Who ate all the pies?' has long been the taunt from the terraces at the expense of a slightly rotund player. And how many of us have wistful memories of a grandmother's blackberry and apple or gooseberry pie: the fruit encased in sweet pastry and dusted with sugar, the juice oozing out in little pools? In 1799 the poet Robert Southey even wrote an ode to 'Gooseberry-pie'; while Jane Austen summed up that warm feeling of comfort and wellbeing we associate with a good pie in a letter she wrote to her sister Cassandra in 1815: 'I am glad the new cook begins so well. Good Apple Pies are a considerable part of our domestic happiness.' Pie crops up everywhere in our everyday expressions: we describe someone's attitude as 'nice as pie', something improbable as 'pie in the sky', and when everything is as it should be, it is in 'apple-pie order'. A little word it may be, but it sweeps through British history and geography, embracing a vast array of recipes from everyday to extravagant.

The earliest Neolithic pies were made of rough paste wrapped around meat and baked in pits heated by the ashes from fires. In medieval times, pork or mutton were baked inside thick, hard, lidded pastry cases. Most open tarts and covered pies of the time were made inside these sturdy 'coffins', most likely designed to hold the filling together rather than to be eaten. In the Tudor courts, where such coffins were often elaborate, towering affairs, there was a tradition of birds in pies, celebrated in the nursery rhyme 'Sing a Song of Sixpence':

> Sing a song of sixpence a pocketful of rye,
> Four and twenty blackbirds baked in a pie.
> When the pie was opened, the birds began to sing,
> Oh, wasn't that a dainty dish to set before the king?

Historians believe it was considered a good courtly joke to put live birds under a lid of pastry, so that when the pie was opened they would fly out – presumably a proper pie with cooked birds would be waiting in the wings. Sometimes whole cooked peacocks or swans, still in their feathers, would be sitting, rather terrifyingly, atop the pies. The elaborate Tudor Christmas pie was an extravaganza of different birds (cooked!), which crops up later as a Yorkshire Christmas pie in the writings of the eighteenth-century cookery writer Hannah Glasse. She specifies a boned turkey, goose, fowl, partridge and pigeon, one inside the other, together with hare, woodcock, moor game and any other wild fowl that might be available, all packed inside a thick pastry crust. Of course, it wasn't only birds that went into the dishes of the wealthy. Pies made with eel-like lampreys were considered a delicacy right through to the seventeenth century, and fish pies were also made which, like their meat counterparts, were usually sweetened.

Although meat and dried fruit and spices were still usually mixed together, pies in which fresh fruit was the hero began emerging in Elizabethan times. The Warden pie, made with 'wardens' pears grown at the Cistercian Abbey of Warden in Bedfordshire, and flavoured with ginger, saffron and sometimes rosewater, became so popular that Shakespeare's Clown in *The Winter's Tale* insists, 'I must have saffron to colour the warden pies'.

The seventeenth and eighteenth centuries saw the real heyday of raised pies: elaborate, high-sided creations, made easier by the advent of sprung metal moulds in intricate designs, which enabled the cook to make a more delicate pastry and turn out pies that looked as though they had been carved with columns, flowers, leaves or coats of arms. Often the moulds were shaped to mirror the ingredients inside.

Meat pies still usually included dried fruits or candied peel and spices – the Devonshire squab pie, made with lamb (not squab pigeon as the name might suggest), contained apples and prunes; while fish pies were sweetened with sugar, offset with verjuice (made from sour grapes or crab apples) or citrus juice. Often there would be a hole in the middle of the pie, into which you would pour a hot liquid towards the end of baking. It might be a custard, or 'caudle', usually egg mixed with wine, sugar and lemon juice; or, in the case of a fish pie, wine and verjuice, spices and sometimes butter.

In Victorian London, oysters from the Thames were plentiful, so they frequently padded out the meat in a steak pie, and eel, pie and mash shops were a favourite in the East End. Mince pies, which had evolved over the centuries, began to resemble those we know today, though they were still made with minced beef along with raisins, currants and suet. Pies were by now so much the food of the people that Alexis Soyer, the celebrity chef of the times who devoted much of his time to trying to improve the food of the poor, noted in his book *A Shilling Cookery for the People* that 'pies in England may be considered as one of our best *companions du voyage* through life'. It was only when potatoes began to be more widely cultivated in the late nineteenth century, offering a cheaper, less time-consuming calorie intake, that the making of pies in the home began to wane.

The provenance of many of our regional pies is shrouded in questions and controversy, none more than in the case of two of our most celebrated pies: the Cornish pasty and the Melton Mowbray pork pie. Both are vehemently championed by those who have argued that any pies bearing the name should only be allowed to be made to strict specifications within a designated region. In the case of Melton Mowbray pies, such campaigning finally achieved Protected Geographical Indication status in 2009, so now any pies bearing the name must adhere to strict criteria.

Pasties have been made since the Middle Ages – in the seventeenth century, the diarist Samuel Pepys dined regularly on venison pasties – though these were usually massive creations made with big hunks of meat, to share with others and eat over several days. In the eighteenth century, the pasty in the form that we know it today – the original convenience food, being a portable meal – became inextricably associated with Cornwall. While at home family-sized pasties were still being made, individual ones were made for children or men going to work in the tin mines or fields. Their initials were marked in the pastry, to avoid them picking up the wrong one. The advantage of the pasty shape was that you could hold it by its ends, which could then be discarded if you had dirty hands. There is also a popular story that miners' pasties were sweet one end and savoury the other.

The subject of what exactly makes up a Cornish pasty arouses high emotion. Some say the pasty should be rough puff, some say shortcrust. However, when it comes to the filling, pasty purists are immovable: forget minced beef or lamb, and don't even think about carrots, peas or swede. The only allowable ingredients are chopped steak – either skirt or chuck – and potato, onion and turnip. The earliest pasties probably didn't include meat at all, as poorer families couldn't afford it. However, skirt (from the underside of the belly of the animal) is considered the perfect cut, as its juice produces wonderful gravy, it has no fat or gristle and it cooks in the same amount of time as the vegetables, which, like the meat, should never be pre-cooked as a pasty acts as its own oven. The only spicing should be black pepper, and the pastry should be crimped around the side – so that the pasty forms a 'D' shape – never over the top.

Stories and superstitions linked to pasties abound. One popular idea was that pasties kept the devil out of Cornwall – he didn't dare go there in case he ended up being put inside one! According to another, the miners would leave the ends for the mischievous sprites who lived underground, to keep them happy and the miners safe. If you were a fisherman, you always left your pasty on dry land for later, since it was considered bad luck to take a pasty on board a boat: if you did so, you wouldn't catch any fish. Again, this superstition harks back to the devil, who somehow got inside the pasties. However, if you broke off the ends and let the wind through, the devil might be let out . . .

Aficionados of the Melton Mowbray pork pie are equally protective of the original recipe against imitations. It is said that Melton Mowbray became the epicentre of pork-pie-making because the local Stilton cheese-makers kept pigs which they fed on leftover whey, so there was a surplus of fresh pork. What characterizes a true Melton Mowbray pie is this use of fresh meat which hasn't been cured, giving it a characteristic grey, rather than pink, colour. The second defining characteristic is the shape. Melton Mowbray is in the heart of traditional hunting country and originally the pies were made as a snack for huntsmen to carry in their saddlebags. Since the pies needed to withstand quite a bit of bumping around, they were baked 'standing free' so they took on a bowed shape which was less likely to break. The lack of a tin also allowed some of the lard in the hot-water crust to burn off, drying it slightly and making the pastry more crisp and durable. So popular were the pies with the hunting fraternity that they also demanded that they be served in their London clubs outside the hunting season. At first the pies had to be transported by stage coach, but the advent of the railways in the second half of the nineteenth century meant that their fame spread like wildfire.

Look at an old-fashioned, bowed pork pie, raised by hand and crimped around the top, and you could be rolling back the years to those early medieval pies – a reminder that as long as Britons have known how to turn flour and water into pastry, they have loved a good pie.

PHILP'S

FAMOUS PASTIES

Est. 1958

E OLDE ORK PIE HOPPE

YE OLDE PORK PIE SHOPPE

THE HALF MOON

HOW TO MAKE ROUGH PUFF PASTRY: Rough puff is simpler and faster to make (as well as less rich) than puff pastry but still has plenty of crisp, light, flaky layers. It's ideal for pie toppings when you want a change from shortcrust.

Sift the flour and salt into a mixing bowl. Add the pieces of cold finely diced butter and stir gently with a round-bladed knife until they are thoroughly coated in flour, without breaking up the pieces. Add the lemon juice to the ice-cold water and stir in enough water to bind the dough, adding it a tablespoon at a time. The dough should be lumpy, soft and moist, but not sticky or wet.

Turn the dough out on to a lightly floured work surface and shape it into a brick by gently patting it with floured fingers. Using a floured rolling pin, roll out the dough (rolling away from you) to a rectangle about 45 x 15cm. Fold the dough in 3 like a business letter: fold the bottom third of the dough up to cover the centre third, then fold the top third down to cover the other 2 layers. Gently but firmly seal the edges by pressing down with a rolling pin. This is the first 'turn'. Wrap and chill the dough for 15 minutes.

Unwrap the dough and turn it so the rounded folded edges are now on the left side, like a book. Roll out and fold in 3 again, wrap and chill just as before, then again give the dough a quarter turn anti-clockwise, and repeat so that it has been rolled out and folded up 3 times. Wrap and chill for 20 minutes, then do one more 'turn' so that the dough has been rolled out and folded up a total of 4 times. Chill for 20 minutes before using.

HOW TO MAKE SUET CRUST PASTRY: This is the most traditional British pastry of all, and is used for both sweet and savoury recipes, whether baked, steamed or boiled. It has a light, moist, spongy texture; when it's baked the crust becomes crisp and crumbly. It's most often used for steamed and baked puddings, roly-polys and dumplings; cooked in a pudding cloth or basin or along with a stew it makes an excellent container or contrast for a well-flavoured, succulent filling. These days suet, made from solid beef fat, is available already shredded and boxed – not so long ago it was sold by the butcher in a lump and needed to be 'skinned', chopped finely by hand or grated and tossed in flour just before it was used. Vegetable fat 'suet' and a low-fat vegetarian 'suet' are also readily available and seem to work just as well as the old-fashioned sort.

This pastry uses self-raising flour, which gives the all-important texture and is best quickly mixed and used. Adding breadcrumbs adds to the lightness, and parsley to the taste.

Put the flour, breadcrumbs, parsley (if using in a savoury recipe) and suet into a mixing bowl and stir until combined. Using a round-bladed knife, mix in enough cold water to make a firm but elastic, soft dough. Turn out on to a lightly floured work surface and knead very lightly and briefly to make a smooth ball of dough. Cover with the upturned bowl and leave for 10 minutes while heating the oven and preparing the filling.

HOW TO MAKE HOT WATER CRUST PASTRY: This is a crisp, firm, robust pastry made and filled in the same way as the medieval pie crust called a coffin or coffer. From the fourteenth century, and perhaps earlier, cooks made tough flour and water pastes to wrap joints of meat to keep them moist during cooking. This paste 'coffin', called a *ciste* in Wales, was chipped off after baking and discarded. Later, fat and spices were added to make the pastry edible.

Hot water crust is quite distinct from our other methods of pastry-making; here the fat, lard or white fat, is melted with water (and often some milk), then mixed while still hot into flour and salt to make a smooth and pliable paste that can be rolled out or moulded or worked, 'raised', by hand, rather like clay, to line or cover a mould. The pastry is strong enough to hold a compact meaty filling and absorb all the meat juices during baking. After baking and cooling, the filling usually contracts and the pastry case can be filled with cold stock to fill up the gaps left. It is usually eaten cold.

To make the pastry, sieve the flour, usually a good strong white flour (not the extra strong Canadian kind) or good-quality plain flour (not the very soft kind used just for cakes and sauces) and salt into a heatproof bowl. Put the fat and water (or milk and water) into a pan and heat gently until the fat melts, without letting the mixture boil. Pour into the centre of the flour and mix vigorously with a wooden spoon to make a soft, paste-like dough. Don't worry if it looks a mess to begin with, it will come together as you beat. When the mixture is cool enough to handle, cut off a piece for the lid and reserve. The large piece can be rolled out or moulded by hand to form a case for the filling. It's important there are no cracks or holes. The trimmings can be used to make decorations: leaves – oak leaves are traditional for pork fillings – tassels, flowers or rosettes, even plaited or twisted ropes.

HOW TO MAKE JELLIED STOCK: To make a tasty stock that will set to a firm jelly is not difficult, but it does take some time. Put the bones from the meat used for the filling, plus a couple of pig's trotters (ask the butcher to split them), into a large pan with a large onion and carrot, roughly sliced, a good-sized bouquet garni (or a bay leaf) and a teaspoon of peppercorns. Add water, 2 or 3 litres, to well cover, then bring to the boil. Skim off any scum on the surface, then cover the pan and simmer gently for 4 to 5 hours. Strain the stock through a colander into a clean pan, discard the flavourings, and boil the liquid rapidly until it has reduced down to about 750ml. Taste and season lightly. Leave to cool, then remove any fat on the surface. When chilled the stock should set; when you want to fill your cold pies it should be cold but still liquid.

HOW TO MAKE A GOOD SEAL: When you've topped your pie with pastry, it's important to create a good seal. This is called 'knocking up' the pastry. Using the flat of a knife, work your way round the edge of the crust, making small cuts (or knocks) into the pastry rim. You can then create a decorative scalloped or fluted edge by placing two fingers on the edge of the pastry and gently drawing a small knife between them.

Beefsteak and Kidney Pie with a Suet Crust SERVES 4–6

Definitely a cold-weather treat: meltingly tender, succulent meat under a proper suet crust, crisp, crumbly and richly flavoured. Beef skirt (also used in the Cornish pasties, page 209) is the best cut for flavour. The kidney should be well prepared – pull away any fat and covering membrane. Snip out the white ducts with kitchen scissors; check that they are completely removed before cutting the kidney into large dice. Beef and pork kidneys will taste stronger than lamb's. If you don't want to cook kidneys, use all stewing steak, either beef or venison. Alternatively, replace the kidneys with an equal weight of button mushrooms or diced carrots.

FOR THE FILLING:
900g diced lean stewing steak
200g diced kidney
2 tablespoons plain flour
¼ teaspoon each salt and pepper
3 tablespoons vegetable oil
2 medium onions, peeled and finely chopped
500ml good beef stock
3 tablespoons chopped fresh parsley

FOR THE SUET CRUST:
200g self-raising flour
50g fresh white breadcrumbs
1 tablespoon chopped fresh parsley
¼ teaspoon salt
100g beef or vegetable suet
about 200ml cold water
beaten egg, to glaze
a large pie dish, about 1.25–1.5 litres
a pie raiser or funnel

To make the filling, toss the pieces of steak and kidney in the flour with the seasoning. Heat the oil in a large, heavy-based flameproof casserole, or a pan with a good lid, and fry the meat in small batches until lightly browned, about 2 minutes on each side. Using a slotted spoon, remove the meat from the pan to a plate. When all the meat has coloured, turn the heat right down and stir in the onions. Cover the pan and cook very slowly, stirring frequently, until the onions are soft and tender – this will take 10 to 12 minutes.

Return the meat to the pan along with the juices on the plate. Add the stock, the parsley and a little more pepper. Bring to the boil, stirring frequently, then cover with the lid and cook very slowly, stirring occasionally, until the meat is very tender – 1½ to 2 hours. Taste and add more salt and pepper as needed. Leave to cool. At this point the filling can be covered and chilled overnight.

When ready to assemble and bake, make the pastry (see page 188). While it's resting, heat the oven to 180°C/350°F/gas 4. Set the pie raiser or funnel in the middle of the pie dish and spoon the beef mixture around it. Roll out the pastry on a lightly floured surface to an oval 3cm larger all round than your pie dish. Dampen the rim of the dish with water, then cut a strip of pastry about 1.5cm wide from around the edge of the pastry and press it on to the rim of the pie dish. Brush this with water, then wrap the pastry around the rolling pin and lift it over the pie dish. Let the pastry gently cover the pie, letting the pie funnel poke through. Using your thumbs, gently press the edges firmly to the rim to seal the pastry topping. Cut off the overhanging pastry with a sharp knife. 'Knock up' the edges of the pastry and make a scalloped or fluted pastry rim (see page 189). Brush the pie with beaten egg to glaze, and cut a couple of steam-holes with the tip of a sharp knife. Bake in the heated oven for 30 to 35 minutes, until the pie is firm and a good golden brown.

West Country Egg and Ham Pie

SERVES 6

This is an old-fashioned pie made from cooked ham or gammon, most often using the leftovers from a cooked piece or joint, plus whole raw eggs, and moistened with a chive egg custard. You can buy a piece of cooked meat or uncooked ham hocks or a knuckle from the butcher. To cook a piece of ham, put it into a large pan of water and bring it up to the boil. Tip off the water and cover with fresh. Add an onion stuck with a clove and a large bouquet garni, then bring to the boil and simmer until tender – allowing about 30 minutes for each 500g plus 30 minutes extra (thin joints will take less time, really thick ones slightly more). Leave in the stock until cool enough to handle, then peel off the skin and fat, and shred the meat. The stock, and any ham scraps, will make good soup (pea and ham, lentil . . .).

FOR THE ROUGH PUFF PASTRY:
275g plain flour
a good pinch of salt
200g unsalted butter, chilled and diced
(or 175g butter plus 25g lard or
white fat, well chilled)
about 200ml ice-cold water
1 teaspoon lemon juice

FOR THE FILLING:
400g cooked ham or gammon,
shredded or diced
5 medium free-range eggs
50ml creamy milk or single cream
a small bunch of fresh chives, snipped
salt and pepper
beaten egg, to glaze

a deep meat pie plate, about 24cm

Make the rough puff pastry (see page 187), then wrap in clingfilm and chill until ready to assemble the pie. Heat the oven to 220°C/425°F/gas 6 and put a baking tray in to heat. On a floured surface, roll out half the pastry and use to line the pie plate, gently pressing the pastry on to the base, up the sloping sides of the plate where the base meets the rim, and on to the rim. Don't trim off any overhanging pastry for now.

Arrange half the ham or gammon over the pastry base. Make 4 slight hollows for the eggs. Whisk 1 of the eggs with the milk or cream, the chives and seasoning: use a little salt and plenty of pepper. Carefully spoon about half this custard over the meat, to moisten. Break the remaining eggs, one at a time, into a cup, then gently slip them into the hollows so they remain whole rather than broken up. Spoon over the rest of the custard and gently cover with the rest of the meat. Brush the pastry rim with water.

Roll out the rest of the pastry to a circle slightly larger than your plate and large enough to cover your pie. Using the rolling pin to support the weight of the pastry, lift it over the pie to completely cover. Press together the 2 layers of pastry on the rim to seal, then trim off the overhanging pastry with a sharp knife. 'Knock up' the edges of the pastry and make a scalloped or fluted pastry rim (see page 189). Brush the pastry with beaten egg to glaze, then make a couple of small steam-holes in the top of the pie with the tip of a sharp knife. Set the pie on the hot baking tray and bake in the heated oven for 15 minutes. Reduce the heat to 180°C/350°F/gas 4 and bake for a further 25 minutes, until the pastry is cooked and golden. Serve warm or at room temperature.

We have been making pies in one form or another since neolithic times. A pie is the perfect way to feed a hungry family, making good use of whatever ingredients are available, however limited. Many regions are very protective of their local speciality. Murray's bakery in Scotland is famed for its Scotch pies and their bakers make them round the clock.

Game Pie SERVES 4–6

This is a richly flavoured pie made from mixed game – typically pheasant, pigeon, partridge, mallard and rabbit, which is now sold already diced at farmers' markets, larger supermarkets and good butchers. For a lighter taste, use half game and half chicken thigh meat. The filling can be made in advance and either stored in the fridge for up to 4 days or frozen.

FOR THE ROUGH PUFF PASTRY:
225g plain flour
¼ teaspoon salt
125g unsalted butter, chilled and diced
about 125ml ice-cold water,
plus ½ teaspoon lemon juice

FOR THE MARINADE:
1 large onion, peeled and coarsely chopped
1 large stick of celery, trimmed
and coarsely chopped
a sprig of fresh thyme
a few fresh parsley stalks
½ teaspoon coriander seeds
½ teaspoon juniper berries, lightly crushed
½ teaspoon black peppercorns
1 bay leaf

500ml red wine
3 tablespoons olive oil

FOR THE FILLING:
1kg boneless mixed game meat, diced
3 rashers of smoked back bacon (about 75g),
diced
25g unsalted butter
1 tablespoon plain flour
150g large mushrooms, thickly sliced
1 sprig of fresh thyme
salt and pepper
1 tablespoon redcurrant jelly
beaten egg, to glaze

a large pie dish, about 1.25–1.5 litres
a pie raiser

Make the rough puff pastry (see page 187), then wrap in clingfilm and chill until needed. Combine all the marinade ingredients in a large bowl. Add the prepared game meat and stir well. Cover and leave to marinate overnight in the fridge. Next day remove the pieces of meat from the marinade. Strain the marinade, reserve the liquid and discard the vegetables, spices and herbs.

Put the bacon and butter into a large flameproof casserole or heavy pan, and cook over a medium heat until lightly coloured. Sprinkle the flour into the pan and stir over the heat for a minute, then add the meat and stir to combine. Pour the reserved marinade liquid into the pan and bring to the boil, stirring gently. Add the sliced mushrooms, the leaves from the thyme sprig and a little seasoning. Cover and simmer gently until very tender – about 1½ hours. Remove the lid and cook uncovered for the last half an hour to reduce the sauce if it seems a bit thin. Stir in the redcurrant jelly, then taste and add more salt and pepper if needed. Spoon into the pie dish and leave to cool. At this point the dish can be covered and chilled overnight.

To make up the pie, roll out the pastry on a floured surface to an oval about 7cm larger all round than your pie dish. Roll the oval of pastry around the rolling pin and gently lay it over the pie so it unrolls without stretching. Press the dough on to the rim to seal firmly. Trim off the excess dough with a sharp knife. 'Knock up' the edges of the pastry and make a scalloped or fluted pastry rim (see page 189). Make a steam-hole in the centre of the pie with the tip of a sharp knife. Chill while heating the oven to 200°C/400°F/gas 6.

Stand the pie on a baking tray, brush with beaten egg to glaze and bake for 15 minutes. Turn the temperature down to 180°C/350°F/gas 4 and bake for a further 20 to 25 minutes, until the pastry is deep golden brown and crisp. Serve hot, with creamy mashed potatoes.

Crumble-topped Fish Pie SERVES 6

The combination of three types of fish – smoked, a firm white, and the richer-fleshed salmon – gives this pie a good depth of flavour and contrast in textures. You could also add some just-cooked peas or button mushrooms, even some cooked cockles or cooked shelled mussels. While there's much to be said for the usual creamy mashed potato topping, the crunchy crumble – made in the same way as you would for a fruit crumble but minus the sugar and plus some good Cheddar – makes a welcome change. Fishmongers and supermarkets now sell fresh and frozen mixtures of fish already filleted, skinned and diced (look out for 'fish pie mix').

FOR THE FISH MIXTURE:
300g white fish fillets, skinned
250g undyed smoked haddock fillets, skinned
250g salmon fillets, skinned
(or 700g prepared fish pie mix)
500ml fish stock
2 tablespoons white wine
1 bay leaf
1 small onion, peeled and quarter quartered
a small bunch of fresh parsley

FOR THE SAUCE:
50g unsalted butter
50g plain flour

150ml single cream
a few drops of anchovy essence or sauce
salt and pepper
150g cooked prawns, or 2 hard-boiled eggs, quartered

FOR THE TOPPING:
175g plain flour
100g unsalted butter, chilled and diced
100g mature Cheddar cheese, finely grated
a good pinch of cayenne pepper

a pie dish or deep baking dish, 1.5 litres

Heat the oven to 200°C/400°F/gas 6. Cut the skinned fillets of fish into 3cm chunks. Put the stock, wine, bay leaf, onion and the stalks from the bunch of parsley into a large pan. Bring to the boil and simmer gently for 5 minutes. Take the pan off the heat and add the prepared fish. Bring back to the boil, then cover the pan, remove from the heat and leave to stand for 5 minutes. Using a slotted spoon, carefully remove the fish from its cooking liquid and leave to cool in a bowl. Keep the cooking liquid.

Melt the butter in a clean pan, then stir in the flour and cook gently over a low heat for a minute, stirring constantly. Remove from the heat and strain the cooking liquid into the pan. Discard the flavourings. Add any liquid from the bowl containing the cooked fish to the pan, then whisk, or stir well, until combined with the butter and flour roux. Return the pan to the heat and bring to the boil, stirring or whisking constantly to make a smooth, thick sauce. Simmer gently for a couple of minutes, then stir in the cream. Taste and add a few drops of anchovy sauce, and a little salt and pepper as needed. Remove the pan from the heat. Finely chop the parsley leaves and stir into the sauce followed by the fish, taking care not to break up the soft flesh. Spoon into the baking dish. Arrange the prawns or eggs on top – this will keep the topping crunchy and prevent it from absorbing too much sauce.

To make the topping, put the flour, butter, Cheddar, cayenne and a little seasoning into the bowl of a food processor and run the machine until the mixture looks sandy. Alternatively, put the ingredients into a mixing bowl and rub in the fat until the mixture looks like fine crumbs.Spoon the mixture evenly over the pie filling, right to the edges of the dish, then bake in the heated oven for 30 minutes, until browned and bubbling. Serve piping hot.

After years of campaigning, Melton Mowbray pies finally achieved Protected Geographical Indication status, so now any pies bearing the name must adhere to strict criteria.

A Melton Mowbray-Style Pork Pie

SERVES 8–10

The thing about pies from Melton Mowbray is that the pork must be fresh, not cured, chopped by hand (though it seems some mincing is allowed these days) and flavoured with anchovy essence as well as the more usual suspect: fresh sage. The pies from the best butchers are hand-raised, moulded by hand over a wooden pie mould called a coffin or coffer to make a free-standing pastry case, but there's no shame in using a springclip tin.

FOR THE FILLING:
1kg boned shoulder of pork, bones saved for the stock
3 rashers of unsmoked back bacon
2 teaspoons chopped fresh sage
1 teaspoon anchovy essence or sauce
salt, pepper and grated nutmeg

FOR THE HOT WATER CRUST PASTRY:
350g strong white plain flour
1 teaspoon salt
85g lard or white fat
185ml water (or half water and half milk)
beaten egg, to glaze

TO FINISH:
about 250ml well-flavoured jellied stock (see page 189), cold but liquid

a 20cm springclip tin
a baking tray

To make the filling, cut about 300g of the meat into neat cubes of about 1cm, and very finely chop or mince the rest – don't use a processor. (You may find it easier to buy 300g lean pork, plus 700g good minced pork with around 20% fat.) Mince or finely chop the bacon. Put all the meat into a bowl with the sage, anchovy essence, a little salt, plenty of pepper and a few gratings of nutmeg. Mix the ingredients thoroughly. Take about a teaspoon of the mixture and fry it, like a mini-burger, then taste and adjust the seasonings, adding more salt and pepper, perhaps some more sage, as needed. The mixture should be tasty, not bland. If possible, cover the bowl and chill overnight for the flavours to develop. If not, cover while making the pastry.

Make the hot water crust pastry (see page 189). When cool enough to handle, cut off a third and keep for the lid. On a lightly floured surface roll out the larger piece of pastry to a circle large enough to line the base and sides of the tin. Lightly flour the surface of the pastry, then fold it in 4 and lift it into the tin. Unfold the pastry and press it on to the base and up the sides of the tin so it overhangs by about 2cm. Take care there are no cracks or holes. The pastry should be about 5mm thick. Pack the meat filling into the pastry case, making sure there are no pockets of air. Heat the oven to 200°C/400°F/gas 6.

Fold the excess pastry neatly over the filling. Brush this rim with a little water. Roll out the remaining pastry to a circle to fit the top of the tin – cut round a plate to get a neat shape if necessary. Lift the pastry over the filling to cover, then press the pastry edges firmly to seal. Pinch the rim to neatly flute it. Make a large steam-hole in the centre of the pie and fit a small cylinder of foil into the hole to keep it open during baking. Brush with beaten egg, then set the tin on the baking tray and bake in the heated oven for 15 minutes. Reduce the oven temperature to 180°C/350°F/gas 4 and bake for a further 2 hours, covering the top of the pie with a piece of foil or greaseproof after an hour to prevent over-browning the crust.

Leave to cool in the tin, then pour the cold stock into the pie through the foil tube. Chill overnight to set fully, then unmould, remove the foil, and serve at room temperature.

Veal, Ham and Egg Raised Pie

SERVES 10–12

The classic recipe – often known as gala pie, as it was traditionally served at miners' galas – is baked in a loaf tin. With the pastry highly glazed and sometimes covered with pastry leaves and rosettes, the finished pie was a magnificent centrepiece for a festive meal. You need to start this several days in advance: begin by preparing the meat, using the bones to make the jellied stock.

FOR THE FILLING:

650g lean 'pink' pie veal, cut into 2cm cubes
250g uncooked ham or gammon cut into 2cm pieces
finely grated zest of 1 large unwaxed lemon
3 tablespoons chopped fresh parsley
1 teaspoon chopped fresh thyme
salt, pepper and cayenne pepper
1 medium onion, peeled and very finely chopped
3 medium free-range eggs, hard-boiled and shelled

FOR THE HOT WATER CRUST PASTRY:

450g strong white plain flour
1 teaspoon salt
150g lard or white fat
275ml water (or half milk, half water)
beaten egg, to glaze

TO FINISH:

about 275ml well-flavoured jellied stock (page 189), cold but liquid

a loaf tin or a special veal and ham pie tin, about 26 x 12.5 x 7.5cm
a baking tray

Put the veal and ham into a mixing bowl with the lemon zest, parsley, thyme, a little salt, plenty of pepper, ¼ teaspoon cayenne and the onion. Mix well until thoroughly combined, then cover and chill for several hours, overnight if possible, for the flavours to develop. It is important that the filling is not bland, so make a tiny burger using a teaspoon of the mixture, fry it, then taste and add more seasoning as needed. Meanwhile make the stock (see page 189).

Next day, cut a long strip of greaseproof paper or baking parchment to fit the base of the tin and up the sides, and use to line the tin. Make the hot water crust pastry (see page 189), and when cool enough to handle cut off a quarter and keep to one side for the lid. On a floured surface, roll the larger piece into a rectangle larger than the base of the tin. Gently fold the pastry in 4 and lift it into the tin, then unfold it and carefully press it up the sides of the tin so it covers the inside evenly. Make sure there are no cracks or holes, and leave 2cm pastry hanging over the rim. Spoon half of the meat filling into the pastry case to make an even layer. Gently bang the tin down on the work surface to eliminate any pockets of air. Arrange the hard-boiled eggs down the length of the tin and cover with the remaining filling, packing it down well – it will shrink down as it cooks. Preheat the oven to 200°C/400°F/gas 6.

Roll out the pastry reserved for the lid to a rectangle slightly larger than the top of the tin and about 5mm thick. Neatly cut the edges. Fold the excess pastry over the filling, then brush this pastry edge with a little water. Using the rolling pin to support the the pastry, lift the lid into place and press the edges together. Trim off any excess. Make 4 steam-holes along the top of the pie and place a small cylinder of foil in each hole to keep it open during baking. Pinch the edges of the pastry around the rim, then glaze the top of the pie with beaten egg. Bake for 15 minutes, then reduce the oven temperature to 180°C/350°F/gas 4 and bake for a further 2 hours. Cover the top loosely with foil or greaseproof paper for the last hour to prevent it from over-browning. Remove from the oven and leave to cool completely. Carefully pour the cold stock into the pie through the foil cylinders. Leave until cold and set, then gently unmould and remove the foil. Wrap in foil and chill overnight.

Cornish Pasties makes 6 pasties

How to make the perfect pasty is the subject of endless argument in Cornwall. This is a modern recipe – old family recipes use suet in the pastry and make a less rich filling. Before you start, put the fats into the freezer for an hour or so until very hard – this makes it easier to grate into the flour and makes the pastry easier to handle. In hot weather the sieved flour should be chilled in the fridge too.

For the pastry:
450g strong white bread flour
a large pinch of salt
100g unsalted butter, chilled in the freezer
100g lard or white fat, chilled in the freezer
about 200ml ice-cold water

For the filling:
200g potatoes (about 6, small to medium)
200g lean best beef skirt
1 small onion, peeled and halved
100g swede, peeled (about 1 small)
salt and pepper
beaten egg or milk, to glaze

2 baking trays, lined with greaseproof paper

Sieve the flour and salt into a mixing bowl. Hold the ends of the blocks of very cold fat in greaseproof paper and grate coarsely into the flour. Stir with a round-bladed knife until just combined with the flour, then stir in just enough of the ice-cold water to bind the dough – it should feel soft but not sticky and should look rather shaggy. With your hand, briefly knead the dough in the bowl until it just comes together into a ball (handle the dough as little as possible), then wrap in clingfilm and chill for at least 30 minutes before using. Well-wrapped dough will keep in the fridge for 24 hours.

Meanwhile, prepare the filling: peel, halve and slice the potatoes to about the thickness of a £1 coin and keep them in a basin of cold water until needed. Trim the meat to remove any gristle, but keep a little of the veining fat for flavour and moisture, then cut into pieces the size of your little fingernail. Finely slice the onion and slice the swede into pieces about the same size as the potatoes, but thinner.

To assemble the pasties, heat the oven to 220°C/425°F/gas 7. Divide the pastry into 6 equal portions, shape each into a ball, then roll out to a neat circle, about 14cm. If the circle is a bit ragged, trim around a plate to make a neat shape. Place the onion along one side of each circle and cover with a layer of swede. Sprinkle with a little salt and plenty of pepper. Arrange the meat along the top and up to the ends (it is important that the meat reaches right to the last corner of the pasty). Season the meat with salt and pepper, then top with a layer of potato and sprinkle with pepper only, no salt, to prevent the pastry tasting bitter. Moisten the edge along one side of the pastry circle. Fold the half nearest to you over to the other side to seal. Press the edges of the pastry together, working from the middle out to each corner. Crimp the seam by folding the pastry over and over on itself to make a rope pattern, working your way along the pastry edge from left to right. Tuck in the end when you reach the far corner.

Place the pasties on the lined baking tray, gently mould with your hands into a neat shape and lightly brush with beaten egg or milk to glaze. Bake for 15 minutes, until nicely browned. Reduce the oven temperature to 180°C/350°F/gas 4 and bake for 15 minutes longer. Turn off the heat but leave the pasties in the oven with the door closed for a further 15 minutes. Remove from the oven and leave to stand for 5 to 10 minutes before eating.

Ruth's Beef Pie SERVES 4

This is a really traditional filling and the cheese in the pastry crust gives it a lovely twist. Season generously to give the pie extra flavour – keep tasting the mixture until you're happy with it.

FOR THE CHEESE PASTRY:
225g plain flour
75g salted butter, chilled and diced
75g Lancashire cheese
1 medium free-range egg yolk
4–6 tablespoons ice-cold water

FOR THE FILLING:
2 tablespoons sunflower oil
1 medium onion, peeled and finely chopped

250g lean minced beef
2 peeled carrots, diced
1 stick of celery, diced
4 tablespoons ale or good beef stock
3 tablespoons tomato ketchup
1 tablespoon Worcestershire sauce
salt and pepper
beaten egg, to glaze

a 20 x 15cm enamel deep pie dish

To make the pastry, put the flour and diced butter into the bowl of a food processor. Run the machine until the mixture resembles fine crumbs. Crumble the cheese into the bowl and pulse until the mixture looks like coarse crumbs. Add the egg yolk and 4 tablespoons of ice-cold water and run the machine until the mixture comes together to form a ball of dough, adding more water, a teaspoon at a time, as necessary, through the feed tube. Remove from the bowl and cut off a third of the dough (for the lid). Wrap both pieces of dough in clingfilm and chill while making the filling.

Heat the oil in a large frying pan, preferably non-stick. Add the chopped onions and cook gently until soft but not coloured. Push the onions to one side, then add the minced beef and cook over a medium heat, stirring constantly, until browned. Turn the heat down to low, then add the diced carrots and celery and stir the mixture well to incorporate the onions. Cook gently, stirring frequently, until the vegetables have softened – about 10 minutes. Add the ale or stock, ketchup, Worcestershire sauce and salt and pepper to taste, stir well, then simmer gently until the meat is tender and the mixture is thick and just slightly moist rather than runny – about 10 minutes. If necessary turn up the heat and stir constantly if the filling seems a bit wet. Taste and adjust the seasoning – the mixture should be nicely savoury, so add more pepper or Worcestershire sauce as necessary. Leave to cool completely.

When ready to assemble, roll out the large portion of pastry on a lightly floured work surface to a rectangle big enough to the line the base and sides of your pie dish. Roll the pastry around the rolling pin and gently drape it over the dish. Carefully press the pastry on to the base and sides of the dish, pressing out any bubbles of air. If necessary patch up any holes with scraps of pastry. Brush the pastry on the rim of the dish with beaten egg. Spoon the cold filling into the dish. Roll out the second portion of pastry to a rectangle about 20 x 15cm to make the lid. Using the rolling pin as a support, lift the pastry over the dish and gently press it on to the dampened rim to seal firmly. Trim off any excess pastry using a sharp knife. Crimp or decorate the rim with your fingers or a pastry crimper. Leave to rest for 10 minutes. Meanwhile heat the oven to 190°C/375°F/gas 5.

Brush the pie with beaten egg to glaze, make a small steam hole in the centre using the tip of a sharp knife, and bake in the heated oven for 25 to 30 minutes, until the pastry is a good golden brown. Serve hot, as soon as possible.

# Stargazy Pie SERVES 6

This pie comes from the West Cornish fishing village of Mousehole and is made to celebrate the legend of Tom Bawcock. He was a local fisherman who put to sea during a lull in winter storms so bad and prolonged that the village was on the point of starvation. The local inn – The Ship – made a pie of many fishes from his catch, and today 23 December is still celebrated as Tom Bawcock's Eve with a great display of Christmas lights, as well as pies made with whole pilchards.

FOR THE SHORTCRUST PASTRY:
200g plain flour
a good pinch of salt
125g unsalted butter, chilled and diced
2–3 tablespoons ice-cold water

FOR THE FILLING:
600g firm white fish fillets, skinned
8 pilchards (or small herrings or sardines), cleaned and boned, heads on
500ml full-fat milk
a bayleaf

a small bunch of parsley
a slice of onion (optional)
50g unsalted butter
50g plain flour
salt and pepper, to taste
3 medium free-range eggs, hard-boiled, shelled and coarsely chopped
3 medium potatoes (about 300g), peeled
beaten egg, to glaze

a large pie dish, about 1.75 litres
a baking tray

Make the shortcrust pastry (see page 148), then wrap in clingfilm and chill while preparing the filling. Rinse the fish fillets, drain then cut into 3cm chunks. Rinse the pilchards, check the cavities are clean, then drain and leave on a plate lined with a couple of sheets of kitchen paper until needed.

Put the milk, bayleaf, the stalks from the bunch of parsley (save the sprigs for later) and the slice of onion, if using, in to a large pan, preferably non-stick, and bring slowly to the boil. Cover the pan, remove from the heat and leave for 10 minutes for the flavours to infuse. Add the pieces of fish fillet to the pan, return it to the heat and bring it back to the boil. Once again, cover the pan and remove it from the heat. Leave to stand for 5 minutes. Using a slotted spoon, lift the fish out of the milk and on to a large plate. Strain the milk into a jug and discard the flavourings. Rinse out the pan, then add the butter and gently melt. Stir in the flour and cook over low heat, stirring constantly, for a minute. Stir in the strained milk and bring to the boil, stirring constantly, to make a thick smooth sauce. Leave to simmer for a minute, stirring frequently, then remove from the heat. Gently stir in the cooked white fish plus any liquid that has drained onto the plate. Finely chop the fresh parsley sprigs, reserve a tablespoon for garnish and stir the rest into the fish mixture. Season to taste with salt and plenty of pepper. Spoon the mixture into the pie dish. Scatter the egg over the fish mixture. Halve the potatoes and cut into slices the thickness of a pound coin. Arrange over the eggs.

Preheat the oven to 180°C/350°F/Gas 4. Roll out the pastry on a lightly floured work surface to a shape the same as your dish but 3cm larger. Brush the rim of your pie dish with a little beaten egg then cut a 1cm strip of pastry from around the edge and press it on to the rim of the dish. Brush this pastry rim with beaten egg then, using the rolling pin to support the weight of the pastry, drape the pastry over the dish to completely cover it. Press the pastry lid on to the pastry rim to seal, then trim off the excess pastry. Crimp the edge with your fingers or a fork. Using a small sharp knife make 8 slits in the pastry lid and gently push a pilchard through each – four fish head-first and four fish tail-first. Brush the pastry with beaten egg, set the pie on a baking tray and bake for 35 minutes until golden brown. Stand for 5 minutes, scatter with the remaining parsley and serve.

Mousehole, in Cornwall, where the legend of Tom Bawcock is still celebrated every 23 December. People queue up to taste the famous Stargazy pie made by the chefs at The Ship Inn.

Jasminder's Chicken Pie SERVES 6

The spinach is a great addition to this classic chicken and mushroom pie. The combination of flavours work really well together.

FOR THE SHORTCRUST PASTRY:
250g plain flour
a good pinch of salt
150g unsalted butter, chilled and diced
6 tablespoons ice-cold water

FOR THE FILLING:
about 2 tablespoons olive oil
3 large skinless chicken breasts (about 550g), diced
150g button mushrooms, quartered
1 small onion, finely chopped

1 clove of garlic, finely chopped
50g unsalted butter
2 tablespoons plain flour
225ml good chicken stock
100ml single cream
salt and pepper
freshly grated nutmeg
2 tablespoons chopped parsley
a 150g bag of washed fresh baby leaf spinach
beaten egg, to glaze

a 25cm round deep pie dish (about 1.75 litres)

Make up the shortcrust pastry either by hand or using a food processor (see page 148), then wrap and chill while making the filling.

Heat 2 tablespoons of the oil in a large preferably non-stick frying pan. Add the diced chicken and fry over a medium heat, stirring constantly, until the meat turns white. Add the mushrooms and continue to fry, stirring frequently, until the chicken is golden brown and cooked through. Using a slotted spoon, remove the chicken and mushrooms from the pan and set aside in a bowl. If necessary add a little more oil to the pan, then add the onion and garlic and stir over a low heat for a couple of minutes until soft but not browned. Add to the bowl with the chicken and mushrooms.

Melt the butter in a large saucepan, stir in the flour and cook over a very low heat for 3 minutes, stirring constantly, until you have a frothy, smooth, straw-coloured mixture. Whisk in the stock and cream, then bring to the boil over low heat, stirring constantly. Simmer gently for 5 minutes, stirring constantly to make a smooth, thickened, creamy sauce. Season to taste with salt, pepper and plenty of grated nutmeg. Remove the pan from the heat and stir in the chicken mixture, plus any juices in the bowl, the parsley and the spinach. When thoroughly combined, taste and adjust the seasoning – you may need to add more pepper or nutmeg.

Spoon the filling mixture into the pie dish and leave to cool completely.

When ready to assemble, roll out the pastry on a lightly floured work surface to a circle slightly larger than your dish and the thickness of a pound coin. Dampen the rim of the pie dish with a little beaten egg. Cut a narrow strip from all around the edge of the pastry and press it on to the rim of the dish. Brush this rim with beaten egg. Roll the pastry around the rolling pin and lift it over the dish. Carefully unroll the pastry so it drapes over the dish, then gently press the pastry on to the pastry rim to seal firmly. Trim off the excess pastry with a sharp knife and crimp the edges with your fingers. Decorate the top with pastry leaves cut from leftover scraps of pastry, stuck on with a little beaten egg. Leave to chill for 15 minutes while heating the oven to 200°C/400°F/gas 6.

Brush the top of the pie with beaten egg to glaze, then make 2 or 3 slits in the pastry to allow steam to escape. Bake for about 25 minutes, until a good golden brown. Serve hot, as soon as possible.

Apple and Bramble Pie

Apples, usually Bramleys, mixed with grated orange or lemon zest, are the most popular filling for this traditional fruit pie. For a change, flavour the apples with ground cinnamon and dark muscovado sugar, or add raisins or another fruit: blackberries or brambles, as here, or try blueberries, cranberries or raspberries. The crust is a classic sweet shortcrust pastry; made with butter and caster sugar, it has a wonderful flavour and light, crisp texture.

FOR THE SWEET SHORTCRUST PASTRY:
225g plain flour
a pinch of salt
60g caster sugar
125g unsalted butter, chilled and diced
about 3 tablespoons ice-cold water

FOR THE FILLING:
900g Bramley or other cooking apples (about 4 large)
200g blackberries
about 3 tablespoons caster sugar, to taste
3 tablespoons water

a deep pie dish, about 1 litre

To make the pastry by hand, sift the flour, salt and sugar into a mixing bowl. Add the diced butter and rub into the flour, using the tips of your fingers, until the mixture looks like fine crumbs. Using a round-bladed knife, stir in enough ice-cold water to bind the mixture to a soft but not sticky dough. If the dough is dry and hard it will crumble as you try to roll it out, but if it is too wet and sticky it will be tough and heavy when baked. (See also page 148.)

To make the pastry in a food processor, put the flour, salt and sugar into the processor bowl and pulse until combined. Add the diced butter and process for about a minute, or just until the mixture looks like fine crumbs. With the machine running, pour in the ice-cold water through the feed tube – the dough should come together in a ball within a minute. If it doesn't come together, and there are dry crumbs in the bottom of the bowl, add more water a teaspoon at a time. (See also page 148.)

Wrap the dough in clingfilm and chill for 15 minutes while preparing the fruit. Heat the oven to 200°C/400°F/gas 6. Peel, core and thickly slice the apples and put them into a mixing bowl. Rinse the blackberries and add to the apples with the sugar. Toss gently until combined, then pile the fruit into the pie dish, mounding it well in the centre so it supports the pastry (if necessary add more fruit), and spoon over the water.

Roll out the pastry on a floured work surface to an oval about 7cm larger all round than the dish. Cut off a strip of pastry about 1cm wide and long enough to fit around the rim of the dish. Dampen the rim of the dish and press the pastry strip on to it. Dampen the pastry rim. Roll the pastry around the rolling pin and lift it over the dish, then gently lay the dough over the dish so it completely covers the pie. Press the dough on to the pastry rim to seal the lid to the dish. Trim off the excess dough – you can make decorations for the top with the leftover pastry. 'Knock up' the edges of the pastry and make a scalloped or fluted rim (see page 189). Stick any decorations to the top of the pastry with water and cut a couple of small steam-holes.

Bake in the heated oven for about 30 minutes, or until the pastry is golden and crisp. Sprinkle with a little caster sugar and serve warm or at room temperature.

Cherry Pie

SERVES 4–6

We have the Babylonians and Assyrians to thank for cultivating the cherry, and the Romans for introducing it to our orchards; there are now over 1,000 cultivated cherry varieties worldwide, and the vast majority are sweet. Kent, the garden of England, has been at the heart of cherry-growing since the sixteenth century, and is once more attempting to wrest the short seasonal market from Italian and French growers. Taste the fruit, then decide how much sugar you need.

FOR THE ROUGH PUFF PASTRY:	FOR THE FILLING:
275g plain flour	650g stoned cherries (about 800g unstoned)
a good pinch of salt	3 tablespoons caster sugar, or to taste
200g unsalted butter, chilled and diced	1 rounded tablespoon cornflour
(or 175g butter plus 25g lard or white fat,	a little milk or egg white, for brushing
well chilled)	sugar, for sprinkling
about 200ml ice-cold water	
1 teaspoon lemon juice	*a deep pie plate, about 23–25cm*
	a baking tray

Make the rough puff pastry (see page 187), wrap in clingfilm and chill until needed.

Heat the oven to 220°C/425°F/gas 7 and put a baking tray into the oven to heat. Put the stoned cherries into a mixing bowl, sprinkle over the sugar and cornflour and toss gently until thoroughly combined. If the cherries are very tart you may need to add a bit more sugar.

Roll out half the pastry to a circle slightly larger than your pie plate and, using the rolling pin to support the weight of the pastry, carefully drape it over the plate, bringing the pastry up and over the sides. Press it gently into the base and the rim. Do not cut off any overhanging pastry yet. Spoon the fruit on to the pastry base. Dampen the pastry rim with a little water. Roll out the rest of the pastry to a circle slightly larger than your plate and, supporting the pastry on the rolling pin, carefully lift it over the pie to cover. With your thumbs press the pastry edges together to seal firmly, then trim off the overhanging pastry with a sharp knife. Make a couple of steam-holes in the centre of the pie with the tip of a knife. 'Knock up' the edges of the pastry and make a scalloped or fluted pastry rim (see page 189).

Brush the pie with a little milk or egg white and sprinkle with sugar. Set the pie on the hot baking tray and bake in the heated oven for 15 minutes. Reduce the temperature to 180°C/350°F/gas 4 and bake for a further 20 to 25 minutes, or until the pastry is crisp and a good golden brown. Serve hot or warm, with cream or ice cream.

Individual Plum Cobbler

MAKES 4 SERVINGS

A cobbler is an old-fashioned sort of pie with a light, fluffy scone topping, rather than the usual pastry covering, over whatever fruit is in season. Here, the fruit is plums – a good way to cook a glut – flavoured with orange, though you could also bake nectarines, peaches, blueberries or tender young rhubarb in the same way.

FOR THE FRUIT FILLING:
750g just-ripe plums
grated zest and juice of 1 large unwaxed orange
1 cinnamon stick, broken into 4
3 tablespoons soft light brown muscovado sugar, or to taste

FOR THE TOPPING:
200g self-raising flour
a good pinch of salt
40g soft light brown muscovado sugar
40g unsalted butter, chilled and diced

1 rounded tablespoon chopped roasted hazelnuts or walnuts
1 medium free-range egg, beaten
5 tablespoons buttermilk
(or use good creamy plain yoghurt mixed with milk)
a little milk, for brushing
a little sugar, for sprinkling

4 small baking dishes
(about 15cm across the top and 4cm deep)
a baking tray

Heat the oven to 180°C/350°F/gas 4. Rinse the plums, then quarter them and discard the stones. Put them into a large bowl with the orange zest and juice, cinnamon and sugar. Toss gently until thoroughly combined, then put to one side while making the topping.

Sift the flour, salt and sugar into a mixing bowl. Add the diced butter and rub into the flour, using the tips of your fingers, until the mixture looks like fine crumbs. Mix in the nuts, then add the beaten egg and buttermilk to the bowl and mix to a soft but sticky dough, using a round-bladed knife. If the dough seems dry and won't come together in a ball, work in a little more buttermilk or milk.

Turn the dough out on to a lightly floured work surface and knead lightly and briefly until less ragged. Roll out about 1cm thick, then cut into strips about 1.5cm wide, using a sharp knife or a pastry wheel.

Spoon the fruit mixture and the juices into the 4 dishes, then dampen the rim of each dish with a little water. Arrange the dough strips over the fruit in a lattice pattern, pressing the ends of each strip on to the rim. Brush the lattice with a little milk and sprinkle with sugar. Set the dishes on the baking tray and bake in the heated oven for 20 to 25 minutes, until the fruit is tender and the lattice topping is golden. Serve warm with cream or custard (see page 290). The cinnamon stick is not meant to be eaten.

TO MAKE 1 LARGE COBBLER:

Spoon the fruit into a deep baking dish or pie dish, about 1.25 litres. Make up the lattice as in the recipe and arrange over the fruit. Brush with milk, sprinkle with sugar and bake for 25 to 30 minutes, or until the fruit is soft and the lattice is golden.

Apple Pie with Cheddar Crust

SERVES 6

A winning combination – 'an apple pie without cheese is like a kiss without a squeeze' – the habit of serving a wedge of warm pie along with a slice of the finest local cheese is at least 300 years old and cheese pastry has long been used instead of regular shortcrust around cheese-making farms. In Yorkshire, the apple filling was often topped with a layer of Wensleydale cheese before the pie was baked. Pick a good mature Cheddar for a tasty, crisp crust.

FOR THE CHEESE PASTRY:	FOR THE FILLING:
300g plain flour	1kg eating apples such as Cox's,
a pinch of salt	James Grieve, Laxtons, Worcester
150g mature Cheddar cheese,	3 tablespoons caster sugar
chilled and finely grated	grated zest of ½ an unwaxed lemon
150g unsalted butter, chilled and diced	25g butter, melted
50ml ice-cold water	caster sugar, for sprinkling
	a deep pie plate, about 26cm
	a baking tray

To make the pastry, put the flour, salt and grated cheese into the bowl of a food processor and pulse several times until just combined. Add the diced butter and run the machine until the mixture looks like fine crumbs. With the machine running, add the ice-cold water through the feed tube. Stop the machine as soon as the dough comes together into a ball. The dough should feel firm; if there are dry crumbs in the base of the processor bowl, add more water, a teaspoon at a time. Flatten the ball of dough into a disc, wrap in clingfilm and chill for 30 minutes, until cool and firm.

Meanwhile, heat the oven to 200°C/400°F/gas 6 and put the baking tray in to heat. Peel the apples. Quarter and core, then cut each quarter into 3 thick slices and put them into a bowl. Add the caster sugar, lemon zest and melted butter and toss gently until thoroughly combined.

Roll out a third of the pastry on a floured surface to a circle slightly larger than your pie plate. Using the rolling pin to support the pastry, gently drape it over the plate. Flour your fingers and press the pastry on to the base, up the sloping sides between the base and rim, and on to the rim, making sure any pockets of air have been pressed out. Don't cut off any overhanging pastry at this stage. Pile the apple mixture on to the plate, mounding it up neatly and leaving the rim clear of filling. Brush the pastry rim with cold water. Roll out the rest of the pastry to a large circle – it has to cover the mound of fruit – then drape it over the rolling pin as before and lift it over the pie. Gently but firmly press the pastry on to the damp rim with your thumbs to seal the two layers.

With a sharp knife trim off any pastry overhanging the rim of the plate. 'Knock up' the edges of the pastry and make a scalloped or fluted pastry rim (see page 189). Cut a couple of steam-holes in the top of the pie with the tip of a sharp knife, sprinkle with a little sugar and bake on the hot baking tray in the heated oven for 15 minutes. Reduce the heat to 180°C/350°F/gas 4 and bake for a further 20 to 25 minutes, until the pastry is golden and crisp. Remove from the oven, sprinkle with a little more sugar and serve warm with custard (see page 290) or cream.

Mince Pies

The only remnant of the medieval recipe is the suet in the mincemeat, though more often than not it is omitted or replaced with a vegetarian alternative. But home-made mince pies are still a real treat in December – some people say that Christmas only begins for them when they sit down on the afternoon of Christmas Eve with a first-class mince pie warm from the oven. Adding ground almonds gives rich shortcrust pastry an even richer flavour, and a good crumbly, light, crisp texture; it is the best pastry for mince pies. You can use icing sugar, which gives the pastry a fine crisp texture, or caster, which makes it slightly more crumbly. The dough is easy to make in a food processor, and can be kept in the fridge for a couple of days before you need it. Mince pies can be frozen before or after baking, and are nicest eaten gently warmed.

FOR THE ALMOND PASTRY:	FOR THE FILLING:
225g plain flour	about 400g best mincemeat
a pinch of salt	1 tablespoon brandy, rum or Amaretto
50g ground almonds	caster or icing sugar, for sprinkling
85g icing sugar or caster sugar	
175g unsalted butter, chilled and diced	*a plain or fluted round cutter, 8–9cm*
1 medium free-range egg yolk	*a star-shaped cutter*
	a mince pie or bun tin

To make the almond pastry, put the flour, salt, ground almonds and sugar into the bowl of a food processor. Pulse several times to combine the ingredients, then add the diced butter and process just until the mixture looks like fine crumbs. Add the egg yolk and process briefly until the mixture comes together to make a ball of soft but not sticky dough. If there are dry crumbs in the base of the bowl, or the dough feels hard and dry, add cold water a teaspoon at a time until the dough comes together. Wrap in clingfilm and chill for 15 minutes, until firm but not hard. If the dough is kept for several hours or overnight, remove from the fridge and leave for 15 minutes before using.

Heat the oven to 180°C/350°F/gas 4 and roll out the chilled pastry on a floured work surface to about 4mm thick. Cut out 12 rounds using the cutter and 12 stars (or smaller rounds or holly-leaf shapes), re-rolling the trimmings as necessary. Press the larger rounds into the depressions in the mince pie tin, gently pressing the dough against the sides with your thumb to remove any air bubbles.

Stir the mincemeat well and mix in the brandy, rum or Amaretto. Put about 1½ teaspoons of mincemeat into the centre of each pastry case. Lay a pastry star on the surface of each pie.

Bake for 20 to 25 minutes, or until firm and just golden; richer pastry tends to brown very quickly, so keep an eye on these mince pies. Leave to cool in the tin for several minutes so the pastry firms up, then carefully unmould and cool on a wire rack. Serve dusted with sugar.

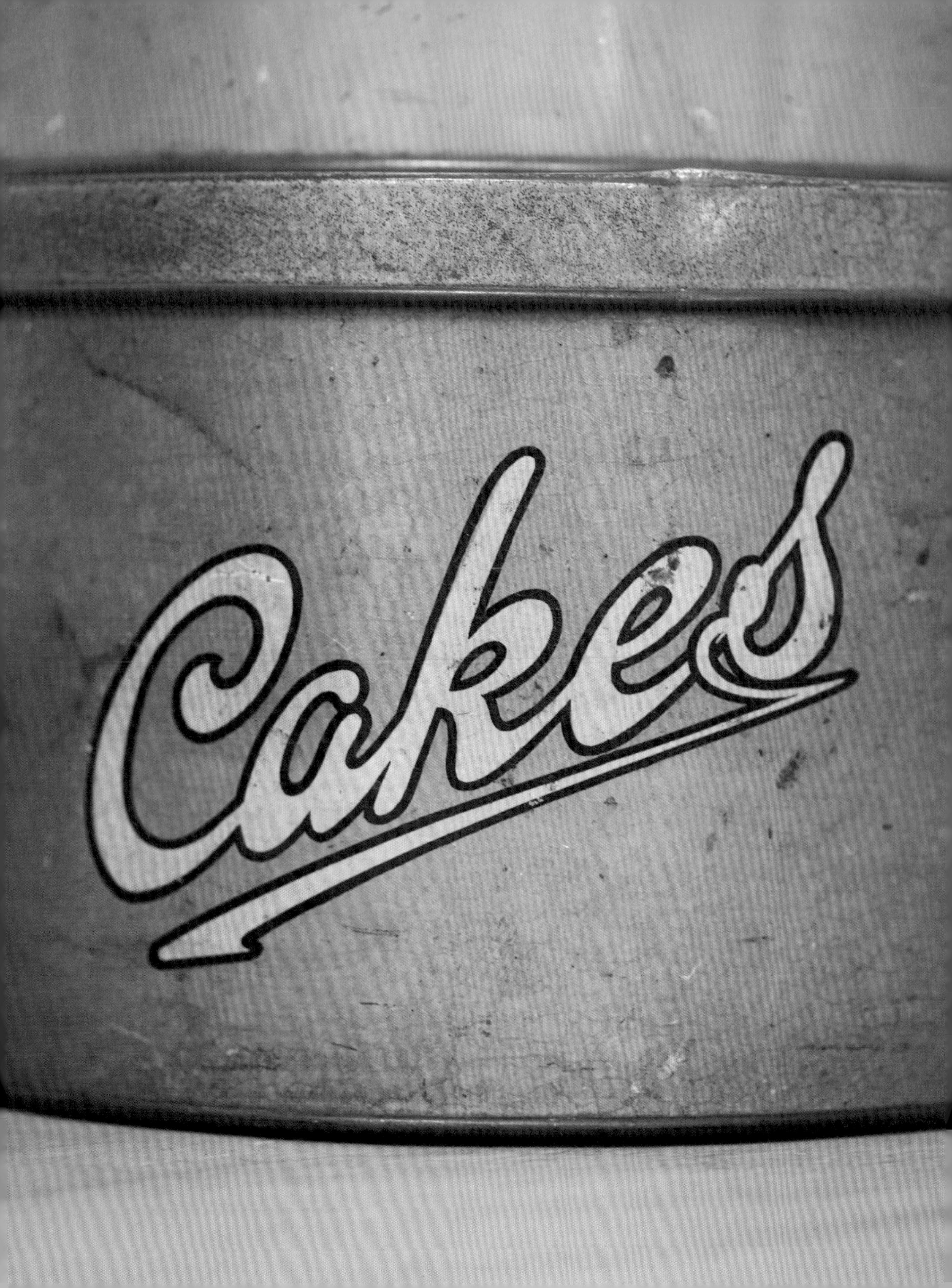
Cakes

Few countries can have given the world as many recipes for cakes in every shape and size as Britain, from traditional styles that are recognizable everywhere to quirky regional confections that have made a small village or town famous. Delve into their origins and a fascinating social and geographical history emerges, since over the centuries, wherever there have been communities, people have baked cakes of some description, inventing or adapting handed-down recipes to make use of local ingredients.

But what, actually, is a cake? It sounds like a silly question: surely everyone knows that a cake is a sweet, soft indulgence that might involve dried fruit, nuts and spices, or something gooey like chocolate or cream? These days, we might define a cake as a baked confection, usually created from four main ingredients – flour, eggs, sugar and butter – but there are myriad variations and methods that produce something we instinctively class as a 'cake', including the likes of Eccles, Chorley and Banbury cakes, which are actually made with flaky or shortcrust pastry filled with dried fruit, or the Scottish black bun, a rich fruit cake encased in pastry. Perhaps what we can say is that while European confectionery often involves showy artistic cakes that people go out and buy, British cake-making has evolved through a cosier craft tradition that is more about the simple joy of sharing a cake baked at home.

The earliest 'cakes' were little more than crude breads which gradually evolved into yeast doughs, occasionally enriched with fruit, honey or seeds. For centuries, the demarcation line between bread and cake wasn't very clear, and it can still be pretty blurred: after all, are Irish barm brack and Welsh bara brith really so different from a fruit cake? Is a teacake really a cake; is gingerbread really bread?

The word 'cake' is believed to be a derivation of the Old Norse 'kaka', which described rough rounds of grain or (especially in Scotland) oats, mixed with water and baked on a stone so they were probably quite brittle, more like biscuits. However the Romans, who were ingenious bakers, learned how to harness wild yeasts, such as barm, which occurs during beer-making, to raise and lighten the dough – hence the name 'barm brack'.

On special occasions such as local fairs, festivals and weddings, these everyday breads were sweetened and titivated, increasingly with the dried figs and dates, almonds and spices that were beginning to be traded from warmer climates. Superstition, religion and customs were inevitably entwined with the ritual of baking. A wealth of stories are told about the origins of the likes of 'dumb cakes', involving the secret, silent carving of initials into the cake, or sleeping with pieces under the pillow to reveal who a young girl would marry. Early wedding 'cakes' were possibly breads which were broken over the bride's head, or sweetened buns stacked up in an ancient version of a *croque en bouche*, over which the newlyweds would attempt to kiss: success meant many children.

Shakespeare, in *Twelfth Night*, alluded to 'cakes and ale' as a symbol of the good life; and the gratifying nature of cakes was often frowned upon by the Puritans of Oliver Cromwell's era, who even tried to ban Christmas feasting. It wasn't until Victorian times that the Christmas cake as we know it became an integral part of the celebrations.

Over hundreds of years, regional recipes, often with evocative names like fat rascals and singin' hinny, the famous Northumberland griddle cake, have been handed down through generations and show the influence of local produce. Lardy cakes, either glossy and plain or layered with dried fruit, were famous in the prime pig-rearing region of Wiltshire, Oxfordshire and Berkshire, where pork lard was plentiful. In the orchard counties of the south of England, apple cakes were popular; while in Ireland, the staple potato was often used to bulk out their own version. The fruit and spice used in Banbury cakes were apparently brought back by Crusaders from the Near East in the thirteenth century. Saffron cakes are a reminder that the spice was once grown prolifically in Britain (think Saffron Walden); while the heavy, dark, spicy gingerbreads and parkin famous around the north-east coast reflect the fact that sugar and spices arrived in the eighteenth century with slaves from the Caribbean who found work locally as servants, and whose recipes have become interwoven in British baking tradition.

Through medieval times until the early seventeenth century, there was often no real distinction between sweet and savoury food, so it wasn't unusual to find beef, dried fruit and spice inside a cake. In wealthier houses, cakes were baked in brick ovens in which a fire would be lit, the ashes would be swept out and the cake/bread baked on the floor of the oven. However, in poorer homes cakes were more likely to be made in pots covered in ashes which sat by the fire, or, particularly in Scotland, Ireland and Wales, using the time-honoured griddle.

The real sea change for the kind of cakes we are more used to today happened in the eighteenth century, and owes much to the shift from yeast as a raising agent to beaten eggs. By then, not only eggs but ingredients such as sugar and butter were more easily accessible, while cake 'rings' or 'hoops' had been in use since the seventeenth century. However, the new-style cakes, still made with heavy flour, required a lot of hard work to get enough air into the mixture. Hannah Glasse, who wrote *The Art of Cookery Made Plain and Easy* in 1747, gave her recipe for pound cake, made with a pound each of sugar, flour, eggs and butter, instructing the reader to 'beat it all well together for an hour with your hand, or a great wooden spoon'.

In the nineteenth century, life became easier with the development of special soft cake flour, which could more easily be mixed with fats, along with raising agents such as bicarbonate of soda and baking powder, and eventually self-raising flour. By then, many homes had cast-iron ranges with ovens for baking; the Victoria sandwich – possibly created as a witty take on the jam sandwich to cheer up the widowed Queen Victoria – was popular; and fashionable 'teashops' were opening up in towns, cities and seaside and tourist spots, such as the Cotswolds. Though mostly an extension of home baking, some reflected the influence of pastry chefs from Europe who were increasingly working in the kitchens of the rich and famous. It was a young Swiss confectioner, Frederick Belmont, who founded one of Britain's oldest tearooms, Bettys in Harrogate, in 1919, when, intending to travel to London, he boarded the wrong train, found himself in the fashionable northern spa town, liked it and stayed.

From the earliest times, when a handful of dried fruit and spice made a workaday yeast cake special, to the advent of the birthday or wedding confection, the making of a cake has said 'well done', 'thank you', 'I love you'. Birthday cakes, which evolved from a German tradition involving candles, first appeared in Britain with Prince Albert, but were the preserve of the rich. In America, however, the same tradition became a home-baking phenomenon that Britain properly latched on to after the Second World War.

You might think cakes depicting everything from Disney movies to football pitches are novelties of recent decades, but back in the 1950s Frederic and Maria Floris, celebrated Hungarian cake-makers and pastry chefs who opened a shop in Soho, were creating fantastical confections for royalty, stars of the West End stage and Winston Churchill, for whom they made huge, elaborate birthday cakes. One of the most famous was in the shape of a hat surrounded by plumage, known as the 'Feather in his Cap Cake'.

Over the centuries, the wedding cake also evolved from its rustic beginnings. The romantic, tiered, white-iced wedding cake first became fashionable in Victorian times – one of the most famous recorded, apparently standing five feet tall and weighing about 225lb, was made for Princess Louise, Queen Victoria's daughter, on her marriage to the Marquess of Lorne.

Sometimes cakes truly define an era. For example, in the sixties, prawn cocktail followed by steak and chips crowned with the decadent Black Forest gateau became the nation's favourite meal; while in the first decade of the new millennium, the cupcake, often garishly iced and served in towering tiers, became the cake of the moment.

It seems that the beauty of the British cake is that as long as there are ingredients like flour, eggs, sugar and fat to be found, enterprising cooks will find a way to transform them into something interesting, from the simple and wholesome to the downright outrageous.

KINGHAM
STATION 1¼

e Inn
urant

HOME MADE CAKES
PARTIES CATERED FOR
MORNING COFFEE
LUNCHES - TEAS

St. Edward

Old Pound House

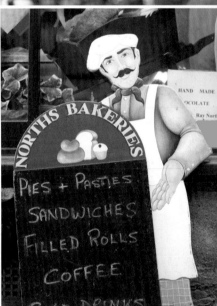

NORTHS BAKERIES

HAND MADE
CHOCOLATE
Ray North

PIES + PASTIES
SANDWICHES
FILLED ROLLS
COFFEE
COLD DRINKS

RENOWNED BAKERY
HUFFKINS
Est 1890
AND TEA ROOMS

WIGGALL'S
CORNER

The Cottage Tearooms

The Cotswolds are famous for cakes and it is claimed
that every village in the area has its own teashop.

Somerset Apple Cider Cake

The ancient art of fermenting pressed cider-apple juice to make cider is still thriving in Somerset. It's hard to miss the orchards and cider farms all across the county – from the small-scale family 'scrumpy' makers to the large commercial producers – as road signs urge you to visit, taste and buy from source. Some of the county's cider farms are over 200 years old and proudly display the old vats or barrels full of slowly maturing cider. You can even see apple brandy being made.

This is a farmhouse recipe for a moist country cake using autumn windfalls or 'rejects', or those apples too tough for the table but too tasty to discard. The cider gives the cake a rich flavour and cuts the sweetness – it is good eaten warm from the oven.

If you would rather not use cider, use 100ml milk instead and toss the diced apples in a teaspoon of ground cinnamon before adding to the mixture.

175g unsalted butter, softened
175g light brown muscovado sugar
3 medium free-range eggs, at room temperature, lightly beaten
250g self-raising flour
100ml cider

about 500g tart eating apples, peeled, cored and diced
2 tablespoons demerara sugar, for sprinkling

a 23cm springform tin, greased with butter and the base lined with greasproof paper

Preheat the oven to 160°C/325°F/gas 3. Using a wooden spoon, electric whisk or mixer, beat the softened butter with the sugar until light and fluffy. Gradually add the eggs, beating well after each addition. Sift the flour on to the mixture and gently fold in, using a large metal spoon, and adding the cider and the apples when the flour is only partially mixed. When thoroughly combined, spoon the mixture into the prepared tin and spread evenly. Sprinkle with the demerara sugar and bake in the heated oven for about 1 hour, until the cake is golden brown and a cocktail stick inserted into the centre comes out clean.

Run a round-bladed knife around the inside of the tin to loosen the cake, then unclip the tin. Cool on a wire rack (or eat while warm). This cake is best eaten within a day of baking.

Sticky Gingerbread

MAKES 1 LARGE LOAF CAKE

A deliciously spicy, sticky dark ginger cake from Scotland and northern England, quickly made by melting and mixing. Nowadays the cake is usually left plain and un-iced, but in early medieval days it was a solid mixture of flour, honey and spices, baked until hard, then heavily decorated with cloves covered in gilt, gilded leaves and as much ornamentation as possible. The recipe has gradually evolved from a work of art to an edible delight. You can still add a decoration of edible gold leaf or white glacé icing after baking, though, if you would like something a little fancier. It is excellent eaten with butter or a wedge of Lancashire cheese. The flavour gets better as it matures, so plan to make this at least a day before cutting.

225g self-raising flour
1 teaspoon bicarbonate of soda
1 tablespoon ground ginger
1 teaspoon ground cinnamon
1 teaspoon ground mixed spice
115g unsalted butter, chilled and diced
115g black treacle

115g golden syrup
115g dark brown muscovado sugar
275ml milk (not skimmed)
1 medium free-range egg, beaten

a 900g loaf tin, about 26 x 13 x 7cm, greased with butter and lined with greaseproof paper

Heat the oven to 180°C/350°F/gas 4. Sift the flour, bicarbonate of soda, ginger, cinnamon and mixed spice into a large mixing bowl. Add the diced butter and rub into the flour mix, using the tips of your fingers, until the mixture looks like breadcrumbs.

Spoon the treacle and golden syrup into a small pan and warm gently until melted and runny but not hot. Set aside until lukewarm. Put the sugar and milk into another pan and heat gently, stirring well to dissolve the sugar. Leave to cool until lukewarm, then whisk the milk into the flour mixture, quickly followed by the treacle mixture and the egg, to make a smooth thick batter, the consistency of double cream.

Put the mixture into the prepared tin. Bake the gingerbread in the heated oven for about 45 minutes, or until a skewer inserted into the centre of the loaf comes out clean. Run a round-bladed knife around the inside of the tin to loosen the loaf, then set the tin on a wire rack and leave the gingerbread to cool completely before turning out. Wrap the loaf in foil and leave for at least a day before cutting; it will get stickier the longer it is kept. Store in an air-tight container.

Madeira Cake

This rich, close-textured sponge cake was designed to accompany a glass of Madeira wine, rather than be made with it. It was all the rage in the nineteenth century among the more leisured upper classes, and was a test of the cook's skill. The cake relies on plenty of beating to achieve its fine, close crumb – luckily an electric mixer makes this easy today – and good butter for its flavour. Seed cake is made in the same way without decoration or icing; well worth getting the bottle or the teapot out for.

250g plain flour
a pinch of salt
1 teaspoon baking powder
175g unsalted butter, soft but not runny
175g caster sugar
3 medium free-range eggs, at room temperature, beaten

finely grated zest and juice of ½ an unwaxed lemon
2 strips of lemon peel, to decorate (optional)

a 20cm round deep cake tin or a loaf tin, greased with butter and lined with greaseproof paper

Preheat the oven to 170°C/325°F/gas 3. Sift the flour, salt and baking powder on to a sheet of greaseproof paper and set aside until needed.

Put the soft butter into a mixing bowl or the bowl of an electric mixer and beat well for a minute with a wooden spoon or an electric whisk or food mixer. When the butter looks lighter and creamier, add the sugar and beat well for about 5 minutes, until the mixture looks very light and fluffy. Gradually add the eggs, beating well after each addition and adding a tablespoon of the sifted flour with the last portion of egg.

Beat in the lemon zest and juice, then sift the remaining flour into the bowl. Using a large metal spoon, gently fold the ingredients together. When thoroughly combined, with no visible streaks of flour, transfer the mixture to the prepared tin and spread it out evenly. Gently bang the tin down on the work surface to dislodge any air pockets, and bake in the preheated oven for 30 minutes. Arrange the strips of lemon peel on top of the cake and cook for a further 30 to 45 minutes, or until firm to the touch.

Remove from the oven and stand the tin on a wire cooling rack. When completely cold, remove the cake from the tin and peel off the lining paper. Store in an airtight container.

SEED CAKE (OPPOSITE, TOP)

A once popular cake that deserves a place on the British tea table once more. Make up the mixture for Madeira cake, omitting the lemon zest and juice, and adding 2 teaspoons of caraway seeds and 1 tablespoon of ground almonds. Leave the top plain.

Cherry Cake

The art of a good cherry cake is to have the fruit evenly distributed rather than clinging to the base. The cake mixture should not be too soft – the ground almonds help here – and the cherries must be thoroughly rinsed, to remove their sticky preserving syrup, and then well dried. This is one of the best of British cakes, well worth baking.

200g best-quality glacé cherries, natural colour if possible	3 medium free-range eggs, at room temperature, beaten
200g self-raising flour	50g ground almonds
a pinch of salt	
175g unsalted butter, soft but not runny	*a 20cm round deep cake tin,*
175g caster sugar	*greased with butter and lined with greaseproof paper*

Preheat the oven to 170°C/325°F/gas 3. Halve the cherries and rinse under the hot tap to remove all their sticky coating. Drain well, then leave to dry between several sheets of kitchen paper.

Sift the flour and salt on to a sheet of greaseproof paper and set aside until needed. Put the soft butter into a mixing bowl or the bowl of a food mixer and beat for a minute until creamy. Add the sugar and beat well until light and fluffy. Gradually add the eggs, beating well after each addition. Using a large metal spoon, fold in the ground almonds.

Tip the cherries into a bowl and toss with a tablespoon of the sifted flour. Sift the rest of the flour into the bowl and carefully fold into the mixture. Finally tip in the cherries, plus any remaining flour in the bowl, and carefully fold together all the ingredients. When thoroughly combined, spoon the mixture into the prepared tin and spread evenly. Make a slight hollow in the centre so the cake will rise evenly, and bake in the preheated oven for 1 to 1¼ hours, until firm to the touch. Remove the tin from the oven and stand it on a wire rack. When the cake is completely cold, carefully remove it from the tin and peel off the lining paper. Store in an airtight container.

Lemon Drizzle Cake

MAKES 1 MEDIUM CAKE

This is one of the simplest cakes to make, but also one of the most irresistible, for it is very lemony. All the ingredients for the cake mixture are mixed together at the same time – this is sometimes called an all-in-one cake method – and the lemon juice and sugar topping is spooned on to the cake straight after baking. It's important for a smooth mixture that the butter is very soft, but not runny, and that the eggs and milk are at room temperature. Look out for unwaxed lemons for the very best flavour.

FOR THE CAKE MIXTURE:
200g unsalted butter, very soft, but not runny
250g caster sugar
3 medium eggs, at room temperature, beaten
finely grated zest of 2 medium unwaxed lemons
250g self-raising flour
½ teaspoon baking powder
100ml milk, at room temperature

FOR THE TOPPING:
100g caster sugar
juice of 2 medium unwaxed lemons
finely grated zest of 1 medium unwaxed lemon

a 20cm springclip tin or deep round cake tin, greased with butter and lined with greasproof paper

Preheat the oven to 180°C/350°F/gas 4. Put the soft butter, sugar, eggs and lemon zest into a large mixing bowl or the bowl of an electric food mixer. Sift the flour and baking powder into the bowl, then pour in the milk. Beat with a wooden spoon, or an electric whisk or food mixer on medium speed, until the ingredients are thoroughly combined and completely smooth.

Transfer the mixture to the prepared tin and spread evenly. Bake in the heated oven until the cake is a good golden brown and firm and a cocktail stick inserted into the centre comes out clean – 50 to 60 minutes.

Meanwhile, make the topping. Mix the sugar with the lemon juice and zest to make a runny glaze. As soon as the cake is cooked, remove it from the oven and stand the tin on a wire cooling rack. Prick the top of the cake all over with a cocktail stick, then quickly spoon the lemon topping over so that it trickles down into the holes. Leave to cool completely before removing the cake from the tin and discarding the lining paper. Serve cut into thick slices.

Lea's Pistachio and Cranberry Cake

MAKES 1 MEDIUM CAKE

A delightfully subtle, sophisticated cake with an exquisitely light, moist sponge, finished with a simple glacé icing that's full of flavour. It is not difficult to make, though you will need 3 mixing bowls plus an electric whisk, and a processor to grind the pistachios to a fine powder.

FOR THE SPONGE:
225g unsalted butter, softened
225g caster sugar
5 medium free-range eggs,
at room temperature
185g plain flour, sifted
115g shelled unsalted pistachios,
finely ground
110g soft-dried cranberries
1 tablespoon orange flower water

FOR THE ICING:
115g icing sugar, sifted
10g unsalted butter
1 tablespoon orange flower water
a few drops of orange oil

TO DECORATE:
1 tablespoon shelled unsalted pistachios
1 tablespoon soft-dried cranberries

*a deep 20.5cm springclip tin,
greased with butter and the base
lined with greaseproof paper*

Preheat the oven to 180°C/350°F/gas 4. Put the soft butter and sugar into a large mixing bowl and beat with a wooden spoon or an electric whisk or mixer until very pale, with a fluffy texture.

Separate the eggs, putting the yolks into a heatproof mixing bowl and the whites into a large, spotlessly clean and grease-free bowl. Set the bowl containing the yolks over a pan of steaming water – don't let the base of the bowl touch the water – and whisk, using a hand-held electric whisk, until the yolks turn into a very thick, pale mousse. Lift the whisk out of the bowl; if a distinct ribbon-like trail of mixture falls back into the bowl, stop whisking and remove the bowl from the pan. Whisk for about 3 minutes more, or until cool; too warm and it will melt the creamed butter mixture. Gradually beat the yolks into the butter mixture.

Add the flour, ground pistachios, cranberries and orange flower water to the bowl and fold into the mixture. Whisk the egg whites until firm, but not quite at stiff peak stage. Add a large spoonful to the cake mixture and mix in to slacken the heavy batter. Using a large metal spoon, gently fold in the rest of the egg whites in 3 batches. When thoroughly combined, spoon the mixture into the prepared tin. Make a small hollow in the centre of the cake so it rises evenly, and bake for 1¼ to 1½ hours, or until a skewer inserted into the centre of the cake comes out clean. If necessary, cover the cake with a sheet of greaseproof paper to prevent it becoming too brown. Remove the cake from the oven and set the tin on a wire cooling rack. Leave for 5 minutes, then run a round-bladed knife around the inside of the tin to loosen the sponge and carefully unmould. Leave to cool completely.

To make the icing, put the icing sugar, butter, orange flower water, and a few drops of orange oil (to taste) into a small pan. Set over a very low heat and stir gently until smooth and melted. If the icing is too thick to pour, add a few drops of water. Pour the warm icing over the cooled cake. Chop or crush the pistachios, using a pestle and mortar, and scatter over the cake. Dot with the cranberries.

Swiss Roll

This is a British classic – a whisked sponge made from just three ingredients, rolled up with a brightly coloured jam filling to give spiral slices. The key to success is proper whisking: the eggs, which must be at room temperature, and the caster sugar need to be whisked with either an electric hand mixer or a large free-standing mixer for at least 5 minutes, until the colour changes from bright yellow to a very pale, creamy colour and the volume increases about five-fold, to a thick, mousse-like foam. If you only have a rotary whisk it's best to stand the mixing bowl over a pan of steaming hot water (don't let the base of the bowl touch the water) while you whisk. Try not to overcook the sponge or it may crack when rolled. This is not a huge problem – it won't alter the nice home-made taste, just the appearance. This version has an additional cream layer.

3 medium free-range eggs, at room temperature
75g caster sugar
75g plain flour
a pinch of salt

6 tablespoons raspberry or strawberry jam
200ml double or whipping cream
extra sugar, for sprinkling

a 20 x 30cm Swiss roll tin, greased with butter and lined with greaseproof paper

Heat the oven to 220°C/425°F/gas 7. Put the eggs and sugar into a large bowl or the bowl of a food mixer and whisk on high speed, using an electric hand whisk or electric mixer, until the mixture is very thick, pale and mousse-like. This will take at least 5 minutes. To test whether the mixture is ready, lift out the whisk; if a very distinct ribbon-like trail of mixture falls back into the bowl, you can stop whisking.

Sift the flour and salt on to a sheet of greaseproof paper, then sift half of it a second time straight into the bowl. Using a large metal spoon, very gently fold the flour into the foamy egg mixture. Sift the rest of the flour into the bowl and fold in until you no longer see any specks or streaks of flour, particularly checking the bottom of the bowl.

Transfer the mixture to the prepared tin and spread evenly. Bake in the heated oven until golden brown and springy to touch – about 9 to 10 minutes. While the sponge is cooking, dust a sheet of greaseproof paper with caster sugar. As soon as the sponge is cooked, flip it out on to the paper and lift off the tin. Carefully peel off the lining paper. With a large sharp knife, make a shallow cut about 2cm in from one of the short sides, then gently roll up the sponge from the end with the cut, using the greaseproof paper to help you. The cut will make rolling easier. Set the rolled-up sponge on a wire cooling rack and leave to cool completely.

When ready to fill, whip the cream. Unroll the sponge, trim off the edges, then spread with the jam. Top with the cream, spreading to within 3cm of the edges. Gently re-roll. Sprinkle with sugar to finish and eat immediately.

Coffee Walnut Cake

MAKES 1 LARGE CAKE

Another cake that's better home-made: a buttery yet light sponge cake with a rich coffee taste and aroma, crunchy walnuts and a bittersweet coffee icing laden with more nuts. The best coffee to use is a well-flavoured instant, rather than a liquid made from ground beans or the traditional Camp essence. The cake will cut more easily and the flavour will be stronger if it is left for a day before eating. As usual with sponge cakes made by the creaming method, it's a good idea to take the butter and eggs out of the fridge an hour or so before you start.

FOR THE SPONGE:
175g unsalted butter, softened
175g caster sugar
3 medium free-range eggs, at room temperature, beaten
75g walnut pieces, chopped smaller
175g self-raising flour
½ teaspoon baking powder
1 tablespoon instant coffee granules, dissolved in 1 tablespoon boiling water

FOR THE FILLING AND TOPPING:
125g unsalted butter
300g icing sugar
3 tablespoons instant coffee granules, dissolved in 2 tablespoons boiling water
4 tablespoons cream (whipping, single or double)
25g walnut pieces, chopped smaller
walnut halves, to decorate

2 x 20.5cm cake tins, greased with butter and the bases lined with greasproof paper

Heat the oven to 180°C/350°F/gas 4. Put the softened butter and sugar into a bowl and beat with an electric whisk, mixer or wooden spoon until light and creamy. Scrape down the sides of the bowl from time to time with a rubber spatula. Gradually add the eggs, beating well after each addition. Add the nuts to the bowl, sift the flour and baking powder on to the mixture and pour in the dissolved coffee. Using a large metal spoon, carefully fold the ingredients together until thoroughly combined. Divide the mixture between the 2 tins and spread evenly. Bake in the heated oven for 20 to 25 minutes, until the sponges are a good golden brown and spring back when lightly pressed. Run a round-bladed knife around the inside of the tin to loosen the sponges, then turn out on to a wire rack and leave to cool completely.

To make the filling and topping, heat the butter in a small, heavy pan until it starts bubbling. If you like a more nutty-flavoured icing, cook the butter for a minute or so more until it turns a light brown colour. Meanwhile sift the icing sugar into a large heatproof mixing bowl. Pour the hot butter on to the icing sugar, quickly followed by the dissolved coffee and the cream. Beat well with a wooden spoon until the mixture is very smooth, then work in the chopped nuts. Leave until thick enough to spread and almost set (in warm weather you will need to chill it in the fridge).

Use half the mixture to sandwich the 2 sponges. Set the cake on a serving plate and spread the rest of the mixture over the top. Decorate the top with walnut halves. Store in an airtight container and eat within 4 days.

Jasminder's Parrot Cake

MAKES 1 LARGE CAKE – CUTS INTO 12

There's plenty of exotic fresh fruit in this quick-to-make cake – juicy ripe mango, fragrant passion fruit, pineapple and bananas, and plenty of chopped nuts. This cake is full of flavour yet very light and not too sweet – the cream-cheese filling and frosting is a perfect contrast to the sponge.

FOR THE SPONGE:
250g plain flour
250g caster sugar
1 teaspoon bicarbonate of soda
1 teaspoon ground cinnamon
200ml sunflower oil
3 medium free-range eggs
50g pecans, roughly chopped
50g walnut pieces, roughly chopped
2 ripe medium bananas
1 ripe large mango
2 passionfruit
85g pineapple, drained and finely chopped
1 unwaxed orange

FOR THE FILLING AND FROSTING:
175g good-quality full-fat cream cheese or soft cheese
55g unsalted butter, softened
400g icing sugar

TO DECORATE:
2 passionfruit
1 ripe medium mango
8 walnuts

2 x 20.5cm cake tins, greased with butter and the bases lined with greaseproof paper

Preheat the oven to 180°C/350°F/gas 4. Sift the flour, sugar, bicarbonate of soda and cinnamon into a large mixing bowl. Whisk the oil and the eggs together until thoroughly combined. Peel and mash the bananas with a fork – they should still have some texture. Peel the mango and slice the flesh away from the stone, then mash, in the same way as the bananas, so it keeps some texture. Halve the passionfruit and scoop out the pulp and seeds. Add to the bananas along with the mango. There should be about 375g of fruit – if there is too much, remove some of the banana.

Add the pineapple to the other fruit. Finely grate the orange zest and set aside for the filling, then squeeze the juice from the orange and add 2 tablespoons to the oil mixture. Add the oil mixture, nuts and prepared fruit mixture to the flour mixture and mix thoroughly with a wooden spoon. Pour the cake mixture into the 2 prepared tins, to fill them evenly. Bake for 35 minutes, until the cakes are golden brown and firm to the touch. Run a round-bladed knife around the inside of the tins, then turn them out on to a wire rack and leave to cool.

Meanwhile, prepare the cream cheese filling and frosting. Beat the cream cheese, butter and reserved grated orange zest with an electric whisk or mixer until smooth. Sift the icing sugar into the bowl and work in, using a low speed. Once the sugar has been thoroughly combined, whisk on high speed for a couple of minutes to make a light and creamy thick frosting. Chill for about 20 minutes, or until firm enough to spread.

To assemble the cake, put one of the sponge cakes on a serving plate, top crust down. Spread with half of the cream cheese filling. Add a second sponge and spread with the remaining cream cheese frosting, swirling it with a round-bladed knife. Halve the passionfruit and scoop out the pulp and seeds. Peel the mango, slice the flesh away from the stone, and cut into neat slices. Decorate the top of the cake with the prepared fruit and walnuts.

Battenberg Cake

MAKES 1 MEDIUM CAKE

This cake was named in honour of the marriage in 1884 of Queen Victoria's granddaughter, Princess Victoria of Hesse-Darnstadt, to Prince Louis of Battenberg (they later changed their name to the more English-sounding Mountbatten). It is thought to represent either traditional German two-tone cakes or the four Battenberg princes (Louis, Alexander, Henry and Joseph).

FOR THE SPONGE:
175g unsalted butter, softened
175g caster sugar
3 medium free-range eggs, at room temperature, beaten
½ teaspoon vanilla extract
175g self-raising flour
1 tablespoon milk
a few drops of pink or red food colouring

TO FINISH:
350g white marzipan
8 tablespoons good-quality apricot jam

a 20 x 15cm Battenberg tin or an 18cm-square cake tin, greased with butter and the base lined with greaseproof paper, and divided in two halves with tin foil

Preheat the oven to 180°C/350°F/gas 4. Put the butter and sugar into a bowl and beat with a wooden spoon or an electric whisk or mixer until light in colour and very creamy in texture. Mix the eggs and vanilla, then gradually add to the butter mixture, beating well after each addition. Sift the flour into the bowl, add the milk and gently fold the ingredients together using a large metal spoon. Divide the mixture in half. Spoon one half into 2 sections of the Battenberg tin, or into half of the divided square tin (make sure the foil divider is folded over the side of the tin so it is well secured), and spread evenly. Add the food colouring a few drops at a time to the second portion of mixture, mixing it in well so there are no streaks; the colour will tend to darken on baking, so don't overdo it. Spoon this pink mixture into the remaining sections of the Battenberg tin or the other side of the divided tin. Spread evenly, then bake for 25 to 30 minutes, until firm to the touch. Remove from the oven and run a round-bladed knife around the inside of the tin and the dividers to loosen the sponge, but do not unmould. Stand the tin on a wire rack and cool completely.

Carefully turn out the sponge and remove the lining paper. If the cakes have risen unevenly in the oven, trim them with a long sharp knife so that the short sides are exactly square. If using the square tin, cut each sponge in half lengthwise. If you would like to make an 8-sectioned cake (see picture opposite) cut each strip in half lengthways to make 4 strips of each colour. Brush off any crumbs. Roll out the marzipan on a work surface lightly dusted with cornflour or icing sugar to a rectangle measuring 20 x 30cm. Heat the apricot jam with a tablespoon of water, then push through a sieve to make a smooth purée. Brush one long side of one strip of pink cake with jam and set it jam side down on the marzipan, so it is lined up along one short side. Brush the 3 other long sides of this strip with jam and set a yellow-coloured strip, lightly brushed on the long sides with jam, next to it and another one, also brushed with jam, on top of it. Lightly brush jam on the last pink strip and place it on top of the yellow one to make a two-layered chequerboard pattern. (Repeat these steps to make a 4-layer pattern.) Wrap the marzipan neatly over and around the whole cake, leaving the ends visible. Trim off the excess marzipan and slice off the ends to neaten. The top can be left plain, or pinched along the edges decoratively. Store in an airtight container.

Cornish Clotted Cream Cake

MAKES 1 MEDIUM CAKE

The south-west of England is the spiritual home of clotted cream: golden yellow and thick enough to spread like butter, it is particular to Devon and Cornwall. The writer Alan Davidson suggests that the recipe for turning milk into clotted cream dates back 2,000 years and is connected to the local tin industry: Phoenicians trading in tin, among other commodities, introduced it along with their other favourite foods. Until very recently, clotted cream in a tin or can was a popular holiday gift sent through the post. This easy whisked recipe produces a very light, moist, plain cake, flecked with vanilla seeds, that's nice either just as it is or served with a vanilla cream or compote of red fruits for dessert.

2 medium free-range eggs, at room temperature
225g caster sugar
½ a vanilla pod
1 x 225g tub of clotted cream
a good pinch of salt

200g self-raising flour
crème fraîche or double cream mixed with a few vanilla seeds, to serve (optional)

a 20cm springclip tin or deep round cake tin, greased with butter and lined with greaseproof paper

Preheat the oven to 180°C/350°F/gas 4. Put the eggs and sugar into a large bowl. Split the vanilla pod along its length with the tip of a sharp knife and scrape the sticky black seeds into the bowl (reserve some of the seeds to mix with the serving cream, if using). The pod can be used to make vanilla sugar – just add it to a jar filled with caster sugar – or to infuse milk for a custard or ice-cream. Using an electric whisk or mixer, or a rotary whisk, whisk the eggs and sugar until they are very thick and mousse-like and the whisk leaves a thick trail when lifted out of the mixture.

Stir the cream until smooth, and gently stir into the mixture with the salt. Sift the flour into the bowl and carefully fold in with a large metal spoon. When thoroughly combined, transfer the mixture to the prepared tin and spread evenly.

Bake in the preheated oven for 50 to 60 minutes, until the cake is a good golden brown and firm, and a cocktail stick inserted into the centre comes out clean. Leave for 5 minutes to firm up, then carefully remove from the tin, discard the lining paper and leave to cool completely on a wire rack. Store in an airtight container.

Carrot Cake

MAKES 1 LARGE CAKE

Carrot cake is usually thought of as an American import, but carrots have been used in Britain for puddings and cakes since the Middle Ages; along with parsnips and beetroots, they became a particularly useful ingredient for adding sweetness and colour to recipes in the eighteenth and nineteenth centuries. These recipes were dusted down during the Second World War, when sugar and fat were in scarce supply. Chocolate cake made with a little cocoa powder along with plenty of beetroot for dark colour, moistness and flavour became quite popular. This is a more indulgent cake, with walnuts, spices and a creamy topping and filling flavoured with orange.

FOR THE SPONGE:
225g self-raising flour
1 teaspoon baking powder
1½ teaspoons ground cinnamon
¼ teaspoon grated nutmeg
½ teaspoon ground mixed spice
½ teaspoon ground ginger
225g soft light brown muscovado sugar
grated zest of ½ an unwaxed orange
100g walnut pieces
3 medium free-range eggs, beaten
150ml sunflower oil
250g grated carrots (about 3 medium carrots)

FOR THE FILLING AND TOPPING:
200g full-fat cream cheese
50g unsalted butter, softened
150g icing sugar, sifted
grated zest of ½ an unwaxed orange
2 teaspoons orange juice

TO DECORATE:
grated orange zest and walnut pieces (optional)

2 x 20.5cm round tins, greased with butter and the bases lined with greaseproof paper

Preheat the oven to 180°C/350°F/gas 4. Sift the flour, baking powder and all the spices into a large mixing bowl. Using a wooden spoon, mix in the sugar, orange zest and nuts followed by the beaten eggs, sunflower oil and grated carrots. When thoroughly combined, divide the mixture between the prepared tins and spread it out evenly. Bake in the preheated oven for about 25 minutes, or until a cocktail stick inserted into the centre of each cake comes out clean. Turn the cakes out on to a wire rack and leave to cool completely.

To make the filling and topping, beat together all the ingredients with a wooden spoon until very smooth and creamy. In warm weather you may need to chill the icing until firm enough to spread. Spread almost half of the mixture on to one of the cakes. Top with the second cake and spread the remaining mixture over the top. The cake can be decorated with extra orange zest and walnut pieces or left plain. Store in an airtight container in a cool spot.

Miranda's Chocolate Brownie Meringue Cake

MAKES 1 LARGE CAKE – CUTS INTO 12

This looks and tastes spectacular: layers of well-flavoured but light brownie with a hazelnut meringue topping, sandwiched with a vivid raspberry pink cream.

FOR THE BROWNIE BASE:
200g good-quality dark chocolate
200g unsalted butter, softened
250g icing sugar
3 medium free-range eggs, at room temperature, beaten
110g plain flour

FOR THE MERINGUE TOPPING:
4 medium free-range egg whites, at room temperature
¼ teaspoon cream of tartar
200g caster sugar
100g chopped roasted hazelnuts

FOR THE FILLING:
300ml whipping cream, well chilled
100g icing sugar
300g fresh raspberries

TO FINISH:
200g fresh raspberries
100g toasted hazelnuts, roughly chopped
100g shelled unsalted pistachios

2 x 20.5cm sandwich tins, greased with butter and the bases lined with greaseproof paper

Preheat the oven to 190°C/375°F/gas 5. Roughly chop the chocolate, set 20g aside for later, and put the remaining 180g into a heatproof bowl. Set the bowl over a pan of steaming water and leave to melt gently, stirring frequently. Don't let the base of the bowl touch the water. When melted and smooth, remove the bowl from the pan and leave to cool until needed.

Meanwhile, beat the soft butter with the icing sugar until very light, creamy and fluffy; you can do this with a wooden spoon or an electric whisk or mixer. Gradually add the eggs, beating well after each addition. Gradually beat in the flour. When the mixture is very smooth, gradually beat in the cooled, melted chocolate. When thoroughly combined, stir in the reserved chopped chocolate. Divide the mixture between the prepared tins and spread it out evenly. Bake for 8 minutes – the mixture will not be cooked but will have started to form a crust. While the mixture is baking, whisk the egg whites with the cream of tartar in a bowl until stiff peaks form. Whisk in the sugar in 4 batches, to make a smooth and glossy thick meringue. Fold in the chopped hazelnuts.

Remove the cake tins from the oven and reduce the temperature to 170°C/325°F/gas 3. Divide the meringue equally between the two brownie-filled tins, and gently spread it evenly over the still-soft mixture to cover evenly. Smooth and flatten the surface of the meringue in one of the tins, and 'peak' the meringue in the other using a skewer or the tip of a knife – this will be the top of the cake. Return the tins to the oven and bake for a further 25 minutes, until the meringue is firm to the touch. Remove from the oven and leave to cool before unmoulding.

To make the filling, whisk the cream until soft peaks form, then add the icing sugar and 200g of the raspberries. Whisk briefly, to make a thick pink cream. Fold in the remaining 100g of raspberries. Run a round-bladed knife around the inside of each tin to loosen the cakes. Turn out the flat-topped meringue cake on to a serving plate, meringue-side down. Spread with the raspberry cream. Top with the second cake, with the peaked meringue side uppermost. Decorate with raspberries, hazelnuts and pistachios.

Victoria Sandwich Cake

MAKES 1 LARGE CAKE

This is a classic vanilla-scented creamed-butter sponge cake, named after Queen Victoria. Earlier sponge cakes were made by whisking eggs with sugar by hand for a long time until foamy, then folding in flour to form a feather-light cake mixture – like the Swiss roll on page 248. Victorian bakers added butter, melted or beaten with the sugar, to make a richer, firmer cake. Sandwiched with plenty of raspberry or strawberry jam and dusted with sugar, it is part of a traditional afternoon tea, along with fresh scones (page 72). Add fresh berries and whipped cream for a glamorous special treat.

FOR THE SPONGE:
175g unsalted butter, softened
175g caster sugar
3 medium free-range eggs, at room temperature
½ teaspoon vanilla extract
175g self-raising flour
1 tablespoon milk, at room temperature

FOR THE FILLING:
150ml double or whipping cream, well chilled

4 rounded tablespoons good jam: raspberry, strawberry or blackberry, home-made if possible

OPTIONAL:
200g berries: raspberries, strawberries (hulled and sliced if large) or blackberries

TO FINISH:
icing sugar, for dusting

2 x 20.5cm round tins, greased with butter and the bases lined with greaseproof paper

Heat the oven to 180°C/350°F/gas 4. Put the softened butter and sugar into a bowl and beat with an electric whisk or mixer, or a wooden spoon, until very light and creamy. Scrape down the sides of the bowl from time to time with a rubber spatula.

Beat the eggs and vanilla with a fork until well mixed, then gradually add to the butter mixture, beating well after each addition. Sift the flour on to the mixture, add the milk and carefully fold in with a large metal spoon.

Divide the mixture between the 2 tins and spread evenly. Bake in the heated oven for 20 to 25 minutes, or until the sponges are a light golden brown and spring back when gently pressed. Run a round-bladed knife around the inside of the tins to loosen the sponges, then turn them out on to a wire rack and leave to cool completely.

Whip the cream until it thickens and stands in soft peaks – go carefully to avoid overbeating as this will ruin it. Set one sponge upside down on a serving plate and spread with the cream. Top with the jam. (If using fresh berries, layer the jam, then berries and then the cream.) Gently set the second sponge, golden crust side uppermost, on top and gently but firmly press down to sandwich the cakes. Dust with icing sugar. Keep cool until ready to serve. Store in an airtight container in the fridge and eat within 2 days.

Death by Chocolate

This is an incredibly rich but light chocolate cake. It's made without flour, and unlike many recipes it doesn't have cocoa powder or ground almonds either. You do need an electric whisk or mixer for whisking the eggs with the sugar to a thick mousse. It's also worth choosing good chocolate, as there is nothing to mask the flavour. As with most chocolate cakes, it tastes even better the next day.

FOR THE SPONGE:
300g good-quality dark chocolate
150g unsalted butter, diced
5 medium free-range eggs,
at room temperature
½ teaspoon vanilla extract
100g caster sugar

FOR THE TOPPING:
200g good-quality dark chocolate
100ml double cream

a 22cm springclip tin, greased with butter and the base lined with greaseproof paper

Preheat the oven to 180°C/350°F/gas 4. Break up the chocolate and put it into a heatproof bowl with the butter. Set over a pan of steaming hot but not boiling water and leave to melt, stirring frequently. Don't let the base of the bowl touch the surface of the water or the chocolate may become too hot and seize up (i.e. become a thick, clumpy mess rather than a smooth fluid). Once the chocolate has melted, remove the bowl from the pan and leave to cool while you whisk the eggs.

Break the eggs into a large mixing bowl, add the vanilla and whisk for a few seconds just to break up. Add the sugar and whisk on full power until pale, very thick and mousse-like and about 5 times the original volume. This will take about 5 minutes. To test if the mixture is ready, lift out the whisk – if a thick, ribbon-like trail of mixture falls back into the bowl and is still visible after 5 seconds you can stop whisking. Pour the chocolate mixture on to the egg mousse and very gently, but thoroughly, fold the two together, using a large metal spoon. Take your time, and make sure there are no pockets of chocolate at the bottom of the bowl.

Pour the mixture into the prepared tin and bake in the preheated oven for 35 to 45 minutes, until just firm to the touch – the centre should still be slightly moist under the crust, as the cake will continue cooking after it comes out of the oven. If the cake is overcooked it won't cut as neatly. Stand the tin on a wire cooling rack and run a round-bladed knife around the inside to loosen the sponge. Leave until completely cold before removing the tin. The cake will rise to the top of the tin during baking but will sink on cooling.

Invert the cake on to a serving plate – it is easier to ice the flat base. Don't worry if it looks a bit messy at this point. To make the topping, finely chop the chocolate and put it into a large heatproof bowl with the cream. Set over a pan of steaming hot but not boiling water, again making sure the base of the bowl doesn't touch the surface of the water. Leave for a minute or so until the chocolate is half melted, then remove the bowl from the pan and beat the chocolate well until glossy. Pour the topping evenly over the cake and let it trickle down the sides; you can help it a little, though if you work it too much you will lose the shine. Leave until firm, preferably overnight, before serving.

You can also cover the cake with whipped cream, slightly sweetened and flavoured with a little kirsch or vanilla, and decorate it with fresh cherries.

Fairy Cakes

These are small, light, delightful and hard to resist; individual sponge cakes baked in tiny paper cases, then decorated with a swirl of sweet buttery icing, nothing overwhelming or over-indulgent, just fun. The easy all-in-one sponge mixture can be flavoured simply with vanilla, or with cocoa, and topped with a light fluffy butter icing or a richer buttercream. Finish with a dusting of icing sugar or cocoa, or go mad with sprinkles and edible decorations.

175g unsalted butter, very soft but not runny
175g caster sugar
3 medium free-range eggs, at room temperature, beaten
½ teaspoon vanilla extract
150g self-raising flour, plus 3 tablespoons cocoa powder, for chocolate cakes, or 175g self-raising flour for plain vanilla cakes
½ teaspoon baking powder
2 tablespoons milk

TO FINISH:
butter icing (see page 268)
or buttercream (see page 269)
icing sugar, cocoa or sprinkles

mince pie, bun or muffin trays lined with greaseproof paper
bun or muffin cases
a piping bag fitted with a 1.5cm plain tube, for decorating (optional)

Preheat the oven to 180°C/350°F/gas 4. Put the soft butter, sugar, beaten eggs and vanilla into a mixing bowl or the bowl of a food mixer. Sift the flour, the cocoa if using, and the baking powder into the bowl. Add the milk, then mix thoroughly using a wooden spoon, electric whisk or mixer to make a smooth, thick cake batter.

Spoon the mixture into the paper cases so they are evenly filled – each one should be about half full. Bake in the preheated oven until the sponge springs back if you gently press it – 12 to 15 minutes for small fairy cakes, 15 to 20 minutes for larger cup cakes. You may need to rotate the trays halfway through the baking time so the cakes cook evenly.

Remove the cakes from the trays and leave on a wire cooling rack to cool completely before icing and decorating.

TO MAKE BUTTERFLY CAKES:

Slice off the domed top from each cake, using a sharp knife. Cut each small disc of sliced-off sponge in half to make two semi-circles. Pipe or spoon a little butter icing into the centre of each little cake and gently push the semi-circles into the icing to resemble wings. Dust with icing sugar, cocoa or sprinkles.

How to make butter icing

This is an extremely versatile icing that can be used to decorate most cakes. It can easily be coloured by beating in a few drops of edible food colouring. (Pour a little colouring into the bottle cap and use drops from that rather than pouring it straight from the bottle.)

125g unsalted butter, very soft but not runny	3–4 tablespoons milk
	1 teaspoon vanilla extract
400g icing sugar	or 3 tablespoons cocoa powder

Put the soft butter into a mixing bowl and beat with a wooden spoon, or an electric whisk or mixer, until very creamy in colour and texture. Sift the icing sugar into the bowl. Add the milk and the vanilla or cocoa and beat (use low speed if using an electric whisk or mixer) until very smooth and thick.

The icing can be spread on top of the cakes or spooned into a piping bag fitted with a star tube and piped in swirls or rosettes.

To make a coffee icing, replace the milk with cold strong coffee.

For a richer mocha icing, use strong coffee instead of milk and cocoa powder instead of vanilla.

How to make buttercream

This is a much richer, creamier and lighter version of butter icing, but you do need a sugar thermometer for the best results. Once you've tried this topping and filling, you may find it hard to go back to butter icing.

85g caster sugar	150g unsalted butter, very soft but not runny
4 tablespoons water	1 teaspoon vanilla extract, or 75g dark
2 medium free-range egg yolks	chocolate, melted, or 1–2 tablespoons strong coffee

Put the sugar and water into a small, heavy-based pan and heat gently, without boiling, until the sugar dissolves. Bring to the boil and boil until the temperature reaches 110°C or 225°F on a sugar or cooking thermometer (about 5 minutes). Don't let the syrup start to caramelize.

Meanwhile, put the egg yolks into a bowl and mix briefly. Stand the bowl on a damp cloth to keep it from slipping, then pour the hot syrup into the bowl in a thin, steady stream, whisking continuously with an electric whisk (or use a large free-standing electric mixer). Keep whisking until the mixture becomes very thick and mousse-like, pale in colour and completely cold. Gradually whisk in the soft butter, followed by the vanilla, cooled melted chocolate, or cold coffee to taste. Spoon or pipe on to the cakes. In warm weather, chill the decorated cakes just until the icing is firm.

Scripture Cake

MAKES 1 MEDIUM TO LARGE CAKE

A fruit cake recipe popular in late Victorian days which required a certain knowledge of the Bible, this was written in the form of a puzzle. Each ingredient is discovered by looking up the relevant Bible passage (these use the Authorized version). The result is an excellent farmhouse-style cake; the original recipe used wholemeal flour, which gives quite a hearty result – light brown flour is much lighter but still adds a nice flavour to complement the figs. There is a good proportion of cake to fruit as well, so it is not too rich. The top can be left plain or sprinkled with coarse sugar crystals or crushed, unrefined sugar cubes before baking.

225g Judges 5:25, last clause	350g 1 Kings 4:22
225g Jeremiah 6:20	1 teaspoon 11 Chronicles 9:9
1 tablespoon 1 Samuel 14:25	1 teaspoon Amos 4:5
3 Jeremiah 17:11	a pinch of Leviticus 2:13
225g 1 Samuel 30:12	6 tablespoons Judges 4:19
175g Nahum 3:12	
85g Numbers 17:8	*a 20cm round deep cake tin, greased with butter and lined with greaseproof paper*

Preheat the oven to 170°C/325°F/gas 3.

Using a wooden spoon, electric whisk or mixer, beat the Judges 5:25, last clause, with the Jeremiah 6:20 and the 1 Samuel 14:25 until creamy, lighter in colour and fluffy. Gradually beat in the Jeremiah 17:11, beating well after each addition (following Solomon's advice in Proverbs 23:14 to beat well). Stir in 1 Samuel 30:12. Using kitchen scissors chop up the Nahum 3:12, discarding the stalks, and stir into the mixture with the Numbers 17:8. Mix 1 Kings 4:22 with 11 Chronicles 9:9, Amos 4:5 and Leviticus 2:13 and fold into the mixture with Judges 4:19, using a large metal spoon. When thoroughly combined, spoon the mixture into the prepared tin and spread evenly. Bake in the preheated oven for about 2 hours, or until a skewer inserted into the centre of the cake comes out clean. If the top browns too quickly, cover with a sheet of greaseproof paper.

Stand the tin on a wire cooling rack and leave to cool completely before turning the cake out of the tin and removing the paper. Wrap in foil and keep for a couple of days before cutting.

Judges 5:25, last clause = unsalted butter, softened   *Jeremiah 6:20* = light brown muscovado sugar   *Samuel 14:25* = honey   *3 Jeremiah 17:11* = medium free-range eggs, at room temperature, beaten   *1 Samuel 30:12* = raisins   *Nahum 3:12* = soft-dried figs   *Numbers 17:8* = blanched almonds, roughly chopped   *1 Kings 4:22* = light brown plain flour   *11 Chronicles 9:9* = ground mixed spice   *Amos 4:5* = baking powder   *Leviticus 2:13* = salt   *Judges 4:19* = milk

Dundee Cake

MAKES 1 MEDIUM TO LARGE CAKE

Dundee has a reputation for fine baking and for making the richest and most luxurious of fruit cakes. Thanks to its busy port, sought-after ingredients such as sugars, spices, dried fruits, nuts and citrus arrived from overseas and fine white wheat flour from England. This cake dates from the seventeenth century and was a favourite at the court of Mary, Queen of Scots. According to legend, the Queen had a sweet tooth, though she disliked cherries, so her bakers pleased her with a cake made of expensive and uncommon ingredients and no cherries.

275g plain flour
a good pinch of salt
½ teaspoon baking powder
50g ground almonds
225g unsalted butter, soft but not runny
225g light brown muscovado sugar
4 medium free-range eggs, at room temperature, beaten
grated zest of 1 unwaxed lemon

1 tablespoon whisky
350g sultanas
250g currants
50g chopped mixed candied peel
18 blanched almond halves

a 20cm round deep cake tin, greased with butter and lined with greaseproof paper
a baking tray

Preheat the oven to 180°C/350°F/gas 4. Sift the flour, salt, baking powder and ground almonds into a bowl and set aside until needed. Put the butter into a large mixing bowl or the bowl of a food mixer and beat until very creamy, using a wooden spoon or an electric whisk or mixer. Scrape down the sides of the bowl, add the sugar and beat thoroughly until the mixture is paler in colour and very light. Gradually add the eggs, beating well after each addition. Add a tablespoon of flour with each of the last 2 portions of egg to prevent the mixture from curdling. Beat in the lemon zest and whisky.

Mix a tablespoon of the flour with the fruit and chopped peel to prevent the fruit sticking together in a clump, then add half the remaining flour to the bowl and gently fold into the creamed mixture with a large metal spoon. Fold in half the fruit mixture, followed by the remaining flour and then the rest of the fruit. When thoroughly combined, spoon the mixture into the prepared tin and spread evenly. Dip your fingers into cold water, then press them lightly over the surface of the cake: this helps prevent the crust from becoming too hard. Press the almond halves on to the cake in neat circles.

Tie a folded newspaper around the outside of the tin, then stand the tin on top of another folded newspaper on the baking tray and bake in the preheated oven for 40 minutes. Reduce the oven temperature to 170°C/325°F/gas 3 and bake for a further 1¾ hours, or until a skewer inserted into the centre of the cake comes out clean. Stand the tin on a wire cooling rack and leave overnight or until completely cold before turning out and removing the lining paper. Wrap in foil and keep for a week before cutting.

Parkin

A dark and moistly sticky cake with a shiny top from the north of England. It is made by the melting and mixing method in much the same way as gingerbread (page 62), except for the addition of oatmeal. The recipe varies from place to place, and depends on what ingredients are to hand, but along with the flour, ginger, oatmeal, black treacle and golden syrup, the fat can be lard, dripping or, as here, butter. The sugar can be light or dark brown muscovado or caster, and the liquid milk, water, stout or ginger beer. It can also be flavoured with a little chopped mixed peel, stem ginger or almonds. Whichever way you make it, for the best taste and texture wrap the cooled cake in foil and store it for a week before cutting – traditionally parkin is stored in a wooden box.

225g plain flour
a good pinch of salt
1 tablespoon ground ginger
1 tablespoon baking powder
225g medium oatmeal
100g unsalted butter
100g dark muscovado sugar
175g golden syrup

175g black treacle
1 medium free-range egg
4 tablespoons milk
25g chopped stem ginger
or mixed peel (optional)

a 20cm square cake tin, greased with butter and lined with greaseproof paper

Preheat the oven to 180°C/350°F/gas 4. Sift the flour, salt, ginger and baking powder into a large bowl. Stir in the oatmeal.

Gently heat the butter, sugar, syrup and treacle in a medium-sized pan, stirring frequently until melted and smooth. Beat the egg with the milk until just combined. Pour the melted mixture and the egg mixture into the bowl. Add the chopped ginger or peel if using, then mix everything together with a wooden spoon to make a thick batter. Put into the prepared tin and spread evenly.

Bake in the preheated oven for about 45 minutes, or until firm to touch. Remove from the oven – the top may have sunk slightly – and run a round-bladed knife around the inside of the tin to loosen the cake. Stand the tin on a wire cooling rack, leave to cool completely, then turn the cake out and wrap it in foil. Keep for a week to mature before cutting.

Eccles Cakes

This is a recipe to show off a baker's skill at pastry. Eccles cakes were apparently first sold in 1793 by James Birch, who had a shop on Vicarage Road in Eccles, but they seem to have developed from a type of mince pie, flavoured with brandy or rum and stiffened with a bit of calves'-foot jelly. They were certainly very popular, and by 1818 were being exported to the New World. Home-made flaky pastry encases a sweet, buttery, spicy mix of currants and chopped peel. At one time they were made with fresh blackcurrants and chopped mint, until dried fruit became widely available. The brittle topping is made by brushing the pastry with egg white, then dusting with sugar. They are best eaten fresh and warm.

1 quantity of flaky pastry (see page 281)

FOR THE FILLING:
25g dark brown muscovado sugar
25g unsalted butter, softened
75g currants
15g chopped mixed peel, chopped finer
a little grated nutmeg

TO FINISH:
1 medium free-range egg white
caster sugar, for sprinkling

a 9cm cutter or a small saucer
1 or 2 baking trays, lightly greased with butter

Make up the flaky pastry. While it is chilling, make the filling: beat the sugar and softened butter until creamy, then mix in the currants, chopped peel and several gratings of nutmeg.

Roll out the pastry to a square with sides of about 30cm. Cut out 9 discs using the cutter, or cut around the saucer. Pile the trimmings on top of each other, rather than kneading them together, then re-roll and cut out 2 or 3 more discs. Divide the filling between the pastry discs, spooning it into the centre. Gather the edges of the pastry together to cover the filling. Turn the little cakes over on to the work surface, so the gathered side is facing down, and gently roll them out so they are flatter and about 7.5cm across, with the currants visible through the pastry. Arrange on the baking trays, then score the cakes in a lattice pattern with the tip of a sharp knife. Chill for 20 minutes.

Meanwhile preheat the oven to 220°C/425°F/gas 7. Beat the egg white with a fork until frothy, and lightly brush the tops of the cakes with it. Sprinkle with plenty of caster sugar and bake immediately in the preheated oven for about 15 minutes, until puffed up and a good golden brown colour. If necessary, turn the trays round during baking so the cakes cook evenly. Cool on a wire rack.

How to make flaky pastry

This is a good pastry skill to master. The pastry can be used in sweet or savoury dishes and is great for when you want to make something a bit more special.

225g plain flour | 85g unsalted butter, chilled
¼ teaspoon salt | 1 teaspoon lemon juice
85g lard or white fat, chilled | 90ml ice-cold water

Sift the flour and salt into a mixing bowl. Mash the lard or white fat and the butter together on a plate, so they are thoroughly combined, pliable but still cold. Spread them into an even layer, then divide into 4 equal portions. Remove one portion, cut the fat into flakes and add to the flour. Wrap the plate with the 3 remaining portions in cling film and chill until needed.

Using your fingertips rub the fat into the flour until the mixture looks like fine crumbs. Make a well in the centre of the mixture. Add the lemon juice to the water and stir in with a round-bladed knife to make a soft but not sticky dough, adding more water a teaspoon at a time if necessary. Knead the dough in the bowl for a few seconds then wrap it in clingfilm and chill for 30 minutes.

Roll out the dough on a lightly floured work surface to a rectangle about 15 x 45cm. Cut another portion of the fat into small flakes and this time dot the flakes evenly over the top two-thirds of the pastry rectangle. Fold the bottom third of the rectangle up to cover the fat-dotted middle third, then fold down the fat-dotted top third to make a three-layer sandwich of dough plus flakes of fat. Seal the open edges of the sandwich with the side of your hand, then wrap and chill the dough for 20 minutes.

Set the chilled piece of dough on the lightly floured work surface so that the side with the rounded fold is by your left hand – rather like a book – with the open edge on your right hand. Roll out the dough to a rectangle, just as before, then dot the top two-thirds with another portion of fat cut into flakes. Fold up, wrap and chill as before. Then repeat one last time, roll out the dough, dot with the remaining fat, fold up, wrap and chill for 20 minutes (or up to a day) before using.

Fat Rascals

MAKES 6 LARGE BUNS

No trip to a Bettys Café Tea Room in Yorkshire is complete without a fat rascal, served warm with butter. It is probably their most popular cake – they make 1,000 every day – and they even send them by post to those who can't visit in person. The recipe is a well-kept secret but is based on an Elizabethan Yorkshire bun, rather like a rock cake or a North Riding turf cake (so called because it was made up from scraps, odds and ends, bits of dough, lard and whatever was at hand at the end of the day and baked on a griddle over a turf fire).

250g self-raising flour
½ teaspoon ground cinnamon
a little grated nutmeg
75g caster sugar
100g unsalted butter, chilled and diced
125g mixed dried fruit and chopped peel
1 medium free-range egg, beaten
about 125ml crème fraîche (or double cream
plus ½ teaspoon lemon juice)

TO DECORATE:
1 medium free-range egg, beaten
12 glacé cherries
6 blanched almonds

a large baking tray, greased with butter

Preheat the oven to 200°C/400°F/gas 6. Sift the flour, cinnamon and about 3 gratings of nutmeg into a mixing bowl. Stir in the sugar. Add the diced butter and rub into the flour with your fingertips until the mixture resembles fine crumbs. Stir in the dried fruit and peel with a wooden spoon. Add the egg and crème fraîche (or double cream mixed with lemon juice) and mix to a firm dough. If there are dry crumbs at the bottom of the bowl or the dough won't come together, add more crème fraîche or double cream a teaspoon at a time.

Divide the mixture into 6 equal portions and roll each into a neat ball. Set on the prepared baking tray and brush the tops with beaten egg to glaze. Press on 2 cherries for eyes and an almond for the gnarl (a cross between a grimace and a snarl), and bake in the heated oven for 20 to 25 minutes, until the cakes are a good golden brown and firm to the touch. Cool briefly on a wire rack and eat warm the same day.

REFINED
BRAND

Puddings

TRADE SINCE 1846 MARK

What is a pudding?

A good question, since 'pudding' is a word that we tend to bandy about quite loosely to cover everything from the savoury Yorkshire pudding or black pudding to anything sweet that we eat at the end of a meal. For some, pudding is synonymous with school dinners: baked rice puddings with thick brown skins, ripped back to allow for a big dollop of jam; roly-polys and spotted dick with thick yellow custard – the kind of stodgy, sweet and filling food that was out of fashion for a while but is now riding high on a wave of nostalgia for its comforting, yet slightly sinful, charms. However, these days, 'Anyone for pudding?' could equally be an offer of ice cream, fruit salad, trifle or chocolate cake. Purists, however, would say that it is the steamed (originally boiled) or baked pudding which should rightly bear the name; and it is those puddings that are baked in the oven that feature in this chapter.

In Britain, the beginning of the heyday of puddings was undoubtedly the late seventeenth and early eighteenth century: George I was known as The Pudding King, because it was during his reign that sweet steamed and baked puddings first became popular. Even in those days, pinning 'the pudding' down to a definition proved tricky, as one François Maximilien Misson, a foreign visitor to England in the 1690s, clearly found. While praising the British pudding as 'an excellent thing', he wrote in his memoirs:

> The Pudding is a dish very difficult to be described; flour, milk, eggs, butter, sugar, suet, marrow, raisins etc. are the most common ingredients of a pudding. They bake them in an oven, they boil them with meat, they make fifty different ways: Blessed Be He That Invented Pudding for it is a manna that hits the palates of all sorts of people.

The marrow Monsieur Misson referred to was probably not the vegetable, but bone marrow, often used instead of butter to enrich a pudding; and the boiling with meat most likely refers to the practice of popping a pudding, wrapped in a cloth, into the pot in which meat was boiling, so that it cooked at the same time – rather than the combining of sweet and savoury ingredients which had been the habit until the seventeenth century. Purely sweet dishes were beginning to emerge, making good use of the sugar that was being imported from the Caribbean cheaply enough for most households to afford, as well as dried fruits, candied peel and spices, orange zest and juice, chestnuts or almonds, and flavourings such as rosewater and orange flower water.

At this point in history, puddings first began to fall into two categories: boiled (steaming didn't come to the fore until the twentieth century) or baked. Two culinary advances conspired to ease the making of both types: first, the old reliance on animal gut was transformed with the advent of the pudding cloth or bag – its use is recorded for a Cambridge or College Pudding in 1617. This meant that a boiled pudding (usually based on suet and/or breadcrumbs) could easily be made without having to acquire a sausage skin (these had to be fresh, so were only available when animals were being slaughtered).

The second change, for those who could afford it, was the advent of ovens which could be built into the chimney breast of a family home, in which you could bake your puddings, as opposed to boil them. Since these home ovens were not as hot as a baker's oven, you could make lighter confections such as milk puddings and delicate custards, again usually highly spiced with nutmeg and mace and sweetened with dried fruits. This was the era in which Queen of Puddings was popular, with its custard base topped with jam and meringue; and there is a story that in 1630 at Trinity College, Cambridge, some thirty years before *crème brulée* became famous in France, they first made Burnt Cream – a thick baked custard topped with sugar which was burned to a crunchy caramel, using a branding iron bearing the college crest.

Often puddings were baked in dishes lined with pastry, or 'puff-paste' as it was known. Sometimes there was even some latticework of pastry over the top, blurring the lines between puddings, tarts and pies.

The importance of puddings in the fabric of British life, particularly in country communities, was perfectly highlighted in the famous eighteenth-century diaries of Parson Woodforde of Weston Longville, Norfolk, who, in keeping with the trend of the time, recorded the details of the plentiful meals he enjoyed at home and when eating out locally. In the four years between 1788 and 1802 alone, he records over 280 puddings, both savoury and sweet, the majority of which are plum or fruit puddings, made with the likes of damsons, gooseberries, apples and oranges. Often several puddings would be eaten at one meal, but what is evident is that such puddings were meant for sharing, often between the gentry and their tenants, the parson and his flock. They were built for comfort, rather than ostentation.

By now the idea of pudding had almost become a metaphor for being British or, perhaps, more specifically, English. Writers of the time observed that the English were known as a nation of 'pudding-eaters', and in 1750 William Ellis noted in his book *The Country Housewife's Family Companion*:

> *Pudding is so necessary a part of an Englishman's food, that it and beef are accounted the victuals they most love. Pudding is so natural to our harvest-men, that without it they think they cannot make an agreeable dinner.*

While French cooks had begun to take charge in the kitchens of some rich houses, many of the gentry would have none of it. John Bull, the cartoon rotund country squire created in 1712 by Dr John Arbuthnot to define Britishness, would undoubtedly have preferred a good old-fashioned solid pudding to extravagant French frippery. Puddings even began to denote a political divide: if you were a Whig, you preferred the newer, lighter French desserts; while Tories stuck stubbornly to stodgier British puddings.

Perhaps one of the most treasured of British custard-based puddings over the years has been bread and butter pudding. Contemporary chefs have transformed the traditional recipe into something light and ethereal, substituting bread for fluffy panettone and adding all kinds of ingredients from marmalade to chocolate, but the version that has stood the test of time is a much more solid, comforting affair, which raises the simple combination of leftover bread, custard and raisins or sultanas into something deeply satisfying.

Surprisingly, the other classic British pud, the fruit crumble, is relatively modern – it first became popular during the Second World War when there was too little fat, flour and sugar available to make pastry, but enough to give a topping to fruit – a triumph of the British tradition of make-do-and-mend, while still coming up with a treat that has remained a favourite ever since, to be embellished and enriched in times of plenty. Perhaps, after all, that is what best defines a British pudding: not a set of ingredients, but an experience that is at once comforting and homely, with the potential to be a little decadent and naughty; a recipe for success that the British instinctively seem to understand.

How to make custard

MAKES 500ML – SERVES 4 TO 6

Home-made egg custard, flavoured with good vanilla, is a real treat and doesn't take long to make. It can be served warm, at room temperature or chilled, and will keep for a couple of days in the fridge. The word 'custard' comes from 'crustade', meaning a custard-filled tart with a crust, popular in the Middle Ages, though the thin runny sauce we know has been partnered with our favourite puddings for only 150 years or so.

450ml creamy milk
(Jersey or Guernsey milk is good)
1 vanilla pod

4 medium free-range egg yolks,
at room temperature
2½ tablespoons caster sugar

Pour the milk into a medium-sized pan, preferably non-stick. Split the vanilla pod in half along its length to reveal the tiny specks of seeds, scrape a few into the milk with the tip of the knife, then add the pod to the pan. Bring to the boil, then remove from the heat, cover and leave to infuse for 15 minutes.

Meanwhile, put the egg yolks into a heatproof mixing bowl with the sugar and beat well with a wooden spoon for a minute, until smooth and light. Remove the vanilla pod from the milk (it can be rinsed, dried thoroughly, then used to make vanilla sugar). Stand the bowl on a damp cloth to prevent it from wobbling, then pour the warm milk on to the yolks in a thin steady stream, stirring constantly. Tip the mixture back into the pan and stir constantly over a medium heat until it thickens enough to coat the back of the wooden spoon; don't let the mixture come to the boil or the eggs will scramble. As soon as the custard has thickened, pour it into a serving jug. Serve as soon as possible, or sprinkle the surface with a little sugar, to prevent a skin forming, then once cooled, cover and chill.

Rhubarb and Strawberry Crumble SERVES 6

A fruit crumble is much like a pastry-topped pie, but a lot quicker and easier to make. The crumbly topping is made in the same way as shortcrust pastry, but without the water to bind the crumbs of butter, flour and sugar. The recipe seems to have become popular in Britain during the Second World War, but it is very like the cinnamon streusel topping found on cakes in Germany as well as the American baked fruit crisp. Demerara sugar makes the mixture slightly crunchy; for more texture, replace the ground almonds with porridge oats and maybe a good pinch of cinnamon. Tender, sweet young rhubarb makes a well-flavoured, juicy filling for a crumble to follow a meaty main course; you could also use halved or quartered plums or apricots in season, or a combination of sliced pears and raspberries, or the traditional late-summer mix of Bramley apples and blackberries.

FOR THE CRUMBLE TOPPING:
100g plain flour
100g demerara sugar (or caster sugar)
100g unsalted butter, chilled and diced
100g ground or finely chopped almonds,
or porridge oats

FOR THE FILLING:
about 450g trimmed tender young
rhubarb stems
about 200g strawberries, not overripe, hulled
3 tablespoons sugar, or to taste
1 tablespoon water
2 tablespoons flaked almonds,
to decorate (optional)

a large, shallow ovenproof baking dish,
about 1.5 litres

Heat the oven to 180°C/350°F/gas 4. Mix the flour with the sugar in a mixing bowl. Add the butter and toss in the flour. Using a round-bladed knife, cut the butter into smaller pieces and rub into the flour, using the tips of your fingers, until the mixture looks like coarse crumbs. Stir in the almonds or oats. Set aside while making the filling.

Rinse the rhubarb and cut across into pieces about 2cm long. Wipe the strawberries. Leave small ones whole, halve medium-sized ones and quarter any giant berries. Gently mix both fruits with the sugar and tip into the baking dish. Sprinkle over the water. Scatter the crumble topping over the fruit without compacting the crumbs. Scatter with the flaked almonds, if using, and bake in the heated oven for 30 to 35 minutes, until the top turns a good golden brown and the fruit juices start to bubble. Leave to stand for 15 minutes before serving with custard (page 290) or ice cream.

Seville Orange Marmalade Pudding

MAKES 1 MEDIUM PUDDING – SERVES 6

Baking a sponge pudding seems so much easier than steaming it, particularly if you are using the oven for the main course anyway. For a good, rich flavour use a tangy, thick-cut marmalade, home-made if possible, and avoid any that looks pale or watery and tastes very sweet.

100g unsalted butter, softened
100g caster sugar
grated zest of 1 medium unwaxed orange
2 medium free-range eggs, beaten
125g self-raising flour

2 tablespoons fresh orange juice
3 tablespoons home-made or good-quality thick-cut orange marmalade

a 750ml ovenproof-glass pudding basin or dish, or a deep baking dish about 22.5 x 12.5cm, greased with butter

Heat the oven to 180°C/350°F/gas 4.

Put the soft butter, sugar and orange zest into a mixing bowl or the bowl of a food mixer. Beat with a wooden spoon or an electric whisk or mixer until light and fluffy. Gradually add the eggs, beating well after each addition. Sift the flour into the bowl and gently stir into the mixture along with the orange juice, using a large metal spoon. Gently warm the marmalade and pour into the prepared basin or dish. Spoon the sponge mixture on top and spread evenly.

Bake in the heated oven for 35 to 40 minutes, or until a skewer inserted into the centre of the pudding comes out clean. Remove from the oven and leave to stand for 5 minutes. Run a round-bladed knife around the inside of the basin to loosen the pudding, then quickly invert it on to a warm serving plate. Serve immediately, with custard (see page 290).

Bread and Butter Pudding

SERVES 6

A simple treat. You can use any slightly stale good bread, but challah, barm brack and bara brith (see pages 110, 121, 133) make the most luxurious bread and butter pudding. The rich, creamy custard is flavoured with grated lemon and orange rind and is barely sweetened. Before serving, the pudding is dusted with icing sugar and briefly glazed under a very hot grill.

7 slices of good-quality bread, not too thickly sliced
40g unsalted butter, very soft
50g sultanas
300ml single cream
300ml whole milk
35g caster sugar

4 medium free-range eggs
grated zest of 1 unwaxed orange and 1 lemon
icing sugar, for dusting

a pie dish or baking dish, about 1.25 litres, greased with butter

Cut the crusts off the bread, then spread with the soft butter. Cut into pieces to fit the dish, slightly overlapping to make a single layer. Scatter with the sultanas as you go.

Gently heat the cream with the milk and sugar, stirring to dissolve the sugar, but do not allow it to come to the boil.

Beat the eggs in a heatproof jug or bowl with a lip, then slowly stir in the warm creamy milk and the grated zests. Pour over the bread and leave to stand for about 1 hour. Towards the end of this time, heat the oven to 160°C/325°F/gas 3.

Stand the dish in a large roasting tin and pour enough warm water into the tin to come halfway up the sides of the dish. Carefully slide the roasting tin into the oven and bake for about 40 minutes, until just set (the time will depend on the depth of the mixture).

Lift the dish out of the roasting tin. Heat the grill to its hottest setting, thickly dust the top of the pudding with icing sugar and quickly flash under the grill until golden and shiny. Serve while still warm.

Sticky Toffee Pudding

Credit for this must go to Francis Coulson and Brian Sack. In the 1970s they put it on the gourmet menu at their luxurious hotel, Sharrow Bay, in the Lake District, and it quickly became the most requested dish. They were generous enough to give the recipe to any diner who asked, and to add that they had merely updated a simple local sweet dried- fruit sponge recipe. As with other Lake District recipes, this one uses dried dates and muscovado sugar, two popular baking ingredients in the north-west.

FOR THE SPONGE:
175g stoned chopped dates
1 teaspoon bicarbonate of soda
300ml boiling water
75g unsalted butter, softened
175g caster sugar
2 medium free-range eggs, at room temperature, beaten
175g self-raising flour
½ teaspoon vanilla extract

FOR THE SAUCE:
200g soft dark brown muscovado sugar
100g unsalted butter
150ml double cream
1 vanilla pod

an 18cm square cake tin, greased with butter

Put the dates and bicarbonate of soda into a medium pan. Pour over the boiling water – the mixture will foam up. Set the pan over a medium heat and simmer for 1 minute, then take off the heat and leave to cool for 15 minutes.

Meanwhile, heat the oven to 180°C/350°F/gas 4. Put the butter and sugar into a mixing bowl and beat until light and fluffy, using a wooden spoon or an electric whisk or mixer. Gradually add the eggs, beating well after each addition. Gently stir in the flour (switch to a spoon if you've been using a whisk), followed by the date mixture and the vanilla extract. Pour the mixture into the tin and bake for about 35 minutes, until springy to the touch.

While the pudding is baking, make the sauce. Put the sugar, butter and cream into a medium pan, preferably non-stick. Split the vanilla pod down its length and add to the pan. Heat gently until the butter has melted, then bring to the boil and simmer for about 5 minutes, until thick and toffee-coloured.

Spoon a little of the sauce over the cooked pudding to coat the surface, and return it to the oven for a couple of minutes more so the top turns sticky. Remove from the oven, cut the sponge into squares, pour the rest of the hot sauce into a jug and serve immediately.

Spiced Pears in Port

SERVES 4

We've been cooking fruit in sweet, spicy red wine since the twelfth century. Pears that failed to ripen were boiled until tender, then sliced and combined with cinnamon, ginger, saffron, sugar and red wine to give a spiced sweet-and-sour dessert. Mulberries were also used and, later on, peaches and figs; you can replace the pears here with halved stoned peaches, nectarines or plums, or halved figs. Any leftover cooking syrup can be stored in a screw-top jar in the fridge and used to bake more fruit. The cinnamon stick can be replaced with a couple of star anises for a change of flavour.

500ml ruby port
3 rounded tablespoons honey
75g caster sugar
2 strips of lemon zest

1 cinnamon stick, about 3–4cm long
4 medium to large pears, not too ripe

an appropriately sized flameproof and ovenproof baking dish, with a lid or foil to cover

Heat the oven to 180°C/350°F/gas 4. Pour the port into the baking dish, add the honey, sugar, lemon zest and cinnamon stick, and bring to the boil on top of the stove. Leave to simmer for 5 minutes, then remove from the heat. If your dish isn't flameproof, use a pan to make the port syrup, then pour it into the baking dish.

Peel the pears and arrange them in the hot port syrup. Cover tightly with a lid or foil, and bake in the heated oven for 50 minutes, until tender when pierced with the tip of a knife. Remove the dish from the oven and leave to cool. Serve at room temperature or chilled, with crème fraîche or ice cream. Store in the fridge.

Baked Alaska

A heavenly combination of cold ice cream, warm meringue, red summer fruits and fresh sponge cake. The trick to keeping the ice cream from melting in the hot oven is to use basic physics – insulation. Tiny air bubbles trapped in the whisked sponge base and in the meringue keep the centre cold while the exterior heats up. Nobody quite knows where the recipe came from, although one much like this, called 'Florida, Alaska', was made popular by the chef Charles Ranhofer late in the nineteenth century, when Americans fell in love with ice cream. Forward planning is the key. Once all the elements are ready, the individual Alaskas take only a few moments to assemble and 3 minutes to bake. This recipe uses a cooked meringue, made by whisking the egg whites and sugar over hot water until thick, satiny smooth and glossy, as it will keep for several hours before use.

500ml good vanilla ice cream
375g fresh or frozen mixed summer fruits (raspberries, blackberries, red and black currants, strawberries, etc.)
1 tablespoon caster sugar
1 jam-filled Swiss roll (see page 248)

FOR THE MERINGUE:
4 medium free-range egg whites, at room temperature
½ teaspoon vanilla extract
200g caster sugar

a large freezer-proof plate or baking tray, lined with greaseproof paper

Remove the ice cream from the freezer, and when soft enough make 6 scoops and set them on a freezer-proof plate or baking tray lined with a sheet of greaseproof paper. Return to the freezer for at least 30 minutes, until very firm.

Prepare the fresh fruit by removing any stems, stalks and hulls. Halve any large strawberries. If you are using frozen fruit, defrost it. Mix the fruit with the tablespoon of sugar, cover and set aside at room temperature until needed.

Cut the Swiss roll into 6 thick slices and arrange them well apart on the lined plate or baking tray. Cover until needed.

Make the cooked meringue: put the egg whites and vanilla extract into a large heatproof bowl. Whisk with an electric whisk until frothy, then whisk in the sugar. As soon as they are combined, set the bowl over a pan of simmering water, making sure the water doesn't touch the base of the bowl. Whisk until the mixture forms stiff peaks when the whisk is lifted – this will take about 10 minutes. Remove the bowl from the pan and whisk until the meringue cools down to room temperature – 8 to 10 minutes. Cover and keep cool until needed.

When ready to assemble and bake, heat the oven to 230°C/450°F/gas 8. Spoon a little of the berry mixture on to each circle of Swiss roll. Tip the rest of the berry mixture into a pan and warm gently, just until the juices start to run. Keep warm until ready to serve. Set a scoop of ice cream on top of each circle. Working quickly, cover each one with the meringue so that the sponge and ice cream are entirely covered and encased with the meringue 'blanket'. Bake immediately for 3 to 4 minutes, until the meringue is browned. Serve straight away, with the warm berries.

Little Pots of Baked Chocolate

No chapter on puddings would be complete without a hot chocolate sponge recipe, and these little puds make a splendid addition to the British dessert canon. The dark, rich sponge has a gooey, molten chocolate centre that oozes out as you break the crust. As the chocolate is the main ingredient and the star of the show, it's worth indulging in the best you can afford – dark chocolate with around 70% cocoa solids – for the best possible flavour. Serve these as soon as they come out of the oven, with thick cream or proper vanilla ice cream.

300g good-quality dark chocolate
75g unsalted butter, softened
125g caster sugar
1 teaspoon vanilla extract
or 1 tablespoon brandy
4 medium free-range eggs,
at room temperature, beaten
50g plain flour

4 tablespoons milk
icing sugar, for dusting

6 small pudding tins or moulds, about
175–200ml (about 8cm across the top and
5cm across the base), greased with butter,
dusted with flour and the base lined with
a disc of greaseproof paper
a baking tray

Heat the oven to 200°C/400°F/gas 6 and put the baking tray in to heat. Break or chop the chocolate into even-sized pieces and put into a heatproof bowl. Set over a pan of steaming water, making sure the base of the bowl doesn't touch the water, and leave to melt gently, stirring occasionally. Remove the bowl from the pan and leave to cool until needed.

Put the soft butter into a mixing bowl and beat until creamy, using a wooden spoon or an electric whisk or mixer. Beat in the sugar and the vanilla or brandy, beating well until the mixture is light and fluffy. Gradually beat in the eggs, beating well after each addition. Stir in the flour, followed by the melted chocolate – use a large metal spoon, or the lowest possible speed if using an electric whisk. Mix in the milk to loosen.

Divide the mixture evenly between the prepared tins. Set them on the hot baking tray and bake for 10 to 11 minutes, until risen and just firm to touch. Turn out on to serving plates, quickly dust with icing sugar and serve immediately.

NOTE: Once the mixture has been put into the tins they can be covered in clingfilm and chilled for up to 4 hours. Unwrap and bake on the heated tray as above, allowing 11 to 12 minutes – remove as soon as the puddings are just firm, and serve.

Apple and Cinnamon Charlotte

SERVES 6

Baked apple charlotte seems to have been named in honour of Queen Charlotte, in about 1796. Her husband, King George III, was known as 'Farmer George' because of his fondness for growing produce and raising livestock, and became a patron of apple growers. A deep mould (known as a charlotte) or cake tin is lined with fingers of buttered white bread, then filled with stewed apples cooked to a thick purée and stiffened in the old style with crumbs. It is then baked until the bread becomes deliciously brown, sweet and crisp. More modern versions add a few raisins soaked in brandy or rum, or chopped hazelnuts, to the apple mixture.

1kg Bramley or other cooking apples (about 5 medium)	50g fresh white breadcrumbs or slightly stale cake crumbs
grated zest and juice of 1 medium unwaxed lemon	about 8 slices of good-quality white bread, crusts removed
1 cinnamon stick	
100g caster sugar, or to taste	*a deep round charlotte mould or cake tin (not loose-based), or a baking dish, 1.25 litres, about 16–18cm across, greased with butter and dusted with caster sugar*
125g unsalted butter	

Peel, quarter and core the apples. Cut into thick slices and put into a heavy-based pan with the lemon zest and juice, cinnamon stick, sugar and 25g of the butter. Cover and cook gently, stirring frequently, until tender. Remove the lid and cook, stirring very frequently to prevent the mixture from scorching, until the apple pulp is very thick indeed and all the liquid has evaporated. This is important – otherwise the charlotte may collapse when turned out. Taste, and add a little more sugar if necessary. Remove from the heat, leave to cool, then remove the cinnamon stick and stir in the crumbs.

Meanwhile, heat the oven to 180°C/350°F/gas 4. Melt the rest of the butter. Cut the bread to fit the base and sides of your tin or dish. Brush one side of each piece of bread with melted butter and use to line the base and sides, pressing the buttered side against the tin or dish, slightly overlapping. Reserve some pieces to make a lid. Spoon the apple mixture into the bread case. Top with the reserved bread pieces, completely covering the filling. Brush the top with melted butter. If necessary, trim the slices of bread lining the sides with kitchen scissors to make a flat top. Bake in the heated oven for 40 to 50 minutes, until the bread is a good golden brown. Leave to cool for 5 to 10 minutes, then invert on to a serving plate. Serve hot with cream or custard (see page 290), though old recipes recommend a good chocolate sauce.

Lemon Sauce Pudding

MAKES 1 MEDIUM PUDDING – SERVES 4–6

This is a kind of soufflé with a sauce underneath, and is very easy indeed to make. It does need to be eaten as soon as it is cooked for the full effect, but will taste just as good if it has to wait while you finish the main course.

85g unsalted butter, softened
200g caster sugar
grated zest and juice of 2 unwaxed lemons
3 medium free-range eggs, separated
75g plain flour

250ml creamy milk
icing sugar, for dusting (optional)

an 18–20cm baking dish,
about 8cm deep, greased with butter
a roasting tin

Heat the oven to 180°C/350°F/gas 4. Put the soft butter into a mixing bowl, or the bowl of a food mixer, with the sugar and lemon zest and beat with a wooden spoon or electric whisk or mixer, until thoroughly combined. Add the egg yolks one at a time, beating well after each addition. Gradually beat in the lemon juice. Sift the flour into the bowl and mix in with the milk, on low speed if using an electric whisk or mixer, to make a smooth batter.

In another bowl whisk the egg whites until they form stiff peaks. Fold them into the batter in 3 batches, using a large metal spoon. When thoroughly combined, spoon the mixture into the prepared dish. Stand the dish in the roasting tin and half-fill the tin with cold water. Put the roasting tin containing the baking dish into the oven and bake for 40 to 45 minutes, depending on the depth of your dish, until the top is a good golden brown and the pudding is just firm to the touch.

Dust with icing sugar, if using, and serve as soon as possible – the pudding will continue cooking after it comes out of the oven, and if left to stand for too long the sauce will disappear.

Edward's Warm Apple and Plum Pudding SERVES 6–8

This dessert has a lovely contrast of flavours, textures and colours – a warm, indulgent treat!

FOR THE PUDDING:
115g unsalted butter, very soft
175g golden caster sugar
1 medium free-range egg, beaten
150g plain flour
1 teaspoon baking powder
a pinch of salt
1 teaspoon ground cinnamon
½ teaspoon grated nutmeg
100g pecans, finely chopped
4 medium tart eating apples,
such as Granny Smith, peeled,
cored and cut into 1cm-pieces

3 plums, halved, stoned and
cut into 1cm-pieces
2 tablespoons chopped glacé ginger

FOR THE RUM CARAMEL SAUCE:
200g caster sugar
225ml whipping cream,
at room temperature
20g unsalted butter
1 to 2 tablespoons rum, to taste
1 teaspoon vanilla extract

a 22cm springclip tin, greased with butter and the base lined with greaseproof paper

Heat the oven to 180°C/350°F/gas 4. Put the butter into a mixing bowl or the bowl of a large food mixer. Beat with an electric whisk or mixer until creamy, then add the sugar. Beat until light and fluffy, then gradually add the egg, beating well after each addition. Sift the flour, baking powder, salt, cinnamon and nutmeg into the bowl and fold in. When thoroughly combined, add the prepared nuts, apples and plums and the chopped ginger to the bowl and mix in.

Spoon the pudding mixture into the prepared tin and spread evenly. Bake in the oven for 30 to 40 minutes, until the top is golden brown and the sponge springs back when lightly pressed in the centre. Remove the tin from the oven, run a round-bladed knife around the inside to loosen the sponge, and unmould. Serve on a warmed serving plate.

While the sponge is in the oven, make the sauce. Put the sugar into a heavy-based medium pan and set over a low to medium heat. Watch carefully, and as soon as the sugar starts to melt, use a spatula or wooden spoon to gently draw the melted edges into the centre so that all the sugar melts and turns an even dark caramel. At that point, remove the pan from the heat, cover your hand and pour in half the cream, stirring with a wooden spoon – take care the mixture doesn't burn you, as it will bubble up furiously and splatter. Once the bubbling has subsided, stir in the rest of the cream, then return the pan to the heat and stir until the sauce is smooth and any lumps have melted. Remove from the heat and stir in the butter, rum and vanilla. Serve warm, with the warm sponge.

Queen of Puddings

SERVES 4–6

This recipe, described by Sir Kenelm Digby, dates from 1669, but adding breadcrumbs to a rich custard has been part of our cooking tradition since the Middle Ages. It is a delicate, though not bland, confection of egg custard, good fruity jam and hot crunchy meringue, well deserving of its long history as a British delicacy.

600ml Jersey milk
1 vanilla pod
50g unsalted butter
4 medium free-range egg yolks
grated zest of 1 unwaxed lemon
50g caster sugar or vanilla sugar
100g fresh white breadcrumbs
or slightly stale cake crumbs

FOR THE TOPPING:
4 rounded tablespoons good-quality
strawberry jam or conserve, warmed
4 medium free-range egg whites
100g caster sugar

a deep baking dish,
about 1.25 litres, greased with butter

Put the milk and the vanilla pod, split down its length, into a pan with the butter and heat until the milk starts to steam. Remove from the heat, cover and leave to stand for 15 minutes.

Put the egg yolks into a mixing bowl with the lemon zest and sugar and beat with a wooden spoon for a minute until creamy. Stir in the warm milk. Remove the vanilla pod and scrape some of the black seeds into the milk. (The pod can be rinsed, dried and used to make vanilla sugar – or in another recipe.) Stir in the breadcrumbs or cake crumbs, then pour the mixture into the prepared dish. Leave to stand for 15 minutes. Meanwhile, heat the oven to 180°C/350°F/gas 4.

Bake the pudding for about 30 to 40 minutes, until just set – the custard will go on cooking for a few minutes after it comes out of the oven, so don't overcook it; the cooking time depends on the depth of the custard. Remove from the oven and leave to stand for 5 minutes. Carefully spread the warm jam on top of the custard. Put the egg whites into a large bowl and whisk until soft peaks form. Whisk in the sugar to make a thick, glossy meringue. Pile the meringue in top of the pudding and bake for a further 15 minutes, until the top is a good and slightly crunchy golden brown. Serve warm, the same day.

Raspberry Meringue Roulade

MAKES 1 LARGE ROULADE – SERVES 8–10

The first recipe for whipped egg whites and sugar – the meringue – appeared in Britain in 1706, the technique having been discovered by German chefs and quickly taken up by the French. For the best results, the bowl and whisk must be very clean and dry, as any particle of fat (from the yolk or greasy fingers) will make the meringue lose volume and lightness. Lining baking trays and tins with non-stick baking paper will make it easier to peel off baked meringues.

FOR THE MERINGUE:
4 medium free-range egg whites, at room temperature
1 teaspoon lemon juice
225g caster sugar
1 teaspoon cornflour
2 tablespoons flaked almonds

FOR THE FILLING:
250ml whipping cream, well chilled
250g fresh raspberries
(or other prepared fruit)

TO FINISH:
250g fresh or frozen raspberries
1 teaspoon lemon juice
4 tablespoons icing sugar,
or to taste

a 20 x 30cm Swiss roll tin,
brushed with oil and lined
with baking paper (not greaseproof)

Heat the oven to 150°C/300°F/gas 2. Put the egg whites and lemon juice into a spotlessly clean and grease-free bowl and whisk with an electric whisk, a large mixer or a rotary whisk until they form stiff peaks when the whisk is lifted from the bowl. Mix the sugar with the cornflour and whisk into the egg whites a tablespoon at a time, to make a stiff and glossy meringue.

Transfer the mixture to the prepared tin and spread evenly. Scatter the flaked almonds over the top of the meringue and bake in the heated oven for 45 minutes, until risen, golden brown and firm to the touch – the centre will still be slightly soft. Turn the meringue out on to a sheet of non-stick baking paper and lift off the tin. Leave to cool for 10 minutes, then gently peel off the lining paper. Leave until completely cold before filling.

When ready to finish, whip the chilled cream until very thick, almost to stiff peak stage – if the cream is too firm, though, it will be difficult to spread. Spread the cream evenly over the meringue and top with the raspberries. Roll up the roulade from one long side, using one hand to guide the meringue into shape and the other to use the paper to support the meringue and pull it into shape as it rolls up. Once the meringue has become a roulade, use the paper around the roulade to hold it in shape by wrapping it firmly. Chill for an hour before serving. A good accompaniment is some fresh or frozen berries whizzed up with lemon juice and icing sugar to make a thick sauce or purée. The roulade can be made several hours in advance, but is best eaten the same day. To serve, cut the roulade into thick slices and spoon over a little of the raspberry sauce. .

Think of a classic –

or fashionably retro – British finger buffet, and the chances are it will include sausage rolls, little tartlets, cream puffs, maybe even good old cheese straws. Pop into a café for a coffee or a cup of tea and invariably there will be croissants and pains au chocolat on offer, perhaps éclairs, millefeuilles and Napoleons (or, as we know them, cream slices), Danish pastries or even Turkish- or Greek-style filo confections of honey, sweet spices and nuts.

So used are we to all the treats collectively known as pastries, or pâtisserie, we scarcely think about their origins, and it is hard to imagine the smug one-upmanship that wealthy British families around the turn of the seventeenth century enjoyed when offering their guests some new, intricate little fancy rustled up by their modish French chef. Food enjoys its fashions as much as anything else, and this was the era when French food first became all the rage amongst socialites. They began to shun the more solid style of British baking in favour of a whole range of lighter, frothier delights, from the earliest 'kickshaws' and little puff-pastry 'somethings' that took their name from the French 'quelques choses' to more elaborate centrepieces.

Although the French influence on culinary terminology and tastes dates back to the Norman Conquest, it was in the reign of Charles II, 'The Merry Monarch', that it really began to make its mark. Charles, whose mother was the French princess Henrietta Maria, returned from exile in Europe, where he had spent time at the court of Louis IV, to restore the monarchy after a decade of Oliver Cromwell's rule. He brought with him a new taste and fashion for French food that took off particularly amongst Whig peers and the new, moneyed, non-aristocratic landowners who had risen to prominence under Cromwell and were looking for ways to show off their wealth.

In the 1700s many chefs, such as Pierre Clouet, who worked for the Duke of Newcastle, Vincent La Chapelle, who cooked for the Earl of Chesterfield, and Louis Eustache Ude, chef to the Earl of Sefton in Liverpool, were famous for their lavish cuisine, and, just as today, many of them produced recipe books which influenced the way people cooked and baked at home. La Chapelle published *The Modern Cook*, while Ude, who had previously worked as an apprentice in the kitchens of Louis XVI's court and for Napoleon Bonaparte's mother, brought out *The French Cook*.

Artistry was the order of the day. The earliest tough British pastry, most likely designed to hold in a filling rather than to be eaten, had already been supplemented by a finer pastry – a shortcrust, made with eggs and butter. The new fashion was for 'puff paste', which involved thin layers of pastry which would separate and puff up as the hot air spread through them during baking, giving a delicate, light, crumbly texture. Such pastry owed much to the layered pastry typical of the Middle East and the influence of the Ottoman Empire in Vienna, where coffee shops serving elaborate pastries had become famous during the seventeenth century. The Viennese in turn influenced Italian and French chefs, and a big debate exists to this day as to whether it was the Italians who introduced many a fancy pastry to the French court when Catherine de' Medici married the future Henri II of France in the sixteenth century.

Whatever their exact route, over the eighteenth and nineteenth centuries not only puff-pastry creations, but éclairs, profiteroles and cream puffs made with choux pastry, luxurious chocolate 'pyes' and gateaux made with meringue were embraced in British kitchens, some of which sported separate pastry rooms; and 'petits fours', miniature versions of such fancies, became all the rage.

Some of the most influential French chefs, such Alexis Soyer of the Reform Club, Auguste Escoffier and, perhaps most notably, Antonin Carême, considered to be the pastry king, all worked in London at some point in their careers. Carême and Soyer vie for the title of the first 'celebrity chef', but the colourful Carême, author of several books on pâtisserie, is credited with creating many of the pastries that have become absorbed into the British repertoire, from vol-au-vents to millefeuilles. From tough beginnings, abandoned as a child during the French Revolution, Carême forged a starry career in which he gained international fame cooking for the likes of Napoleon, Tsar Alexander I of Russia and Rossini as well as George IV, then Prince Regent, who brought him over to England to dazzle guests at the Brighton Pavilion.

Not everyone in Britain was enamoured of the influence from Europe, and in the eighteenth century many of the political and satirical writers of the day lambasted the *nouvelle cuisine* as frivolous and suspicious, if not downright traitorous, stalwartly championing the traditional plainer style of British pudding as represented by women cookery writers such as Hannah Glasse. And of course at first only the wealthiest could afford such extravagance. However, by the time Isabella Beeton published her *Book of Household Management* in 1861, she was showing families with social aspirations but more constrained budgets how to instruct their cooks to keep up with the trends of the time. As well as her recipe for 'Very Good Puff-Paste', made with flour, butter and water, she also acknowledges the French chefs, including 'Soyer's Recipe for Puff-Paste' together with a 'French Puff-Paste or Feuilletage Founded on Monsieur Ude's recipe' – both of which are made with the addition of eggs.

What is evident from Mrs Beeton is that new ideas of pastry could be used in a very British way. For example, she includes recipes for puff-pastry sausage rolls – a variation on earlier farmworkers' lunches of sausages baked in bread dough. Around the country, bakers were also taking on board new styles of pastry. In Coventry, God Cakes were sold at Christmas or Easter for godparents to give to their godchildren: these were triangular envelopes of puff pastry (the triangle shape may or may not have represented the Holy Trinity), filled with jam or mincemeat.

As always, fashions in food were reflected in contemporary literature, none more potently than in 'The Garden Party', the famous short story by Katherine Mansfield. A pivotal moment in this day in the life of the privileged children of the Sheridan family is the delivery of 'beautifully light and feathery' cream puffs from Godber's, who, we are told, were famous for them. The idea of cream puffs 'so soon after breakfast' is brushed off and two minutes later they are 'licking their fingers with that absorbed inward look that only comes from whipped cream'.

Fortunately, today we have a much more egalitarian view of pastries, and while dedicated pastry chefs still vie to spin the most fantastical creations in international pastry competitions, most of us are just thankful to four centuries of European and British baking for melding together to give us our breakfast croissants, our sausage-roll snacks and our naughty but nice confections of pastry and cream.

How to make puff pastry

This is the lightest, richest, flakiest and trickiest of all pastries. What makes it so delicious is its butteriness; this pastry is made with as much butter as flour, and what makes it so flaky is the way the butter is rolled into the flour and water dough to make literally hundreds and hundreds of layers. The lightness is the result of the water in the dough turning to steam in the oven and puffing up the fragile layers.

A few tips: as with the other pastries in this book it is important not to develop the gluten in the flour (as in bread-making) – you don't want overworked, over-stretched pastry that shrinks in the oven, so stick to the chilling times. Don't let the butter get warm and start to ooze out of the dough, or it will be hard to handle and end up greasy and heavy. Keep the pastry trimmings to make cheese straws or pie tops. Stack the trimmings on top of each other then re-roll, don't knead them together as for shortcrust pastry. It's not easy to get right the first, or even the second, time – it will taste great, though. It's difficult to make in really small quantities, but the dough can be kept in the fridge for 4 days, or frozen.

300g plain flour
½ teaspoon salt
300g unsalted butter, cold

1 teaspoon lemon juice
about 140ml ice-cold water

Put the flour and salt into the bowl of a food processor and pulse a few times, just to combine and aerate the flour. Cut 50g of the cold butter into small pieces and add to the bowl, then process until the mixture looks like fine crumbs. Mix the lemon juice with the water and add to the bowl through the feed tube, with the machine running, to make a ball of slightly moist dough. Turn out on to a lightly floured work surface and cut a deep cross in the top of the dough ball. Wrap and chill for 15 minutes.

Sprinkle a little flour on the remaining piece of butter, then set it between 2 sheets of clingfilm. Pound it with a rolling pin until half its original thickness. Remove the film, fold the butter in half, then cover with film and pound again. Keep doing this until the butter is still very cold but pliable. Beat it into a square with sides about 13cm.

Put the ball of dough on a floured work surface and roll out in 4 directions, to make 4 flaps with a thick square in the centre. Put the butter, lightly dusted with flour, in the centre and fold the flaps of dough over to enclose it. Gently press the seams with the rolling pin to seal the butter in. Turn the dough upside down and lightly press with the rolling pin to flatten it – don't squeeze the butter out. Gently roll out the dough to a rectangle about 54 x 18cm. Then fold the dough in 3 like a business letter: fold the bottom third up to cover the centre third, then fold the top third down to cover the other 2 layers and make a neat square. Lightly press the edges with the rolling pin to seal. This is your first 'turn'. Lift up the dough and give it a quarter turn anti-clockwise so that the folded, rounded, edge is by your left hand. Roll out the dough to a rectangle and fold it in 3 again, just as before. This is your second 'turn'. Wrap in clingfilm and chill the dough for 15 minutes, then give it 2 more 'turns'. Wrap and chill the dough as before (at this point the dough can be kept in the fridge for 4 days or frozen). Before using, give the dough 2 more 'turns', to make a total of 6.

How to make choux pastry

This pastry, which is made in a saucepan, is actually a soft dough of butter, water, flour, salt and eggs. It is dropped in spoonfuls or piped on to a baking tray; in the oven it rises and puffs up to make a crisp, hollow container. It is the pastry used for éclairs and profiteroles.

To make the pastry, first measure the ingredients carefully according to the recipe requirements. Sift the flour on to a sheet of greaseproof paper. Put the water, salt and butter into a medium-sized pan and heat gently until the butter has completely melted – don't let the water boil and begin to evaporate. Then quickly bring the mixture to the boil and tip in all the flour in one go. Remove the pan from the heat and beat furiously with a wooden spoon – don't worry, the mixture will look messy at first but will soon come together to make a smooth, heavy dough.

Put the pan back on a low heat and beat the dough for about a minute to slightly cook the dough – it should come away from the sides of the pan to make a smooth, glossy ball. Tip the dough into a large mixing bowl and leave to cool until tepid. Beat the eggs until combined, then gradually beat them into the dough with an electric whisk or mixer, or a wooden spoon, beating well after each addition. The dough should be very shiny and paste-like, and fall from a spoon when lightly shaken.

Sprinkling the baking sheet with a little water just before it goes into the oven helps the choux to rise. Bake until thoroughly crisp – if the centre is soggy the pastry will collapse as it cools.

Special Sausage Rolls

Warm from the oven and full of charm, home-made sausage rolls are one of our best-loved treats. You can use shortcrust pastry, flaky, rough puff or puff (see pages 148, 281, 187, 322), though puff pastry makes them special enough for a party. For a change, roll out the pastry on a work surface lightly sprinkled with black poppy seeds. For the filling, look out for well-flavoured sausages at your local farmers' market or the meat counter of a good supermarket. These days, the range is huge and interesting: from a well-spiced Cumberland, to pork, honey, apple and thyme, to spicy pork and chilli, pork and caramelized onion, Toulouse, venison, duck and orange, lamb with mint and onion . . . You can add your own touch to the filling with a little of your favourite chutney (a spicy peach or mango works well), or a smear of mustard. Sun-dried tomatoes (the chargrilled ones in oil have a nice flavour), soft, ready-to-eat dried apricots, or even sweet, slightly hot pepperdew peppers from a jar, cut into strips, work well with plainer fillings.

½ quantity of puff pastry (see page 322), or 375g shop-bought butter puff pastry

FOR THE FILLING:
450g really good-quality sausagemeat, or sausages, skins removed

a little spicy chutney, honey mustard or wholegrain mustard, a few sun-dried tomatoes or ready-to-eat dried apricots
beaten egg to glaze

2 baking trays, lined with greasproof paper

Roll out the pastry on a lightly floured work surface (or one sprinkled with poppy seeds) to a rectangle about 46 x 24cm. With a large floured sharp knife, cut the pastry along its length to make 2 long rectangles – take care not to drag the knife and distort the edge.

Using your hands, mould the sausagemeat into 2 long rolls about 3cm thick and the length of your pastry strips (you can work in sections if this is easier).

Next, spread the chutney or mustard down the centre of each pastry strip, using a round-bladed knife. Spread the chutney fairly thickly, as you would when making a cheese and chutney sandwich, but spread the mustard as you would spread the butter. With kitchen scissors, snip the sun-dried tomatoes or apricots into strips about 5mm wide and arrange down the centre of the pastry. Set the roll of sausagemeat on the pastry along a line halfway between the edge and the centre. Brush the long edges of the pastry very lightly with beaten egg. Fold the pastry over the sausagemeat to completely cover it, and so that both long edges meet neatly. Press this edge neatly to seal, then 'knock up' the edge with the back of a small knife, making tiny horizontal cuts in the pastry seam. Using your fingers and the back of a knife, draw the pastry edge between 2 fingers to make a scalloped pattern (see page 189).

Heat the oven to 225°C/425°F/gas 7. Brush lightly with beaten egg. With the tip of a sharp knife, score the top of the pastry. Cut the pastry rolls on a slight diagonal into lengths about 5 to 6cm long. Set the sausage rolls on the prepared baking trays, slightly apart, and bake in the heated oven for 15 to 20 minutes, until a good golden brown. Transfer to a wire rack and leave to cool for 5 to 10 minutes. Serve warm.

Little Goat's Cheese and Tomato Tarts

MAKES 4 INDIVIDUAL TARTS

Farmers' markets have played an enormous part in changing, and increasing, the range of food we eat. Smallholders and local growers can try out new varieties and types of produce, find out what works and is viable, and what is not so popular. Shoppers get to try before they buy and can talk to the people who grow and harvest the food they put on the table – a short chain from fork to fork. This recipe celebrates the enthusiasm for new, unusual and heritage varieties of tomatoes – from the massive, bulgy Marmande to tiny orangey Sungold, gorgeously striped Tigerella and tiny plum tomatoes – and cheese. Here, the tomatoes are paired with a fresh, creamy goat's cheese.

½ quantity of puff pastry (see page 322) or 375g shop-bought butter puff pastry
3 tablespoons good olive oil
1 small clove of garlic
a few sprigs of fresh thyme
salt and pepper

150g soft goat's cheese
about 300g tomatoes – a selection of shapes, sizes and colours, depending on what is available

a large baking tray

Make the pastry, or make sure if using ready-made that it's thoroughly defrosted. Roll out the pastry on a lightly floured work surface to a rectangle about 20cm wide and 30cm long. Trim off all the edges then cut into 4 strips or cut out 4 large discs using a cutter. Set the 4 pieces of pastry on the baking tray and prick the centre with a fork. Chill for 20 minutes.

Meanwhile, heat the oven to 220°C/425°F/gas 7. Measure the olive oil into a small bowl. Finely chop the garlic with some of the thyme leaves (keep some back to garnish) and mix into the oil with a little salt and several grinds of pepper. Divide the goat's cheese into 4 portions (slices or rough crumbs). Rinse the tomatoes and cut into wedges – a large Marmande tomato will cut into 16, baby tomatoes can be cut in half or left whole. You will need about 8 wedges or bits of tomato for each piece of pastry.

Arrange the tomatoes on top of the pastry, leaving a 1cm border all the way round. Make sure they are not mounded up in the centre or the cheese will fall off in the oven. Brush very lightly with a little of the olive oil mixture. Top with the pieces of goat's cheese and a few sprigs of thyme. Bake in the heated oven for 15 to 18 minutes, or until the pastry is crisp and golden brown around the edges, and the goat's cheese is just starting to colour. Slide the tarts on to individual serving plates and spoon over the rest of the olive oil mixture. Serve immediately with a salad.

Hot Cheese Straws

Lovely with a drink before a meal or to serve with soup, cheese straws are simple to make. Don't overdo the mustard, as it can overpower the cheese. Parmesan works well, as it is a hard but well-flavoured cheese that doesn't ooze fat in the oven and ruin the pastry.

½ quantity of puff pastry (see page 322), or 375g shop-bought butter puff pastry
2 tablespoons mild mustard (Dijon or honey mustard)
100g finely grated Parmesan cheese

1 teaspoon sweet mild paprika
½ teaspoon dried red chilli flakes, or to taste

2 baking trays, lined with greaseproof paper

Roll out the pastry on a lightly floured work surface to a rectangle about 20 x 50cm. Using a round-bladed knife, spread the mustard evenly over the pastry, right to the edges. Combine the cheese with the paprika and chilli flakes and scatter over the pastry in an even layer. Gently but firmly press the mixture on to the mustard-covered pastry. Using a large sharp knife, cut the pastry into 20 even strips each 20cm long and 2.5cm wide. Avoid dragging or pulling the dough, as this will spoil the flaky layers of pastry.

To make the twists, hold one end of a pastry strip and then, with the other hand, twist the straw several times. Put it down on the work surface and gently roll it with your hands, like a sausage, so the spiral tightens. Set it on the prepared baking tray and repeat with the rest of the strips. When all the strips have been twisted into straws, scatter over any cheese that has dropped off as you have shaped them. Chill for 20 minutes, meanwhile heating the oven to 200°C/400°F/gas 6.

Bake in the heated oven for 15 to 18 minutes, until crisp and a good golden brown. Transfer to a wire rack – the straws will be quite fragile – and leave to cool. Serve warm the same or the next day.

Salmon in Pastry

In 1726 John Nott's recipe for a whole salmon, seasoned with slices of fresh ginger and plenty of butter, and wrapped in pastry, appeared in his book *The Cook and Confectioner's Dictionary*. Scottish salmon was available to the gentry and upper middle classes, thanks to improved transport. It was important that it was 'served prettily' – shown off, in other words.

FOR THE ROUGH PUFF PASTRY:
450g plain flour
½ teaspoon salt
250g unsalted butter, chilled and finely diced
1 teaspoon lemon juice
about 250ml ice-cold water

FOR THE FILLING:
2 x 500g skinned whole salmon fillets
50g slightly stale white breadcrumbs

75g chopped fresh parsley
25g chopped fresh chives
grated rind and juice of
1 medium unwaxed lemon
50g unsalted butter, melted
salt and pepper
1 egg, beaten

a large baking tray, lined with non-stick baking paper

Make the rough puff pastry (See page 187). Wrap and chill for 20 minutes.

Meanwhile, rinse the fish fillets and pat dry. Check that all the small 'pin' bones have been removed, then lightly season the fish and set aside while making the filling. Put the breadcrumbs, parsley, chives, lemon rind and juice, the melted butter and a little seasoning into a bowl. Mix well until thoroughly combined. Prepare the baking tray and set aside.

Divide the pastry into 2 portions, one slightly larger than the other. Roll out the smaller portion on a lightly floured surface to a rectangle 5cm longer and 5cm wider than the larger of the salmon fillets (they may be very similar in size). Using the rolling pin to support the pastry, lift it on to the prepared baking tray. Set a salmon fillet on the pastry, skinned side down. Spread with the breadcrumb mixture, then cover with the second fillet, skinned side uppermost, to resemble a whole (headless) fish. Roll out the second portion of pastry to a rectangle 10cm longer and wider than the first. Brush the pastry edges all around the fish with beaten egg, then, using the rolling pin to support the weight, lift the pastry over the fish and gently drape it over. Gently press the pastry down to remove any bubbles of air and to firmly seal together the pastry edges. 'Knock up' the edges (see page 189) then scallop or pinch the edges to decorate. Decorate the top of the pie with small leaves or fish, cut from the pastry trimmings and stuck on with dabs of beaten egg. Chill for 30 minutes.

Meanwhile, heat the oven to 190°C/375°F/gas 5. Brush the pastry with beaten egg and bake for 20 minutes, then reduce the temperature to 180°C/350°F/gas 4 and bake for a further 25 minutes, until the pastry is a good golden brown and crisp. Transfer to a serving plate and serve warm, with lemon wedges.

TO MAKE THE ORIGINAL FILLING: Fill the cavity between the fillets with 2 pieces of stem ginger, drained and finely chopped, a squeeze of lemon juice, a little seasoning, and the butter, cut into thin slices.

Little Pheasant Pies

MAKES 4 PIES

This is an attractive way to use cooked pheasant, chicken or turkey, while wild mushrooms add a contrast of taste and texture – a mixture of varieties works best, and will really boost the flavour. Tarragon is the classic herb for poultry, adding a subtle, slight, sweet anise flavour that lifts the sauce out of the run-of-the-mill.

½ quantity of puff pastry (see page 322), or 375g shop-bought butter puff pastry

FOR THE FILLING:
350g cooked pheasant, free of skin and bones
150g wild mushrooms, wiped clean

FOR THE SAUCE:
25g unsalted butter
2 tablespoons plain flour
300m good chicken stock, hot

3 tablespoons cream
(single, double or whipping)
a couple of sprigs of fresh tarragon, chopped
lemon juice, to taste
salt and pepper
beaten egg, to glaze

4 small baking dishes, about 250ml, and about 15cm across the top and 4cm deep
a baking tray, lined with greaseproof paper

Roll out the pastry on a lightly floured work surface to a square with sides about 31cm. Using one of the baking dishes as a guide, cut out 4 circles of pastry large enough to cover the top of the dishes. Set on the baking tray, then cover and chill until needed.

Shred the pheasant into fairly large pieces. Thickly slice or quarter the mushrooms. To make the sauce, melt the butter in a medium-sized pan and stir in the flour. Stir over a low heat for a minute, then stir in the hot stock. Bring to the boil, stirring or whisking constantly, to make a thick, smooth sauce. Reduce the heat and simmer gently for 2 minutes, stirring frequently. Stir in the mushrooms and simmer for a minute. Stir in the pheasant, cream and tarragon, then add a squeeze of lemon juice, a little salt and plenty of pepper. Taste and add more lemon juice and seasoning as needed. Spoon into the 4 dishes and leave until completely cold. (Once cold the dishes can be covered and chilled overnight.)

When ready to bake the pies, heat the oven to 200°C/400°F/gas 6. Brush the rims of the baking dishes with a little beaten egg, then carefully set a disc of pastry over the top of each dish, pressing the pastry on to the rim to seal. With the tip of a small sharp knife, lightly score the pastry lids in a diamond pattern, then brush with beaten egg to glaze. Cut a small steam hole in the centre of each pie, then set the dishes on a baking tray and bake in the heated oven for 25 to 30 minutes, until the pastry is well-risen, golden brown and crisp. Serve immediately.

LITTLE VEGETABLE PIES

Replace the pheasant with a mixture of vegetables: 150g shelled broad beans cooked in boiling water for 2 minutes, drained, run under a cold tap and drained again; 200g asparagus spears, cooked in boiling water for 1 minute, drained, then cut into 6cm lengths; and 100g baby carrots, trimmed, cooked for 2 minutes, then drained and sliced in 4 lengthways. Make up the sauce using a good vegetable stock and add sliced mushrooms. Finish with the vegetables, cream and tarragon, then season and add lemon juice to taste. Complete and bake the pies as above.

Cream Slice or Millefeuille

Not for nothing is this the pastry of 'a thousand leaves'. And if you make puff pastry you'll soon realize why; each layer is made up of 729 leaves – all those rolls and folds on page 322 soon multiply up. So this is a recipe to show off the pastry – it is simply baked in a sheet, then sliced in 3 and layered with cream and fruit. You can use fresh berries, as here, or a few well-drained slices of pears baked in wine (see page 300).

½ quantity of puff pastry (see page 322), or 375g shop-bought butter puff pastry
4 tablespoons good-quality strawberry jam
150ml double cream, well chilled

175g small ripe strawberries
icing sugar, for dusting

a large baking tray, lightly greased

Roll out the pastry on a lightly floured work surface to a square with sides about 31cm. Using a large, sharp knife, neatly trim the edges, trying not to drag the knife or pull the pastry as this will distort the shape. Using the rolling pin to support the weight of the pastry, lift it over and on to the baking tray so it is upside down (the pastry, that is). Prick it all over with a fork, then chill for 20 minutes while heating the oven to 220°C/425°F/gas 7.

Bake the pastry sheet for 12 to 15 minutes, or until well risen, golden and very crisp – the pastry must not be undercooked or it will be soggy. Transfer to a wire rack and leave to cool completely.

When ready to assemble, cut the pastry into 3 equal strips, using a sharp knife, each 10 x 30cm. Cut these strips into 6, so you have 18 individual strips of pastry, each approx 6 x 10cm. Put 1 strip on a serving plate and spread with the jam. Whip the cream until stiff. Spread half of it over the jam. Spread the rest of the whipped cream on a second pastry strip and set this on top of the first. Wipe and hull the strawberries; leave them whole if small, but quarter or thickly slice larger berries to make serving easier. Gently arrange the berries on the cream and cover with the last pastry strip. Dust with plenty of icing sugar and serve.

SAVOURY MILLEFEUILLE

Asparagus plus a little blue cheese makes a substantial filling for a savoury millefeuille. Pick a blue cheese that is well flavoured – Oxford Blue or Cashel Blue – or you could use a fairly dry and piquant goat's cheese.

Roll out and bake the pastry and leave to cool. Slice into 3 strips. Break off the very ends of 400g of asparagus spears, then steam them or cook them in boiling water for 4 to 5 minutes, until just tender but still with some bite. Leave the asparagus to cool, then slice each spear into 3, on the diagonal. Set one strip of pastry on a serving plate and spread with 2 tablespoons of half-fat crème fraîche. Scatter over a teaspoon of snipped chives and top with half the asparagus. Season with a little salt and plenty of pepper and crumble over 100g of cheese. Spread another 2 tablespoons of crème fraîche over a second strip of pastry, scatter with snipped chives as before, and set it on top. Gently arrange the rest of the asparagus on top of the crème fraîche, then season and add the rest of the crumbled cheese. Finish with the final strip of pastry. Garnish the top of the pastry with snipped mustard cress, and serve.

Maids of Honour

A historical treat! These sweet little tartlets filled with a rich almond cream are thought to have been invented for Henry VIII in 1525 and enjoyed by his court, including the Queen's maids of honour, at Richmond Palace.

½ quantity of puff pastry (see page 322), or 375g shop-bought butter puff pastry
50g unsalted butter, very soft
100g caster sugar
2 medium free-range egg yolks
3 tablespoons double cream

finely grated zest of 1 medium unwaxed lemon
100g ground almonds
1 tablespoon plain flour

a 7.5cm plain round cutter
a 12-hole mince pie tin or bun tray
a baking tray

Roll out the pastry fairly thinly – about 2mm thick – to a rectangle about the size of your mince pie tin or bun tray. Cut out rounds of pastry using the plain cutter. Pile up the trimmings, then re-roll and cut more rounds until you have 12. Place a pastry round in each hole in the pie tin or bun tray, gently pressing it on to the base and up the sides so there are no pockets of air, and making sure the edge of the pastry is higher than the rim of the hole. Firmly press your thumb down in the centre of each pastry round and prick the base of the pastry with a fork to stop it bubbling up in the oven, then chill the pastry cases for 30 minutes.

Meanwhile, heat the oven to 200°C/400°F/gas 6. Cut 12 small squares of greaseproof paper, crumple them up, smooth them out again and carefully fit one into each pastry case. Fill with baking beans or cubes of stale bread, then 'bake blind' (see page 151) in the heated oven for 12 to 15 minutes, until the pastry is risen, firm and slightly coloured. Remove the tin from the oven and carefully remove the paper and beans. Leave to cool while making the filling. Reduce the oven temperature to 180°C/350°F/gas 4 and put a baking tray into the oven to heat.

Put the soft butter into a mixing bowl and beat in the sugar, using a wooden spoon. When the mixture looks pale and creamy, beat in the egg yolks. When thoroughly combined, beat in the cream, then the lemon zest and finally the almonds and flour. Spoon the mixture into the pastry cases – if the bases have puffed up a lot, gently press them down. Set the pie tin or bun tray on the heated baking tray and bake the pastries in the heated oven for 15 to 20 minutes, until lightly coloured and just firm to the touch. Remove the tray from the oven and leave to cool for 5 minutes before removing the 'maids' from the tin. Eat warm the same or the next day.

In Regency times this would have been a truly exotic, wondrous and extravagant creation of rare ingredients: chocolate, crystallized flower petals and even almonds covered in real gold leaf. This adapted recipe has a thick chocolate biscuit-like pastry case, and a rich chocolate-truffle filling that slices well. Chocolate pastry needs careful handling – it's easiest to roll it out between a couple of sheets of clingfilm, as touching it with floured hands or a rolling pin can leave white marks which spoil the final result. It's worth mixing a couple of teaspoons each of flour and cocoa and keeping it ready for when you need to handle the dough.

FOR THE CHOCOLATE PASTRY:
150g plain flour
75g cocoa powder
100g icing sugar
150g unsalted butter, chilled and diced
2 medium free-range egg yolks, plus 2 tablespoons ice-cold water

FOR THE FILLING:
300ml whipping cream, at room temperature
250g good-quality dark chocolate
1 tablespoon dark rum

FOR THE TOPPING:
125ml whipping cream, well chilled
1 tablespoon icing sugar
1 tablespoon dark rum

a 22 to 23cm loose-based flan tin

Make the pastry in a food processor: put the flour, cocoa and icing sugar into the bowl and pulse several times to combine. Add the cold butter to the bowl and run the machine just until the mixture looks like fine crumbs. Add the egg yolks and water, then run the machine until the mixture comes together to make a heavy, slightly sticky dough. Cut 2 large squares of clingfilm and set one on the work surface. Scrape the dough out of the bowl and on to the middle of the square. Cover with the second square of clingfilm, then press the dough down between the squares of clingfilm to make a thick disc about 17cm across. Chill for 30 minutes.

Roll out the dough, still between the clingfilm, to a circle about 29cm across and about 1cm thick. Peel off the top square of clingfilm and slide your hand under the bottom square to support the dough. Carefully flip the dough over so it is draped over the flan tin. Peel off the remaining square of clingfilm. Lightly flour your fingers (or use a mixture of flour and cocoa) and press the dough on to the base and up the sides of the flan tin – the dough will be much thicker than the usual pastry case. Run a rolling pin across the top of the tin to cut off the excess dough and neaten the rim. Prick the base well, then chill for 30 minutes.

Meanwhile, heat the oven to 180°C/350°F/gas 4. Line the chilled pastry case with a sheet of crumpled greaseproof paper, fill with baking beans and 'bake blind' (see page 151) for 15 minutes. Remove the paper and beans and bake the empty case for a further 8 to 10 minutes, until it feels crisp and firm. Take care the very rich pastry doesn't scorch – unlike pastry made with white flour it is hard to tell when it is cooked, so keep an eye on it and don't let it become very dark. Remove from the oven and leave to cool in the tin.

Make the filling once the pastry case is completely cold and the cream has come up to room temperature. Break the chocolate into even-sized pieces and put into a heatproof bowl. Set over a pan of steaming water (not boiling), making sure the base of the bowl doesn't touch the surface of the water. Leave to melt gently, stirring occasionally. Remove the bowl from the pan and leave to cool to room temperature – it should still be liquid – stirring from time to time.

Pour the cream into another large bowl, add the rum and whip until very thick, but still floppy – just before soft peak stage. Gently fold the chocolate into the cream in 2 batches, to make a thick, mousse-like mixture. Spoon the mixture into the pastry case and spread evenly, working quickly before the mixture starts to set. Chill until firm (or cover and chill overnight).

When ready to finish the pye, make the topping: whip the cream with the sugar and rum until firm and thick enough to hold its shape. Spread the cream over the filling, or you could spoon it into a piping bag fitted with a star nozzle or tube, and pipe rosettes on to the top. Serve immediately or chill for up to 6 hours (remove from the fridge 30 minutes before serving)

Honeyed Baklava

CUTS INTO 30 PIECES

Layered pastries are thought to have been a speciality of the Turks for around 700 years, and the recipes gradually spread around the Middle East and then to Europe via Vienna. Baklava, with its crisp layers of pastry, nuts and sticky honey syrup, is now found up and down the country. Family recipes for baklava tend to use far more nuts than shop-bought, and are all the better for it.

450g filo pastry, fully defrosted
400g nuts: walnut pieces, unblanched almonds, shelled unsalted pistachios
2 tablespoons caster sugar
1 teaspoon ground cinnamon
175g unsalted butter, melted

FOR THE SYRUP:
325g caster sugar
300ml water
2 small cinnamon sticks
1 tablespoon lemon juice
3 tablespoons Greek honey

a roasting tin or baking tin (not loose-based), about 22 x 30cm, greased with butter

Heat the oven to 180°C/350°F/gas 4. Chop the nuts in a food processor – one type at a time works best – until they look like coarse breadcrumbs. Tip the nuts into a large heavy dry frying pan and stir over low heat for 4 to 5 minutes, until the nuts are just starting to colour. Take care, as they will quickly scorch, so it's best to slightly undercook them. Remove the pan from the heat and stir in the sugar and cinnamon.

Unwrap and unfold the pastry but keep what you are not handling covered with a damp cloth. Cover the base of your roasting tin with 1 layer of pastry – you may need 1 or 2 sheets slightly overlapping, depending on the brand of pastry. Leave the excess pastry hanging over the sides of the tin for now. Brush lightly with melted butter. Continue layering with the pastry and brushing with butter until you have 6 layers of pastry in the tin. Sprinkle with a third of the nut filling. Cover with 2 more buttered layers of pastry. Sprinkle half the remaining filling on top, and cover with another 2 buttered layers of pastry. Sprinkle the remaining nut filling evenly over the top layer.

Fold in any overhanging edges of pastry, lightly brushing with melted butter as you go, then set the rest of the pastry sheets on top, buttering them as before. If necessary, trim and neaten up any untidy or overhanging pastry with kitchen scissors. Using a sharp knife, cut the baklava into diamonds – it's easier to do this before baking. Sprinkle the top lightly with cold water and bake in the heated oven for 15 minutes. Increase the heat to 190°C/375°F/gas 5 and cook for a further 15 minutes, until the pastry is crisp and a good golden brown.

While the baklava is baking, make the honey syrup. Put the sugar and water into a pan and heat gently until the sugar has dissolved. Bring to the boil, then add the cinnamon sticks, lemon juice and the honey. Simmer gently for 10 minutes, until slightly syrupy. Remove from the heat and leave to cool for 10 minutes. As soon as the baklava comes out of the oven, pour the hot syrup over it and leave until fully absorbed and cool before serving. The flavour deepens as the baklava matures, so if possible make it a day or so in advance of serving.

Cream Puffs

These large, delicate puffs of crisp choux pastry filled with a cloud of cream and luscious fruit make a pretty summer treat. Add a raspberry fruit sauce (see raspberry meringue roulade, page 314) or a hot chocolate sauce (see below) for a special dessert.

FOR THE CHOUX PASTRY:
175ml water
a good pinch of salt
75g unsalted butter, diced
100g plain flour
3 medium free-range eggs, beaten

FOR THE FILLING:
250ml whipping cream, well chilled
2 tablespoons icing sugar
1 teaspoon vanilla extract
500g sliced strawberries or raspberries
icing sugar, for dusting

a baking tray, well greased with butter

Heat the oven to 200°C/400°F/gas 6. Make up the choux pastry (see page 323) and spoon the mixture into 8 large mounds, spaced well apart, on the prepared baking tray. Sprinkle the tray, not the puffs, with a few drops of water, and bake in the heated oven for 15 minutes. Then, without opening the door, reduce the oven temperature to 180°C/350°F/gas 4 and bake for a further 15 minutes, until golden and crisp.

Remove the tray from the oven and carefully make a small hole in the side of each puff to allow the steam to escape. Return the puffs to the oven and bake for a further 5 to 10 minutes, or until the pastry is completely crisp. Remove from the oven and transfer to a wire rack to cool.

When ready to serve, whip the cream with the sugar and vanilla until stiff. Carefully split open the puffs horizontally and spoon (or pipe) the cream on to each base. Decorate with the sliced fruit and top with the lids. Dust with icing sugar and serve as soon as possible.

TO MAKE ÉCLAIRS

Spoon the choux pastry into a piping bag fitted with a 1.25cm plain tube and pipe 12 x 10cm lengths on to the prepared tray. Bake as above. When cold, pipe or spoon in the whipped cream. To make the icing, break up 100g of good-quality dark chocolate, put into a heatproof bowl with 2 tablespoons of double cream and melt gently over a pan of steaming water. Remove the bowl from the heat, stir gently, then spread the chocolate icing over the top of the éclairs and leave until set before serving.

HOT CHOCOLATE SAUCE

Break up 100g of good-quality dark chocolate and put into a small pan (preferably non-stick) with 25g of unsalted butter, 2 tablespoons of icing sugar and 100ml of water. Heat very gently, stirring frequently, until melted and smooth. Serve warm.

Index

Thanks

WE WOULD LIKE TO THANK ALL THE WONDERFUL PEOPLE WHO HAVE CONTRIBUTED TO THIS BOOK.

Linda Collister for her brilliant recipes and endless good humour. Sheila Keating for her fascinating insight into the history of baking. Mark Read and Chris Fenner for all their adventures and brilliant photography. Also, Tara Fisher and Al Richardson. Thank you to Jonny Rolfe and Laura Fyfe for the delicious food and also Louisa Carter and Joe Woodhouse. Big thanks to Jo Harris for her beautiful styling. Many thanks to Carol Kemp and Steve Crozier for the lovely chapter openers.

From Penguin, thanks to Lindsey Evans, John Hamilton, Sarah Fraser, Laura Herring, Sarah Hulbert, James Blackman, Jessica Killingley, Katy Szita, Katya Shipster, Thomas Chicken, Emma White, Beatrix McIntyre, Debbie Hatfield, Annie Lee, Helen Campbell, Michele Clarke and Gail Jones.

Thank you to everyone at Love Productions, particularly Anna Beattie, Victoria Watson, Andy Devonshire and Jane Treasure, and all the contestants on the show. To Mel Giedroyc and Sue Perkins, Mary Berry and Paul Hollywood.

From the BBC, thank you to Emma Willis, Daniel Mirzoeff and Louise Burke. And thank you to Claire Potter from Metrostar.

But mostly, thanks to all the brilliant people we have met along the way: to Scone Palace and the groundsman who let us in to see the Highland cows; to the lovely ladies (and men) at Murray's bakery in Perth, Scotland (check out their famous Scotch pies). To Tracey at The Ship Inn for making an amazing Stargazy pie; and to Mr Cotton of Mousehole for letting us take his picture when he had just come in from fishing. To Philps in Hale for their legendary pasties; and to Bob Hill and the millers at Sarre windmill in Kent for letting us explore their mill. To the Bakewell Tart Coffee House and The Old Original Bakewell Pudding Shop. To Huffkins in Burford and the pie-makers of Melton Mowbray. Without all of you, we wouldn't have a great baking heritage to be so proud of.